100 GREATEST GOLF COURSES
—AND THEN SOME

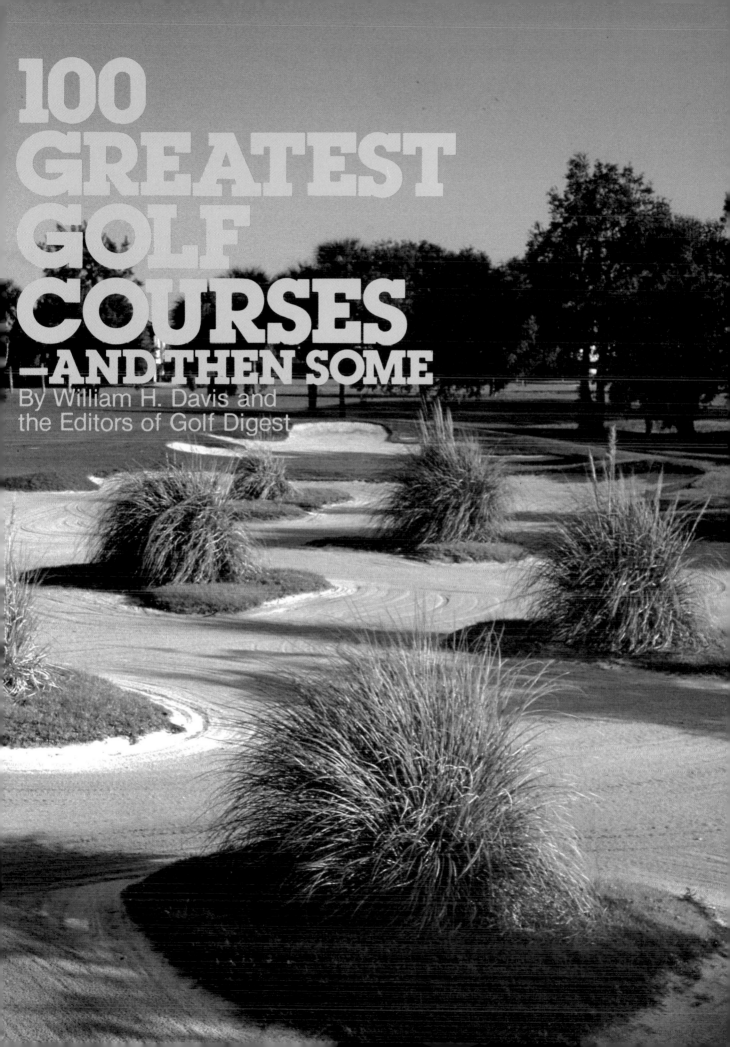

100 GREATEST GOLF COURSES
—AND THEN SOME

By William H. Davis and
the Editors of Golf Digest

Published by Golf Digest/Tennis, Inc.,
A New York Times Company,
495 Westport Avenue,
P.O. Box 5350,
Norwalk, Connecticut 06856

Trade book distribution by Simon and Schuster
A Division of Gulf + Western Industries, Inc.
New York, New York 10020

First Printing
ISBN: 0-914178-571
Library of Congress: 82-081714
Manufactured in the United States of America

Cover and book design by Nick DiDio
Printing and binding by Kingsport Press,
An Arcata Company

*Previous page: the 16th hole at Pine
Tree Golf Club, in Delray Beach, Fla.
The course is a Dick Wilson design and
ranks in the Third Ten of America's 100
Greatest Golf Courses.*

CONTENTS

FOREWORD

One of the enduring appeals of golf is its infinite variety and beauty. Yet until 1974, when *Golf Digest* published a book called *Great Golf Courses of the World,* no one had attempted to assemble a volume devoted largely to strikingly rich color photographs of great golf courses.

One of the reasons is that good golf course photography is hard to come by, particularly in color. Another is that costly, non-instruction golf books are a risky venture.

Great Golf Courses of the World was a surprising artistic and financial success and was sent into four printings. In the foreword of that volume I wrote, "Golf is a constantly changing scene, and until the supply of beautiful open space is crowded from the earth, great new courses will emerge. We hope that your interest will justify our revising and updating this volume accordingly."

100 Greatest Golf Courses and Then Some is not a revise, but a new book with new text and photography. Only a handful of unusual photographs has been republished. The primary editorial focus is on those golf courses that qualify as "greatest," a superlative that over the past 20 years has been given a special meaning by the editors of *Golf Digest* in evolving its biennial listing of "America's 100 Greatest Golf Courses."

Since 1962, when *Golf Digest* undertook to name America's "200 Toughest Courses," the definition and criteria our editors have used to determine noteworthy courses have changed significantly. This list is now called the 100 *Greatest* and its criteria are determined by the Golf Digest National Panel of Selectors, who have increasingly placed emphasis on more qualitative values (see 100 Greatest Golf Courses, starting on page 21).

 hen we suggested that our sister publication in England—Golf World—put together a panel to name the top 25 courses in the British Isles, there was much discussion about the American criteria. Peter Dobereiner, the great golf journalist who serves as a contributing editor and columnist for both *Golf Digest* and Golf World, at first questioned esthetics as a criterion. He wrote, "No limp-wristed poet would sigh with emotion-filled delight at the prospect of the Old Course Hotel as seen from the 17th tee. But as seen through a golfing eye, which translates the new estate into an abstract concept, the view at St. Andrews takes on an awesome beauty."

After he met with the British selection committee, however, he declared "A slightly surprising point of unanimity was the priority given to esthetics. Pro and layman alike insisted that beautiful surroundings provide golf's major appeal; the greatest joy of the game is just to be on the course."

In America, tournament toughness remains a measure of greatness, and it is difficult for a golf course that lacks championship caliber to achieve high ranking. So it is that some dearly loved gems here and abroad are absent from the lists, and appear nowhere in the book. An example is the National Golf Links along Peconic Bay, near Southampton, L.I., where Charles Blair Macdonald designed one of America's first great golf courses. For all of its Scottish flavor and scenic beauty, the quirkiness of some of the holes (short, blind or tricky) caused it to be squeezed from the list of greatest several years ago. Perhaps some day when we more fully return to an appreciation of the old values, the National will reappear on America's list of 100 Greatest (see Tomorrow's Great Golf Courses, pages 8-20).

In England, there are few more-delightful courses than the links at Rye in Kent. It was here that Britain's illustrious golf writer, Bernard Darwin, chose to live and retire for several years before his death in the mid-'60s. He said, "For the few who are artists in using the wind, Rye is a paradise. On only one hole does it blow in your teeth and one where it is straight behind us. At the other 16, the enemy persists in making a flanking attack upon us." I personally have seldom had a more enjoyable and challenging golfing experience than the one day I played Rye, when the winds acted exactly the way Darwin said they would. Yet, like many other fascinating links courses, Rye received little consideration in the top 25 list among the British Isles.

The rankings of golf courses in the United States have rated exceptional interest. If the volume of mail is any criterion, then the 100 Greatest feature easily ranks No. 1 among all ventures undertaken by *Golf Digest.* Hundreds of letters and telephone calls descend on the editors, some praising and some protesting the choices. The list also has inspired some incredible efforts by *Golf Digest* readers to attempt to play the top 100, even though most of these courses are private.

So far as we know, only one person, William Power of Doylestown, Pa, has succeeded. A 64-year-old lawyer, he purports to have played all 100 courses on the 1975 list, and the new ones added in 1977, '79 and '81.

The inspiration for some of the "And Then Some" chapters in this volume came from Frank Cox, a former New York Times vice president, who spent most of his retirement years playing golf all over the world before he passed away in early 1982. He not only had played most of the top 100 in the U.S., but accomplished the record feat of playing 364 different courses in a year (1979).

He maintained regular correspondence with *Golf Digest,* and left a legacy of impressions and recommendations that constitute something of a Michelin Guide for the peripatetic golfer (see "The Frank Cox Gazetteer," pages 268-271).

The standard of greatness on which most of this book is based begins to vary in dealing with golf courses outside the United States, the British Isles, Canada and Australia.

While most of the courses shown or described in the Atlantic Off-Islands section, for instance, fall short of inclusion on any list of the great courses of the world, they are superior by resort-course standards and provide the book with functional and geographic balance.

The "And Then Some" tail to the title of our book also provides license to include a few miscellaneous chapters that we felt would be of special interest to our readers. One of them is the "50 Great Public Courses," which *Golf Digest* commissioned Frank Hannigan, of the USGA, to put together in 1980. The feature created so much interest, we have elected to reprint it.

Two subjects never before published are the "Five Great College Courses" and "The Remaining Personal Golf Courses." In the latter chapter we take readers inside the gates of the very scarce private preserves in the U.S.

100 Greatest Golf Courses and Then Some contains more than 200 color photographs and more than 50 black and white, and the two years it took to put the book together were spent largely in quest of good photos. Part of the lengthy process involved writing to or talking to knowledgeable representatives, usually the club professional for each of the top 100 courses, to determine not only what were the strongest holes but what were the most photographic. Often these club representatives knocked themselves out to locate photographs and we acknowledge their help with appreciation starting on page 272.

Many of these holes, however, had never been photographed in color, if at all. The task of shooting in these situations befell Golf Digest/Tennis staff photographer Steve Szurlej, who traveled from one coast to the other and to the British Isles to obtain for us the type and quality of pictures we wanted.

Capturing superior golf course pictures is a frustrating challenge. The configuration and nuances of most golf holes have a way of eluding the camera's eye. Even when a cherry-picker or helicopter is handy, the picture often gains perspective but loses contour. It has been said, "On a golf course you cannot photograph substance, only mood." But Szurlej defied the rule. We sought photography that was "hole-descriptive" so that readers could get the feeling of how a course, or at least a part of it, not only looks but plays. Szurlej provided this dimension with magnificent success in such photographs as the 16th at the Vintage Club (page 18), and many others.

He often awoke early to capture morning dew and the rising sun, or waited until late evening to catch soft shadows, frequently shot from a 14-foot stepladder. His most unnerving experience came at the new La Quinta Course in Palm Springs, Calif., when he climbed a high rock to get a shot. As he began to position himself, he was joined by a four-foot rattlesnake at his feet. Said Steve, "I began making hissing noises and snapping my fingers trying to scare him away. He finally left of his own accord. Thereafter, I tried to stick with ladders or helicopters."

Writing about great golf courses, particularly those on which no historic events have been played, is very demanding and somewhat unfulfilling journalism. No one wants to hear a play-by-play of the writer's game or a mind-boggling hole-by-hole description of an unfamiliar course.

It took a strong and experienced team of *Golf Digest* editors to get the job done. Ross Goodner, veteran golf journalist and associate editor, not only did most of the writing and reporting for the top 50 courses and Canada, he participated in the planning process from the onset. John May, senior editor, wrote the copy for the second 50, the Atlantic Off-Islands and Mexico Plus South America. His 27 years of staff experience, which has included trips to most of the places he wrote about, made him an invaluable asset.

The major task of editing copy and pulling together all the disparate parts that make up these 280 pages of photographs, captions and artwork was handled by Assistant Managing Editor Roger Schiffman, who also volunteered to research and write the piece on college courses. His stomach for organization of detail is steel-lined.

Creative designers are not generally known for their evenness of temperament, but Nick DiDio, an art director at Golf Digest/ Tennis, is a rare exception. All elements of the book passed across Nick's drawing boards and into the offices of Production Manager Joe Mossa. DiDio's patience was nearly as valuable as his precision in design.

During the closing months of effort, we were fortunate to obtain the assistance of Topsy Siderowf, wife of prominent amateur golfer Dick Siderowf. She served with distinction as a free-lance editorial researcher, arriving on the scene when Jan Van Munching, a regular staff member, became fully occupied with other *Golf Digest* duties. We also were able to gain help in content review from Ron Whitten, co-author with course architect Geoffrey Cornish of the oustanding historical book, *The Golf Course,* published in 1981.

Other staff members providing assistance were Paul Menneg, associate publisher, Jay Simon, managing editor and Jack McDermott, executive editor. *Golf Digest* Editorial Director Nick Seitz showed great forbearance in freeing up his staff members at critical times to work on the project.

We hope these many contributions will help you enjoy the flavor and beauty of the world's great courses, whether or not you ever get a chance to visit them.

TOMORROW'S GREAT COURSES

by William H. Davis

Jerry Pate walked into the locker room after the first round of the 1982 Tournament Players Championship blistering mad. "This is the most unfair golf course I've ever played," he railed.

A handful of other top players, none of whom had broken the new Players Club par of 72, were in assent. Any one of the millions of Americans who watched the tournament on television could see that the Players Club was different from almost anything they had ever seen. Who ever heard of a par 3 with a fairway of water and an island green circled by railroad ties? Who ever heard of an American championship course with deep pot bunkers, rows of grass mounds and vast, sandy stretches of "wasteland" bordering the fairways? Who ever imagined spectators sitting high on natural-grass bleachers overlooking play?

Such noticeably dramatic elements of golf course architecture are the work of Paul "Pete" Dye, of Delray Beach, Fla., who had completed the Players course

less than a year earlier under the supervision of Deane Beman, commissioner of the PGA Tour. Despite plenty of irrigation and rain, the greens lacked the holding characteristics of mature turf, and disquieting bounces were occurring off their undulating surfaces. With a vengeance, Jerry Pate went on to win the first Tournament Players Championship at the Players course with brilliant consistency, and delivered on a threat made earlier to toss both Dye and Beman in the pond at 18 if he conquered the course and won the tournament. It will go down as a memorable splash in the history of golf course architecture.

For many years, golf industry pundits, course designers among them, have been crying for changes in design to meet changing conditions in the game, but they have been slow in coming.

Better players, better equipment and escalating course-maintenance costs have called for courses that essentially would (1) require less care in an age of escalating maintenance costs and potential water shortages, (2) provide more challenge for better players without adding yardage and (3) add pleasure for recreational golfers without unjust punishment for errant play. Such a set of demands contains many built-in conflicts.

While the Players course may not be the prototype for tomorrow's great golf courses, or even for future championship courses, it embodies innovative solutions to challenge better players at a length under 7,000 yards (6,857 from the championship tees). It certainly represents a sharp contrast to the design trends that characterized America's golf courses during the

Perhaps no golf hole has become as widely recognizable so quickly as the par-3 17th at the new Players Club course near Ponte Vedra, Fla. With characteristic innovativeness, Pete Dye adapted classic Scottish-type pilings to the Florida swampland with bold, modern usage. Note the small pot bunker in front of the green.

great new course boom of the '50s and '60s. During that period, designers Robert Trent Jones and Dick Wilson virtually changed the meaning of the word "championship course." It came to mean a trial of 7,000 yards and more, often requiring approach shots of 170 to 220 yards over water to enormous greens. The typical major tournament course was a test of power and putting skill.

For more than 25 years, the Masters has been the most widely seen golf tournament on television. During this time, the Augusta National course has become the symbol of what is beautiful about the game, greatly influencing golf-course architecture. It was created by the immortal Bobby Jones as a "dream golf course," on the site of a lush arboretum. Augusta National was constructed and designed in 1932 by the foremost architect of the era, Dr. Alister Mackenzie of Great Britain, and Trent Jones was brought in for remodeling work in 1949. He enlarged the water hazards on 11 and

The dynamic Robert Trent Jones clan shares a rare moment of relaxation. From left: Bobby, Trent and Rees. The three architects have designed or co-designed 21 courses among the 100 Greatest listing.

12, built a lake on 16, enlarged the greens on eight, 11, 12 and 13, and reshaped or added many bunkers.

In the opinion of many modern critics, Augusta National is today a lavish model of features *not* needed to make a golf course challenging and maintainable at reasonable cost—the vastness of the greens, the "velvet" of the fairways, the plenitude of sand bunkers and the frontal "do-or-die" water hazards.

By contrast, many of the design characteristics of the courses Pete Dye has been building for the past 10 years, as exemplified by the Players Club, are gaining acceptance with the golf course architectural profession. They include natural rough areas, undulating greens and fairways, grass mounds, pot bunkers and

even blind holes. Several of these features can be traced to the great courses of Scotland.

Discussions with the major living architects of *Golf Digest*'s top 100 courses reveal considerable reservations over extensive use of natural, sandy or unkempt rough areas on courses for the average golfer. There is general agreement, however, that golf course architecture is returning to some of the old Scottish and English penal values to help contain the better player. Each designer simply interprets these values in his own way and carries them out with his own style.

The American Society of Golf Course Architects sees the use of more natural elements, such as native grasses, bushes and flowers, as one of the most significant trends in course design.

Joe Finger of Houston, Tex., designer of five of *Golf Digest*'s 100 Greatest Courses, concurs. He states, "I'm a firm believer that golf courses in general must go back toward the less-manicured, more-natural type of construction. Not only are the initial costs less, but annual maintenance costs are smaller."

George and Tom Fazio, who also are responsible for designing five of the top 100, along with several new contenders, are long-time advocates of the natural look. Tom, however, voices grave concern about the emerging trend toward more unkempt rough areas, particularly when they extend beyond 100 yards. "They not only have the potential for slowing up play," he notes, "they make you tense." He cites Pine Valley as an example of an extreme offender. Says Fazio, "A great course is strong for the better player, but playable for the majority." Therein lies one of the great conflicts in designing a course to meet today's needs. If you build courses with extensive low-maintenance rough areas, you discourage the high-handicap and beginning golfer. You also offend many developers, who insist upon well-manicured rough areas near building lots.

It is severe green contouring of Pete Dye's Players Club that has aroused the most controversy with tour players. Drive to a limited landing area. Approach to a restricted pin position. Dye calls it "target golf." Peter Dobereiner, contributing editor of *Golf Digest*, believes the trend has emerged just in time. Following the 1982 Tournament Players Championship, he wrote: "There are target areas on all those contoured greens that will deflect the ball toward the hole, no matter which pin position may be used. It is the player's responsibility to identify those target areas, and it is the architect's job to use every trick of optical illusion to make such identification as difficult as possible. That is the very soul of golf, and in its expression, as at the Players Club, it puts the emphasis on tactical planning and shot-making and reduces the tyranny of the putter.

"In recent years the game has grown bland. Does the Players Club represent a new era in tournament golf? Rather it is a revival, a reaffirmation that golf is a game of flair and imagination and cunning and wit and sensitivity and character and risk."

The original Scottish courses, St. Andrews (circa 1754) and Carnoustie (1842), abound with severe natural and man-made hazards from which the golfer has great difficulty extracting himself in one stroke. The most common of these is the deep "pot bunker,"

One of Robert Trent Jones' most highly regarded courses is Troia, 35 miles south of Lisbon, Portugal, on a sand peninsula in the Sado River. Here is the par-4 15th hole, which shows what Jones himself terms as a similarity to Spyglass Hill, another one of his courses.

"Large islands of flowers—80,000 of them—surround the seventh green at Sentryworld, a 156-yard showcase hole at the Sentry Insurance Company's new course, in Stevens Point, Wis., designed by Trent Jones Jr. Bent-grass fairways are featured between cleared rows of evergreens.

Trent Jones Jr. has designed a lovely course in the Colorado Rockies, the Keystone Resort. Some of the holes run through a dense forest of lodgepole pines before breaking into a wide meadow with striking views of the mountain peaks.

which, like many other penal obstacles of early origin, fell out of favor in the early 20th century, with a shift toward ''strategic'' design. On the rare occasion when you see them in the U.S., such as on the famous par-3 10th hole at Pine Valley, they are accorded profane, ungentlemanly nicknames.

It has taken the pot bunker about 50 years to return to the scene of American golf, and its growing reappearance still arouses controversy. It is a common hazard on a Pete Dye course, particularly at the Players Club. The United States Golf Association, influenced by its committee and former president Frank ''Sandy'' Tatum Jr., added two pot bunkers to Pebble Beach for the 1982 Open; one on four and the other on 16. The bunker on 16 was designed to increase the need for driving accuracy out about 250 yards on the relatively short, 403-yard par 4. It was placed just inside the right rough at the corner of the dogleg. A larger, far-less severe, shallow bunker was allowed to remain farther into the rough. This ordinarily would represent an affront to those theorists who feel that punishment should

fit the crime—that the more offline you hit, the more severe the penalty. As it developed, the pot bunker on 16 well served its purpose. In the final round, Tom Watson, one stroke ahead of Jack Nicklaus, drove into it. He was up against the steep face of the bunker with no way out but safe and sideways. By the time the hole was over he had lost his lead, facing the hard-to-birdie last two holes.

Tom was later asked if he thought it was a fair hazard. ''Certainly,'' he replied. ''People seem to forget that the game was designed as an obstacle course. I hit a bad tee shot and was penalized for it.''

Throughout the history of the game, it has been the course architects who have shaped the look and the spirit of golf. Certainly, no American golf course architect has had more influence over the game than Robert Trent Jones. For many years, he was alone among the designers called upon to suggest modifications of Open championship sites, where fairways are traditionally narrowed to 30-35 yards, and the rough is

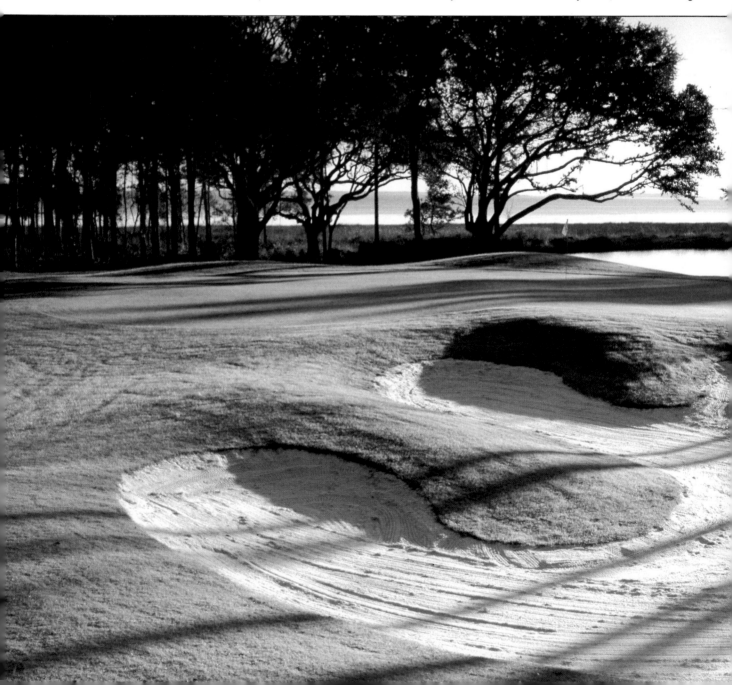

uncut till it is ankle-deep at four to six inches. He was singled out for turning major championships into driving-and-putting contests, often by tournament professionals with rancor more severe than Jerry Pate's toward Pete Dye and Deane Beman.

The most historic example was at Oakland Hills, near Detroit, where for the 1951 Open Jones filled in all the bunkers within 220 yards of the tee markers and replaced them with new ones at about 250 yards. He also intensified the bunkering around several greens. Ben Hogan's locker-room epithets were unprintable, but the course brought out the best in him, and in his own words he "brought the monster to its knees." At the 1970 Open at Hazeltine near Minneapolis, touring pro Dave Hill publicly labeled the Jones-designed course a "cow pasture" and was fined by the United States Golf Association.

Trent Jones, a top amateur around the Rochester (N.Y.) area in his youth, had studied especially to be a golf course architect by combining engineering and agronomy courses at Cornell University in his home state. Not surprisingly, he brought more science to course design than anyone before him. He provided the game with a new dimension, and it wasn't just length. He introduced huge tees, whose alternate tee markers could stretch a golf hole 50 yards. His big, undulating greens often provided a half dozen pin positions, and he guarded them with eye-appealing hazards.

Jones created a truly American style—a look of beauty and expanse, and he began exporting it with great success around the world. Some of the most beautiful courses in the most romantic places bear his design label: Dorado Beach in Puerto Rico, Mauna Kea in Hawaii and Pevero at Costa Smeralda on the Island of Sardinia, to name only a few.

Trent Jones, at age 76, is well aware of the game's changing needs. He is back working for Oakland Hills to help prepare it for the 1985 Open. He is planning to move some of those bunkers he moved in 1951 still another 20 yards farther from the tees, because today's big hitter can carry the ball that much longer. He glibly quotes the PGA Tour statistics, noting that the average of the top 10 long drivers is now 268 yards. "That's why Pine Valley is never out of date," Jones observes, leaving it to you to figure out that Its natural sand hazards occupy swaths long enough along the sides of fairways to catch errant shots of any length.

Despite his appreciation of such native-type courses, Jones seldom strays from good grooming. He recently completed, however, the Troia Golf Course on a peninsula jutting out into the Atlantic Ocean south of Lisbon, Portugal—where several holes run along windswept sand dunes, and natural vegetation flourishes. It may become one of the great links courses in Europe.

Pete Dye, whose most celebrated design is the Tournament Players Club course, near Ponte Vedra, Fla., has, in the eyes of many, returned to the old Scottish values. He has repopularized the use of railroad ties, pot bunkers and severe mounding, resulting in what he calls, "target golf."

While Trent Jones' work and influence in the United States is waning, both of his sons, Bob Jr., of San Francisco, and Rees, of New Jersey, are in the golf course design business. Each, in his own way, is striving for individuality, both having learned the lessons of flexibility their father taught them.

Bobby, as he is known to his friends, hangs out his shingle as Robert Trent Jones II and designs courses all over the world with the promotional flair of Trent Sr. He has completed more than 50 courses, some of them overseas, and has 25 on the drawing board or under construction. One of Bobby's finest achievements is at Keystone, in the Colorado Rockies, where he recently forged a course from an old ranch and an adjoining pine forest. Keystone has a natural, somewhat unkempt feeling. After playing three holes through lodgepole pines, you come out upon the ranch. Here Bobby has allowed the yellow ranch grass to serve as rough for a hundred or more yards in front of many tees. On the backside of the rough is sagebrush. The color contrast of these natural features with newly planted bent and bluegrass presents a striking picture against the mountains.

Keystone notwithstanding, Bobby leans toward lush courses. One of his recent favorites is Sentryworld at Stevens Point in northern Wisconsin, opened in 1982. Here the golf course decorates the headquarters of the Sentry Insurance Company, as the gardens at Versailles beautify the Palace of Louis XIV. While

Sand and water are the golfer's constant companions at the par-3 sixth hole at Oyster Reef on Hilton Head Island. This Rees Jones creation can be played from 157 to 191 yards.

many of the fairways remain lined with beautiful evergreen trees, the rough areas are immaculately cleaned out.

Bobby explains that he is reluctant to let features of nature interfere too strongly with play, noting that architects are committed to design for medal competition. ''We could enjoy more natural hazards if we went back to bogey golf, the way the game was once scored,'' he says.

Pete Dye's La Quinta course, near Palm Springs, Calif., blends the rugged natural beauty of desert mountains with the lush greenery of undulating putting surfaces. This photo shows the importance Dye places on accurate approaches to the greens for the golfer to have a reasonable chance of holing putts.

ees Jones, who in 1974 designed Arcadian Shores, in Myrtle Beach, one of *Golf Digest*'s top 100 courses, considers himself a "purist." By his definition, this means a golf course is not tricked up—no difficult obstacles like deep frontal traps or pot bunkers. Rees Jones likes to build a golf course that will play for everybody, emphasizing the adage, "The guys who play from the tips don't pay for the game."

His idea of a great hole is the 17th at a new course he is designing named Hell's Point in Virginia Beach, Va. It is only 334 yards, but he says, "I like it because it plays like two par 3s."

Early in 1982 his latest of two courses on Hilton Head Island, S.C., was opened. It is called Oyster Reef and is the personification of Rees' strategic style, challenging but not threatening. Approaches are to moderate-size greens of varying contours, guarded by flanking traps to catch off-line shots. It's more position golf than target golf.

Rees is skeptical of the so-called "natural" golf course, as represented by the Players course at Ponte Vedra. "Nothing natural about it," says Rees. "They took down all the trees to create so-called 'natural' areas, instead of leaving more of them wooded. Extensive sand areas make it easier for the better player, tougher for the average golfer."

It would be stretching a point to say that we are moving from the era of Robert Trent Jones to the age of Pete Dye. For one thing, Trent Jr. and Rees will perpetuate the Jones influence in their individual ways, and the tremendous effect of their father's style will be felt for generations. Similarly, early influence is still with us today from the contributions of such great architects of the pre-Jones era as Willie Park Jr. (two), H.S. Colt (five), Donald Ross (13), Alister Mackenzie (three) and A.W. Tillinghast (five), all of whose courses remain in the top 100 in the quantities shown in parentheses.

It also is perhaps an overstatement to identify the modern era so strongly with Pete Dye, when George Fazio and others were "emphasizing" the natural look as early as he. Golf course design, however, like commercial art, is a second level of creativity—creative imitation. Even Pablo Picasso, for all his influence over modern art and expressionism, did not create it.

ye is criticized for giving too many of his courses a look of the "old sod" instead of letting the land dictate the style. Almost everything about his courses evokes strong reaction, particularly an alleged overuse of railroad ties, his trademark. He often uses 6,000-8,000 of them, or equivalent lengths of telephone poles on a new course. Like most of Dye's design features, however, they serve much more than a decorative purpose. The old Scottish railroad ties, or "sleepers" as they were called, were used most frequently to keep the wind from displacing the sand dunes on the time-honored links. They also were used to buttress sand bunkers, such as in the famous Cardinal Bunker at Prestwick (page 202).

It was here and at Royal Dornoch that Pete Dye in 1963 first became imbued with the flavor and practical aspects of the Scottish links courses. Dye transplanted many of these features to America with a special flair. The railroad ties serve as bulkheads to edge lakes and elevate tees. Around traps they help to define the green and the hazard. Dye says that, properly installed, they decrease the need for hand mowing. His critics say they increase it.

Since Pete Dye designed and built Crooked Stick, south of Indianapolis, in 1964, most of his courses have been uncommonly demanding for the mid- to high-handicap golfer. If Jerry Pate and the rest of the field found the new Players Club course difficult, the

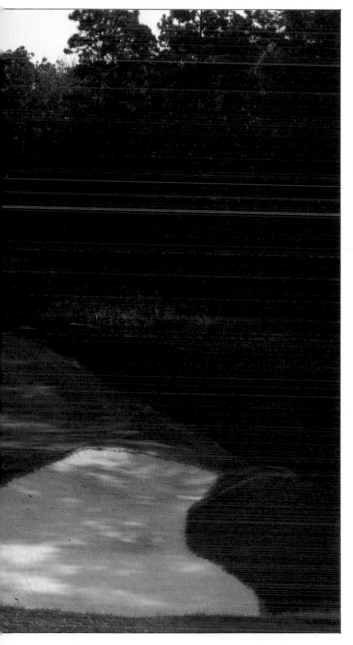

The par-4 15th hole at Pete Dye's Long Cove Club on Hilton Head Island shows the architect's sensitivity toward Scottish-style bunkering and fairway contouring. This course, opened in early 1982, shows Dye's creativity at its best.

average golfer has found it nearly impossible.

Yet this limitation has not prevented Pete Dye courses from breaking into the *Golf Digest* biennial list of America's 100 Greatest Golf Courses faster than any designer before him. It took Crooked Stick seven years before it made the list, but thereafter Dye's recognition came fast. The Golf Club, at New Albany, near Columbus, Ohio, was built in 1967 and entered the rankings in 1969. It took Harbour Town three years—from 1968 to 1971—to make the list, aided by media exposure of the Heritage Classic. Oak Tree, completed in 1976, quickly joined the rankings in 1977. His two courses at La Romana in the Dominican Republic are widely regarded as the most spectacular in the world.

ete Dye seems to be moving more dirt and creating more severe undulations on greens and in selected fairway areas than ever before. His qualities of sharp target demarcation of greens are stronger than his contemporaries'.

An example is his new course on Hilton Head Island,

called the Long Cove Club, opened in early 1982. Most architects would begrudge him the budget freedom he had, but with it he gave full, compelling expression to his style.

Holes six and seven border Route 278, the main Hilton Head road, but they transplant you to another part of the world, probably Royal Dornoch in Scotland,

Jack Nicklaus' new Bear Creek course, between Los Angeles and San Diego (right), reflects Jack's love for the old values of course architecture. The deep bunkering and even a double green are reminiscent of St. Andrews, where Nicklaus won two of his three British Open titles.

The 18th hole of the Wild Dunes course (below), perhaps Tom Fazio's most interesting design to date, combines the rugged terrain of the Atlantic coast with the tranquility of fairway and green.

The 406-yard par-4 16th hole of the Vintage Club (left), designed by Tom and George Fazio, melds nearly every spectacular element nature has to offer—water, mountains, flowers—with the classic undulations and bunkering of a traditional Scottish-style course.

Tom Fazio and Uncle George (right) may be among the foremost designers of tomorrow's courses. Here they inspect one of their most-respected works, the No. 6 and newest course at Pinehurst.

with undulations and elevations that rise to 35 feet. The contrast with the Trent Jones course at Palmetto Dunes along the same road a few miles away marks the startling difference between the old and the new. The Jones course is like an airport runway at sea level.

Pete Dye drew the route map for the Players Club on a napkin, which Deane Beman framed for his recreation room. Careful design planning is not Dye's forte, so it is interesting to imagine how he and the methodical Jack Nicklaus got along when they worked together on the Harbour Town course at Hilton Head 15 years ago. Jack had been employed by Charlie Fraser, the developer, as a co-designer, with Pete Dye's approval. He made some consulting trips to the site, and learned some of the tricks of the trade. This was the beginning of Nicklaus' career in golf course architecture.

Since then, Nicklaus has developed one of the most active course architecture businesses in the country. He has designed two courses in America's top 100—Muirfield Village, near Columbus (pages 86-89), and Shoal Creek, near Birmingham (page 187), plus Glen Abbey near Toronto, in Canada's top 10 (pages 216-217). Muirfield Village and Shoal Creek, constructed five years apart, reflect his changing design thinking. Muirfield Village was built for tournament play in 1974. But Nicklaus acknowledges, "We worked backward to try to accommodate the average golfer. We've continued to make adjustments in this direction." By contrast, Shoal Creek, completed in 1977, is regarded as better balanced than Muirfield, providing more options on approaches to greens, with less-penal results for a missed shot.

icklaus says, "My design ideas change with every course I do." His growing output reflects his flexibility of thought. At Bear Creek, between Los Angeles and San Diego in southern California, Nicklaus has designed a country club development course that can play at more than 7,100 yards and challenge golfers of all levels. It contains the inner mix of American and Scottish features, with pot bunkers and sweeping slopes, and it certainly will gain notoriety as one of the better golf courses on the West Coast.

For a man who has won the Masters five times, Nicklaus professes surprising disdain for the American architecture that existed until the last 10 years. He has said, "There was little emphasis on shot-making and more on turning the courses into turf nurseries."

Yet, Nicklaus has been severely faulted for creating courses with extraordinarily high costs of maintenance, like Muirfield in Ohio and Lakeway in Texas, and many others. At Muirfield, Jack has an excuse. He says it was designed as a championship course requiring high maintenance. The fact is that it incorporates many of the opulent values of Augusta National, but with special shot-making properties that belong only to Jack. His spectator mounds are highly effective and were perhaps a forerunner to what Pete Dye did at the Players Club. Moreover, Jack's mounds blend in far better with the golf course, to the pleasure of many critics who find the grass bleachers at the Players Club out of keeping with the spirit of the game.

icklaus has designed a beautiful private course at Castle Pines, near Denver. Its appeal of high class is already attracting golfers from all over the West. It possesses the very kind of turf-nursery atmosphere that Jack dislikes, but is a long and demanding test. We can look for Jack Nicklaus to greatly influence tomorrow's courses, adopt the best of the appealing features he sees as he plays golf everywhere in the world. No three-time British Open champion could think that Pete Dye's updated Scottish features are valueless, that wastelands are a waste, that lots of roll is too much trickery. The Nicklaus organization is now working on a course near Scottsdale, Ariz., called Highlands at Pinnacle Peak, a site that gives Jack the opportunity to use great, natural desert sand areas to create a links-type course without greatly altering the spirit of the environment. He has gone to the extreme of importing sand for the traps to match the red native soil.

The two golfing greats whom Jack superseded in tournament golf, Arnold Palmer and Gary Player, also are in the golf architectural business. Palmer has joined with Ed Seay, who designed the very distinctive Sawgrass course adjacent to the new Players course and which was the scene of the early Tournament Players Championship. Ed is a highly practical designer whose Sawgrass course was so good that it made the

Golf Digest top 100 in very short order and inspired Pete Dye to outdo him. He knows how to use dunesland and marshland, and his thinking is pretty well summed up in the statement, "We don't have a trademark. If people recognize our work, that means we've got lazy and done something wrong." The variety in their work can be seen in such diverse Palmer-Seay courses as Kapalua in Hawaii, Broadmoor South in Colorado and Saddlebrook in Florida.

A few years ago Gary Player teamed up with Ron Kirby, a designer from Atlanta, Ga., and a long-time employee of the Trent Jones organization. With these credentials, the Kirby-Player team began to design courses around the world. Among their new courses is the one at Sun City in South Africa, site of the world's first $1 million tournament, played in 1981. In the United States Kirby-Player have designed a course near the lovely Winter Park (Colo.) resort that may turn out to be one of the great courses in the Rockies.

ne of the most outspoken of the top architects is Joe Finger. Many of his courses in the Southwest and West, where water is often in short supply, reflect his philosophy of low-maintenance rough areas. He is practicing what he preaches at such courses as Burning Rock, near completion in Grand Junction, Colo., and the Laredo Country Club course at Laredo, Tex. At these courses, he is using native grasses in the roughs and from the tees to the fairways, a distance of about 100 yards.

Finger's affection for the natural Scottish look extends to the manicuring of traps. He prefers shaggy to sharp edges, using fescues or blue grasses in Northern climates and zoysia in the South. He advocates, however, far fewer sand traps, pointing out that judicious use of grass bunkers can make a golf course more beautiful with lower maintenance. He says, "They can be mowed short for regular play so as not to unduly penalize the average golfer. But let them grow three to four inches, and even the best players will find them more difficult to 'get up and down' than from sand."

Other than Pete Dye, the greatest influence on today's and tomorrow's courses is and probably will continue to be the team of George and Tom Fazio. There isn't a great architect who doesn't give credit to the land when he has been able to design a great golf course. George Fazio has always had a keen instinct for selecting dramatic land with special playing and esthetic values—for spotting the natural advantages on a piece of property and using them well.

robably, George is best known for designing Jupiter Hills in Florida, where he created a course with an unusual variety of holes, aided by some mounds of relatively high elevation for otherwise flat Florida terrain. He says he used one hill 14 times simply by adding six to 10 feet of soil in different places.

Yet he opposes overworking any site and feels, as do many of his design colleagues, that Pete Dye moves too much soil—700,000 cubic yards or more per course. He also opposes changing the character of the land. "Whatever we have in this country is better than Scotland or the Swiss Alps."

Tom Fazio strongly subscribes to his uncle's philoso-

phy that a course should be as natural as possible. He has been more adventuresome, however, in creating unusual visual effects. These are strongly in evidence at the new Vintage Club course in Palm Springs, Calif., which is nothing less than spectacular. Tom has managed to accentuate the natural beauty by moving some of the rock formations in and around water holes and other conspicuous locations. He also has employed some mounds and steep pot bunkers.

he course Tom may become best known for is Wild Dunes, near Charleston, S.C., where developer Ray Finch was amenable to relinquishing some of his most valuable ocean-front property for the golf course. As a result, the 17th and 18th sweep along natural ocean dunesland, perhaps more refreshing than anything on the East Coast of the United States. They provide a smashing finish to a course that moves from severely rolling land into natural woods of live oaks and Southern pines, and then across marshland before turning along the ocean.

With designers like the Fazios, the 1970s brought to the world of golf a new look in courses. American architects like Trent Jones Jr. and Sr., exported the expensive American style abroad to foreign landscapes, often where few thought golf courses could be built, and even back to the British Isles. During the same decade Pete Dye accelerated his efforts to import the Scottish links look to such unlikely places as Edmond, Okla. The amalgamation of established American design concepts and the Scottish values we once abandoned already has begun to produce in the '80s some unusual golf courses, several depicted in this chapter. Enlightened golf course designers on both a national and a regional level are responding to new ideas, competition and the changing needs of the times with the most dramatic and practical golf courses ever built.

Today, course architecture requires close familiarity with earth-moving equipment, elaborate irrigation and watering systems, and golf course grasses. In retrospect, it seems incredible that four of the top 10 of *Golf Digest*'s greatest course list were designed by amateurs in the pre-Jones era, using horses and mules pulling scrapers to move and shape land.

There is great hope that tomorrow's courses will be planted with grasses requiring less water, with a stronger resistance to heat and cold, and a higher tolerance of weeds and salt. Plant breeders are trying to develop a Bermuda grass that can survive in Connecticut, and a bent that would grow well in Miami. The USGA, which funds turf research at various universities, recently sponsored a trip to higher regions of South Africa in search of a Bermuda grass with more hardiness. The organization hopes to launch a $5 million program in support of grass research and development over the next 10 years.

Golfers who play American courses can look forward to more challenge, not in length but in shot-making; more surprise, not so much in the hidden as in the overt, and more color contrast between areas where the ball is supposed to land and where it is not. If some of the lushness disappears in places, it will have been for the good cause of lower maintenance, if not for the survival of the game. The end result will be a stimulating and long-overdue change.

AMERICA'S 100 GREATEST COURSES

Golf Digest's selection of America's 100 Greatest Courses is the product of careful research involving almost 200 selectors from every region of the United States. The list is revised every two years and, rather than representing a final judgment, is more a biennial pause for reflection on what makes a great course.

With each succeeding revision, improvements are made in the rating procedure. That is, the selection panel itself is refined, as well as the course listing. Today, that panel includes an impressive cross-section of professionals, amateurs, administrators, local officials, journalists and historians, each of whom relishes his assignment and takes a lively interest in trying out new courses.

The first list, published in 1966, was based solely on the U.S. Golf Association course rating system, which was primarily a measurement of distance. The toughest was Runaway Brook (now The International) in Bolton, Mass., which could be stretched to 8,000 yards.

In subsequent revisions, selectors were asked to rate courses on the basis of the skill of a scratch golfer playing from tees used in formal competition. The list was reduced to 100 and named the "Greatest Tests of Golf," stressing resistance of courses to low scores in competition. Over the years, however, the selectors increasingly placed emphasis on more qualitative values, and the name was changed simply to "Greatest Golf Courses." Today, the panel is guided by the following criteria:

"A great course should test the skills of a scratch player from the championship tees, challenging him to play all types of shots. It should reward well-placed shots and call on the golfer to blend power and finesse. Each hole should be memorable. There should be a feeling of enticement and a sense of satisfaction in playing the course. The design should offer a balance in both length and configuration, and the course should be properly maintained."

Perhaps no course measures up to the above criteria better than Cypress Point, that remarkable thing of beauty perched on the Monterey Peninsula. Over the past 15 years, it has moved gradually in ranking from the fifth 10 to the top 10. Without doubt, many golfers could name dozens of courses that are tougher to score on than Cypress, whose competitive record of 64 is frequently threatened. But are there more than a handful that are greater? Not in the opinion of the panel, despite the fact that the course contains three par 4s of less than 340 yards and an 18th hole so weak that Jimmy Demaret once called Cypress "the best 17-hole course in the world."

Such seeming weaknesses are more than outweighed by some truly classic holes, qualities of play and esthetic values. It is these qualities, these credentials that the selectors feel comprise greatness.

AMERICA'S TOP 50 COURSES

by Ross Goodner

Since *Golf Digest* began singling out courses in the United States for recognition—first for difficulty, then for "greatness"—a place among the chosen few has increasingly become a source of pride for the clubs and their memberships.

This recognition has come to mean so much, in fact, that many golf course architects consider in a sense that they have "arrived" when one of their creations breaks into the 100 Greatest Courses.

Despite *Golf Digest*'s unending efforts to improve the selection panel and refine the selection process, there still is a lot of subjectivity to any such listing. Course design itself is an art, rather than a science, and thus it is impossible to state that one course is, say, the 37th best in the country while another is 38th.

Given this fact of life, the editors have always felt it was best to divide the list of 100 courses into certain broad sub-categories, such as the Top Fifty, Top Ten, etc., and list the courses alphabetically within the grouping.

Herewith, the Top Fifty, as chosen by *Golf Digest*'s national panel of selectors.

OAKLAND HILLS C.C. (SOUTH)	7,067	72	1918
Birmingham, Mich.—Donald Ross/Robert Trent Jones			
OAKMONT C.C.	6,989	72	1903
Oakmont, Pa.—William and Henry Fownes			
OLYMPIC CLUB (LAKE)	6,748	71	1924
San Francisco—Wilfrid Reid			
PEBBLE BEACH GOLF LINKS	6,806	72	1919
Pebble Beach, Calif.—Jack Neville			
PINE VALLEY G.C.	6,765	70	1922
Clementon, N.J.—George Crump/H.S. Colt			
SEMINOLE G.C.	6,778	72	1929
North Palm Beach, Fla.—Donald Ross			
SOUTHERN HILLS C.C.	6,886	71	1935
Tulsa, Okla.—Perry Maxwell			
WINGED FOOT G.C. (WEST)	6,956	72	1923
Mamaroneck, N.Y.—A.W. Tillinghast			

SECOND TEN

(In alphabetical order)	YARDS	PAR	YEAR
AUGUSTA NATIONAL G.C.	7,040	72	1932
Augusta, Ga.—Alister Mackenzie			
BALTUSROL G.C. (LOWER)	7,069	72	1922
Springfield, N.J.—A.W. Tillinghast			
COLONIAL C.C.	7,121	70	1935
Fort Worth, Tex.—John Bredemus			
HARBOUR TOWN LINKS	6,652	71	1969
Hilton Head Island, S.C.—Pete Dye			
LOS ANGELES C.C. (NORTH)	6,811	71	1911
Los Angeles—George Thomas			
MEDINAH C.C. (#3)	7,032	71	1930
Medinah, Ill.—Tom Bendelow			
MUIRFIELD VILLAGE G.C.	7,101	72	1974
Dublin, Ohio—Jack Nicklaus/Desmond Muirhead			
PINEHURST C.C. (#2)	7,020	72	1925
Pinehurst, N.C.—Donald Ross			
RIVIERA C.C.	7,101	71	1926
Pacific Palisades, Calif.—George Thomas/Billy Bell			
SHINNECOCK HILLS G.C.	6,740	70	1891
Southampton, N.Y.—Willie Dunn/William Flynn			

FIRST TEN

(In alphabetical order)	YARDS	PAR	YEAR
CYPRESS POINT CLUB	6,506	72	1928
Pebble Beach, Calif.—Alister Mackenzie			
MERION G.C. (EAST)	6,498	70	1912
Ardmore, Pa.—Hugh Wilson			

THIRD TEN

(In alphabetical order)	YARDS	PAR	YEAR
CASCADES G.C. (UPPER)	6,566	71	1923
Hot Springs, Va.—William Flynn			
CHAMPIONS G.C. (CYPRESS CREEK)	7,166	71	1959
Houston—Ralph Plummer			
FIRESTONE C.C. (SOUTH)	7,173	70	1929
Akron, Ohio—Bert Way/Robert Trent Jones			
JUPITER HILLS CLUB	6,870	72	1970
Jupiter, Fla.—George and Tom Fazio			
OAK HILL C.C. (EAST)	6,964	70	1926
Rochester, N.Y.—Donald Ross			
PINE TREE G.C.	7,121	72	1962
Boynton Beach, Fla.—Dick Wilson			
POINT O'WOODS G. & C.C.	6,884	71	1958
Benton Harbour, Mich.—Robert Trent Jones			
PRAIRIE DUNES C.C.	6,379	70	1937
Hutchinson, Kan.—Perry Maxwell/Press Maxwell			
QUAKER RIDGE G.C.	6,745	70	1916
Scarsdale, N.Y.—A.W. Tillinghast			
THE GOLF CLUB	7,251	72	1967
New Albany, Ohio—Pete Dye			

FOURTH TEN

(In alphabetical order)	YARDS	PAR	YEAR
BUTLER NATIONAL G.C.	7,303	72	1974
Oak Brook, Ill.—George and Tom Fazio			
CANTERBURY G.C.	6,877	71	1922
Cleveland—Herbert Strong			

	YARDS	PAR	YEAR
CHERRY HILLS C.C.	7,185	71	1922
Englewood, Colo.—William Flynn			
C.C. OF NORTH CAROLINA	7,164	72	1963
Pinehurst, N.C.—Ellis Maples/Willard Byrd			
INVERNESS CLUB	6,982	71	1903
Toledo, Ohio—Donald Ross			
LAUREL VALLEY G.C.	7,045	71	1960
Ligonier, Pa.—Dick Wilson			
PEACHTREE G.C.	7,042	72	1948
Atlanta—Robert Trent Jones			
SAN FRANCISCO G.C.	6,623	71	1915
San Francisco—A.W. Tillinghast			
SAUCON VALLEY C.C. (GRACE)	7,044	72	1957
Bethlehem, Pa.—David Gordon			
SCIOTO C.C.	6,917	71	1912
Columbus, Ohio—Donald Ross/Dick Wilson			

FIFTH TEN

(In alphabetical order)	YARDS	PAR	YEAR
BALTIMORE C.C. (FIVE FARMS)	6,675	70	1921
Baltimore—A.W. Tillinghast			
BAY HILL CLUB	7,119	71	1961
Orlando, Fla.—Dick Wilson			
BOB O'LINK G.C.	6,944	72	1916
Highland Park, Ill.—Donald Ross/H.S. Colt/C.H. Alison			
COG HILL G.C. (#4)	6,911	72	1964
Lemont, Ill.—Dick Wilson/Joe Lee			
CONCORD G.C.	7,205	72	1963
Kiamesha Lake, N.Y.—Joe Finger			
CONGRESSIONAL C.C.	7,125	72	1924
Bethesda, Md.—Devereaux Emmet/Robert Trent Jones			
DORAL C.C. (BLUE)	7,065	72	1962
Miami, Fla.—Dick Wilson			
JDM C.C. (EAST)	7,096	72	1962
Palm Beach Gardens, Fla.—Dick Wilson			
LANCASTER C.C.	6,445	70	1920
Lancaster, Pa.—William Flynn			
OAK TREE G.C.	7,015	71	1976
Edmond, Okla.—Pete Dye			

AUGUSTA NATIONAL
Azaleas, dogwoods and the remarkable vision of Bobby Jones

Augusta National is the best-known golf course in the world. All golfers—and countless non-golfers—know that it is the home of the Masters, which is seen by millions on their television sets each April. Ask any of them what the Masters reminds them of, and you'll get a rush of responses like Bobby Jones, Sarazen's double-eagle, the birth of Arnie's Army, the failures of Ken Venturi and Ed Sneed, Eisenhower's cottage, Nicklaus' five victories, the crusty Clifford Roberts, azaleas and dogwoods and the tears of Roberto de Vicenzo.

Because of the welter of memories it evokes—or despite it—Augusta National is so identified in the public mind with the Masters that it's difficult to judge the course on its own. Some in the game think it's overrated, but most of the players feel otherwise.

Augusta National, for a tree-lined course starting its sixth decade, is a relatively wide-open layout. Long hitters are allowed to cut loose through most of a round. The difference between a 75 and a 68 is usually a man's fortunes on the greens. Most of the surfaces are gigantic, presenting an inviting target from well out in the fairway. But, upon closer inspection, they become terrors for putting. An approach to the wrong side of a green can leave an almost certain three-putt. During the 1970s the greens gradually lost some of their firmness and quickness—to the detriment of the course, most felt. But the club overhauled the surfaces completely in 1980 and 1981, restoring most of the fear.

The emphasis on placement and on putting was no accident of birth. After his retirement from competition in 1930, Bobby Jones began to think about creating his own course—and he had definite ideas of what he wanted it to be. Not the least of Jones' attributes was common sense, and he showed it by engaging Dr. Alister Mackenzie as the architect. Mackenzie, fresh from creating Cypress Point in California, was, so to speak, at the top of his game when he joined Jones.

The course itself was a winner from the start, yet it was far different from the Augusta National of today. Over the years several architects, including Robert Trent Jones, Perry Maxwell and George Cobb, were called in to change a green here, add a bunker there. Trent Jones, for example, created an entirely new 16th hole, one that bears no resemblance to the original. But if the course has been modified to fit the times, it has never ceased to be one of the game's great tests, not to mention one of its most beautiful.

Deceptively short for a par 5, at 465 yards, the 13th requires a well-placed drive if the golfer hopes to clear the creek in front of the green with his second shot.

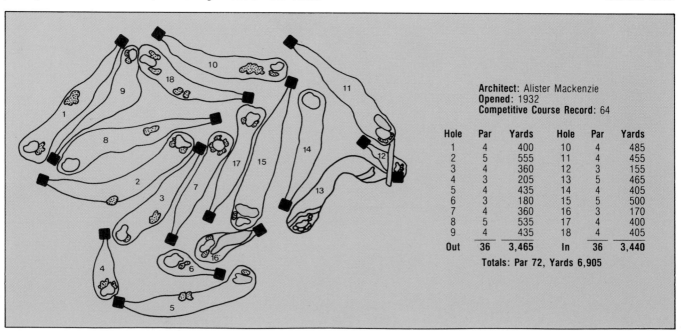

Architect: Alister Mackenzie
Opened: 1932
Competitive Course Record: 64

Hole	Par	Yards	Hole	Par	Yards
1	4	400	10	4	485
2	5	555	11	4	455
3	4	360	12	3	155
4	3	205	13	5	465
5	4	435	14	4	405
6	3	180	15	5	500
7	4	360	16	3	170
8	5	535	17	4	400
9	4	435	18	4	405
Out	**36**	**3,465**	**In**	**36**	**3,440**

Totals: Par 72, Yards 6,905

Three men who were instrumental in the success of the Masters: Bobby Jones, who conceived the tournament; Clifford Roberts, who made certain it ran at peak efficiency, and Arnold Palmer, whose stirring deeds helped make it a major championship.

Year in and year out, the 12th hole—the heart of Amen Corner—is a key to the outcome of the Masters. Variable winds can cause a well-struck shot to fall short into Rae's Creek or sail into a bunker beyond the green.

MASTERS WINNERS		
1934 Horton Smith	284	
1935 Gene Sarazen	282	
(won playoff from		
Craig Wood 144-149)		
1936 Horton Smith	285	
1937 Byron Nelson	283	
1938 Henry Picard	285	
1939 Ralph Guldahl	279	
1940 Jimmy Demaret	280	
1941 Craig Wood	280	
1942 Byron Nelson	280	
(won playoff from		
Ben Hogan 69-70)		
1943-45 no tournaments		
1946 Herman Keiser	282	
1947 Jimmy Demaret	281	
1948 Claude Harmon	279	
1949 Sam Snead	282	
1950 Jimmy Demaret	283	
1951 Ben Hogan	280	
1952 Sam Snead	286	
1953 Ben Hogan	274	
1954 Sam Snead	289	
(won playoff from		
Ben Hogan 70-71)		
1955 Cary Middlecoff	279	
1956 Jack Burke	289	
1957 Doug Ford	283	
1958 Arnold Palmer	284	
1959 Art Wall	284	
1960 Arnold Palmer	282	
1961 Gary Player	280	
1962 Arnold Palmer	280	
(won playoff with 68 from		
Gary Player, 71;		
Dow Finsterwald, 77)		
1963 Jack Nicklaus	286	
1964 Arnold Palmer	276	
1965 Jack Nicklaus	271	
1966 Jack Nicklaus	288	
(won playoff with 70 from		
Tommy Jacobs, 72;		
Gay Brewer, 78)		
1967 Gay Brewer	280	
1968 Bob Goalby	277	
1969 George Archer	281	
1970 Billy Casper	279	
(won playoff from		
Gene Littler 69-74)		
1971 Charles Coody	279	
1972 Jack Nicklaus	286	
1973 Tommy Aaron	283	
1974 Gary Player	278	
1975 Jack Nicklaus	276	
1976 Ray Floyd	271	
1977 Tom Watson	276	
1978 Gary Player	277	
1979 Fuzzy Zoeller*		
Tom Watson,		
Ed Sneed	280	
1980 Seve Ballesteros	275	
1981 Tom Watson	280	
1982 Craig Stadler*,		
Dan Pohl	284	
*Won sudden-death playoff.		

BALTIMORE–FIVE FARMS

Slick greens, sidehill lies and a thinking man's course

Golf was played at Baltimore Country Club as early as 1898. A year later the U.S. Open was held there. So when the Five Farms additional course was built in 1925, it was considered to be merely the suburban branch of the club. However, Five Farms was designed by A.W. Tillinghast and it was apparent from the onset that this was to become another championship test. Three years later, Leo Diegel won the PGA Championship there, ending the four-year reign of Walter Hagen.

Five Farms was built in the rolling Maryland countryside best known for its horse farms. The course isn't long and it doesn't have an abundance of bunkers, but it has slick greens and lots of sidehill lies. And, like all of Tillinghast's courses, it requires considerable thought.

Canadian Sandy Somerville beat Johnny Goodman to win the 1932 U.S. Amateur at Five Farms. In 1965 Britain and Ireland tied the U.S. in the Walker Cup matches there. At about this time Five Farms became the "East" course after the West course was built on the property following the club's sale of its original grounds to the city of Baltimore.

It is said there isn't much sand on the Five Farms Course of Baltimore Country Club, but golfers getting their first look at the 608-yard par-5 14th have been known to think otherwise. Shown here is part of the area called Hell's Half Acre.

Leo Diegel, who won the 1928 PGA Championship at Five Farms to snap Walter Hagen's streak at four, constantly sought relief from putting miseries. The extreme method shown here helped for a while and became widely known as "diegeling."

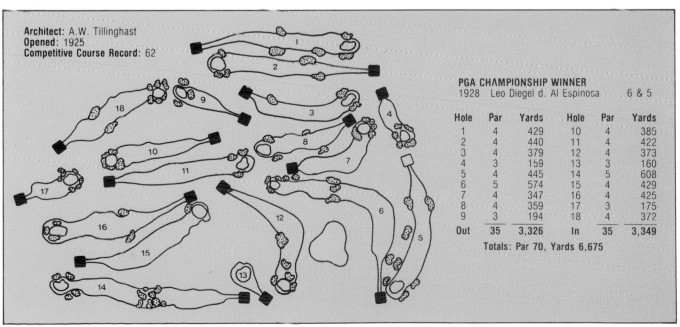

Architect: A.W. Tillinghast
Opened: 1925
Competitive Course Record: 62

PGA CHAMPIONSHIP WINNER
1928   Leo Diegel d. Al Espinosa   6 & 5

Hole	Par	Yards	Hole	Par	Yards
1	4	429	10	4	385
2	4	440	11	4	422
3	4	379	12	4	373
4	3	159	13	3	160
5	4	445	14	5	608
6	5	574	15	4	429
7	4	347	16	4	425
8	4	359	17	3	175
9	3	194	18	4	372
Out	35	3,326	In	35	3,349

Totals: Par 70, Yards 6,675

BALTUSROL–LOWER
A classic course redesigned for modern players

It's no wonder the United States Golf Association repeatedly holds its Open championship at Baltusrol Golf Club, considering the stirring deeds that always seem to take place there.

In 1903 Willie Anderson won the second of his four Open titles at Baltusrol. Then, in 1915, amateur Jerry Travers, driving with an iron because his woods were so unreliable, took the measure of his pro-fessional rivals. Things really got exciting in 1936 when Harry Cooper, the leading shotmaker of the day, completed four rounds over the Upper Course in 284, two strokes under the tournament record. This was seemingly enough to give him a long-overdue Open title, until little-known Tony Manero came in a short while later with 282—and Cooper was thwarted again.

Or how about 1954? Ed Furgol, in the left rough on the 18th hole of the Lower Course, deliberately played to the 18th fairway of the adjoining Upper Course, then pitched back to the green of the Lower and won the ti-

The dashing Johnny Farrell, a fashion-
plate of the 1920s, also won his share of
titles, including the 1928 U.S. Open.
Then he settled down to a long and
distinguished career at Baltusrol.

One of golfdom's great views is the
celebrated fourth hole at Baltusrol with
the handsome clubhouse in the
distance. The hole calls for a shot of 196
yards over water to a huge, two-level
green, and has often been ranked
among America's Best 18 Holes.

tle, by a slender stroke over Gene Littler.

In 1967 it was Jack Nicklaus' turn, even though he almost was upstaged by an unknown Mexican-American named Lee Trevino. Jack, paired with Arnold Palmer the last day, hit two shaky shots on the par-5 18th hole, then hit a colossal 1-iron to the green and holed a 20-footer for a birdie, a round of 65 and a tournament record of 275.

Nicklaus then outdid himself in 1980, opening with a 63 and finishing with a four-round total of 272 to break his own record by three strokes. The victory was his fourth in the Open, tying him with Anderson, Bob Jones and Ben Hogan.

All this derring-do actually took place over three different courses at the New Jersey club. The club began as a nine-hole course in 1895 and got its name from Baltus Roll, a farmer who had been murdered on the spot some 70 years earlier. The course had been expanded to 18 holes by 1901, when the USGA staged its first championship there—the Women's Amateur. That was the course over which Anderson and Travers won their Opens. Then, in 1920, the club engaged A.W. Till-

inghast, one of the game's outstanding course architects, to design two new layouts, a process he was to repeat a few years later at Winged Foot. The Lower has come to be recognized as one of golf's great courses, but many of the club's members speak just as highly of the Upper.

Before the 1954 Open the club brought in Robert Trent Jones to remodel the Lower Course, and his work there ranks with his face-lift jobs at Firestone and Oakland Hills. One of the most notable marks he left on the course is the par-3 fourth hole, a beauty that requires a 196-yard carry over a pond. When the pin is cut in the back left of the green, a close approach shot is almost impossible. Certain club officials felt the hole was too difficult and made their opinions known to Jones during a friendly round after the remodeling was complete. At the fourth, the architect stood by while the others teed off (one of them was Johnny Farrell, the club's professional for more than 40 years), then drilled a shot that hit the green, bounced and rolled into the cup for an ace. There was no further talk about the hole's difficulty.

The demanding 17th hole, the first of two straight par 5s that give Baltusrol its closing wallop, was the scene of an emotional display by Jack Nicklaus as he closed in on his fourth U.S. Open title in 1980.

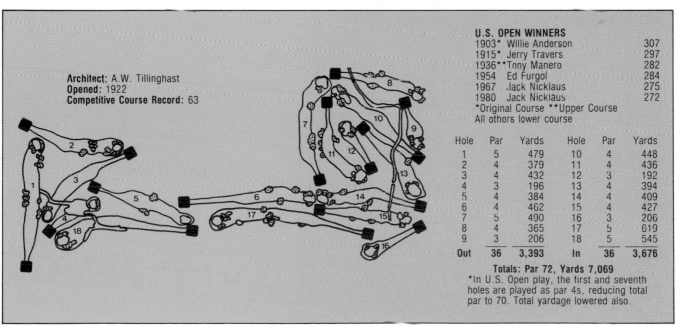

Architect: A.W. Tillinghast
Opened: 1922
Competitive Course Record: 63

U.S. OPEN WINNERS

Year	Winner	Score
1903*	Willie Anderson	307
1915*	Jerry Travers	297
1936**	Tony Manero	282
1954	Ed Furgol	284
1967	Jack Nicklaus	275
1980	Jack Nicklaus	272

*Original Course **Upper Course
All others lower course

Hole	Par	Yards	Hole	Par	Yards
1	5	479	10	4	448
2	4	379	11	4	436
3	4	432	12	3	192
4	3	196	13	4	394
5	4	384	14	4	409
6	4	462	15	4	427
7	5	490	16	3	206
8	4	365	17	5	619
9	3	206	18	5	545
Out	**36**	**3,393**	**In**	**36**	**3,676**

Totals: Par 72, Yards 7,069
*In U.S. Open play, the first and seventh holes are played as par 4s, reducing total par to 70. Total yardage lowered also.

BAY HILL
A difficult layout that finishes with a flurry

Not surprisingly, when Arnold Palmer decides to redesign a golf course he creates one that is tough but fair. That's what happened at Bay Hill, where Palmer took a good Dick Wilson course and made it into a layout that is one of the most demanding tests on the PGA Tour. The club was founded in 1961 by a group of Nashville, Tenn., businessmen, who engaged Wilson to lay out a course in a picturesque orange grove. Palmer first saw the course when he went there for an exhibition in 1965. He was so taken with it that he and a group of partners sought to lease the property. The group eventually signed the lease in 1970 and then exercised an option to buy the course in 1976.

Bay Hill has two lodges, each with 36 guest rooms, and 27 holes of golf on 155 acres that range in altitude from 115 to 170 feet above sea level, a not insignificant elevation for Florida. The 7,065-yard layout features a strong finishing stretch: a 446-yard par 4, a 223-yard par 3 (which is one of Palmer's favorite holes anywhere) and a 456-yard par 4.

Yet good as these holes are, they are unlikely to remain unchanged. Arnie, the Great Tinkerer, is certain to make periodic modifications.

In addition to producing such first-class winners as Andy Bean and Tom Kite, the Bay Hill Classic has also become known for rough early-season weather that wouldn't be out of place at the Crosby Pro-Am. Even Arnie can't control that.

Tom Kite, who has established himself more as a money winner than a tournament winner, made the Bay Hill Classic one of his rare triumphs with a 1982 playoff victory over Jack Nicklaus and Denis Watson.

The home hole at Bay Hill, seen here from behind the green, is one of the more demanding finishing holes. The 456-yard dogleg was toughened when Arnold Palmer moved the previous green and brought water more into play.

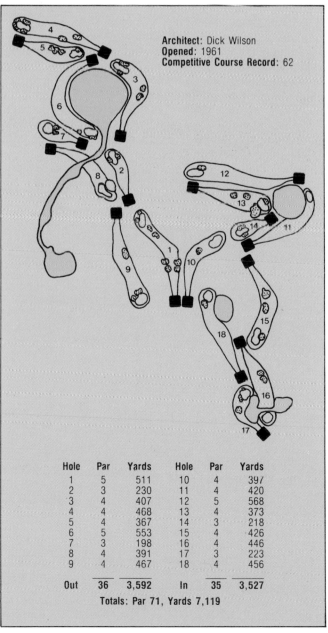

Architect: Dick Wilson
Opened: 1961
Competitive Course Record: 62

Hole	Par	Yards	Hole	Par	Yards
1	5	511	10	4	397
2	3	230	11	4	420
3	4	407	12	5	568
4	4	468	13	4	373
5	4	367	14	3	218
6	5	553	15	4	426
7	3	198	16	4	446
8	4	391	17	3	223
9	4	467	18	4	456
Out	**36**	**3,592**	**In**	**35**	**3,527**

Totals: Par 71, Yards 7,119

BOB O'LINK
A men-only club with a superbly conditioned course

Bob O'Link is one of the nation's few men-only golf clubs that didn't start that way. It opened for play in 1917 as a family club of 100 regular and 25 special members. But in 1921 the club voted to make the facilities open to men only by a vote of 110 to 69. Two weeks later a slate of directors favoring readmission of women was defeated. This was the only opposition slate in the club's history and it has been men-only to this day, except for the time women spectators were allowed on the course during the 1928 Western Amateur.

The club was chartered in March, 1916, bought the Bob O'Link Farm in Highland Park and hired Donald Ross to design a course. He responded with a layout of 6,400 yards at a cost of approximately $50,000.

In 1923 the club bought an additional 36 acres west of the present drainage canal, and over the next two years the course was redesigned by the firm of Colt, Alison and Mackenzie, who put the third through the seventh holes on the new acreage and installed a watering system. Ken Killian and Dick Nugent did some retouching in 1968.

Bob O'Link is a superbly conditioned course whose fairways are so lush that the ball rolls very little after landing. Thus the course plays "long."

Other alterations have been made to the course over the years. In 1960 a lake adjoining the second and eighth holes was constructed as a reservoir and to afford new water hazards. Since then, three other lakes

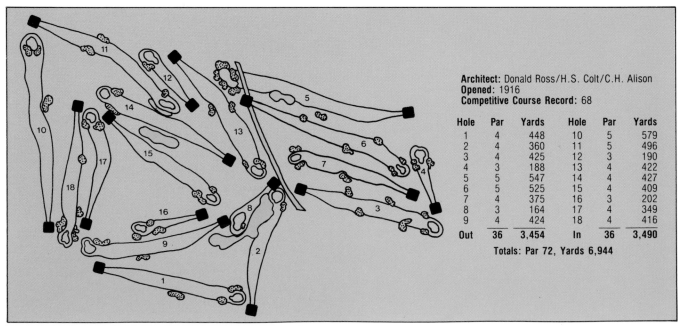

Architect: Donald Ross/H.S. Colt/C.H. Alison
Opened: 1916
Competitive Course Record: 68

Hole	Par	Yards	Hole	Par	Yards
1	4	448	10	5	579
2	4	360	11	5	496
3	4	425	12	3	190
4	3	188	13	4	422
5	5	547	14	4	427
6	5	525	15	4	409
7	4	375	16	3	202
8	3	164	17	4	349
9	4	424	18	4	416
Out	36	3,454	In	36	3,490

Totals: Par 72, Yards 6,944

have been constructed. In 1976 a new green was constructed on the fifth hole across the drainage canal.

Another change, one that will make the course even more demanding, is still developing. Because of the loss of hundreds of elm trees, Bob O'Link has planted more than 10,000 in the last 20 years and, as these mature, the course will become one of the most wooded in the area.

Except for the 1928 Western Amateur, in which Frank Dolp beat Chick Evans in the semifinals and Gus Novotny in the final, the club has hosted no established championships. Still, most of the game's leading players have tested Bob O'Link and the course record is held by Byron Nelson with a 68.

It remains a true golf club. No swimming pool; no tennis courts. Just a beautiful—and demanding—golf course.

There's not a lot of water on the Bob O'Link course, but what there is of it has a strong effect on the golfer's strategy. On the 360-yard second hole, for example, an approach shot over the lake can be downright frightening.

BUTLER NATIONAL
Scene of the highest scores on tour

"Excluding the U.S. Open sites, Butler is the toughest course we play," says touring pro Tom Kite. "If they fixed it up like an Open course, let the rough grow and slicked up the greens, it would be unplayable." Dave Stockton agrees. "If the USGA ever got its hands on this course," he says, "it would be all over." When scoring figures were compiled after the 1975 season, Butler National, the site of the Western Open, had the highest scoring rating for the pro tour, with an average for all rounds played of 75.34. This made it fractionally tougher than Medinah, its neighbor in the Chicago suburbs, which was host to that year's U.S. Open. All this suits Butler National's 150 members just fine. The philosophy of the founders back in 1968 was to create a championship course. That's the message they gave architect George Fazio, and that's what Fazio created.

The club was named for Paul Butler, founder of Butler Aviation and one of the four men who organized the club. The others were Sam Dean, Red Harbour and William Gahlberg.

The course can be stretched to some 7,300 yards, water comes into play on 11 holes and the greens are tough to read. No wonder it has the tour's highest stroke average.

Tom Weiskopf, a supremely talented player who is awesome when he gets everything together, did just that at Butler National when he won the 1982 Western Open with a dramatic birdie on the final hole.

A lake on the left and a creek in front of the green make the 10th at Butler National an extremely demanding par 4. At 448 yards, it requires two strong, accurate shots.

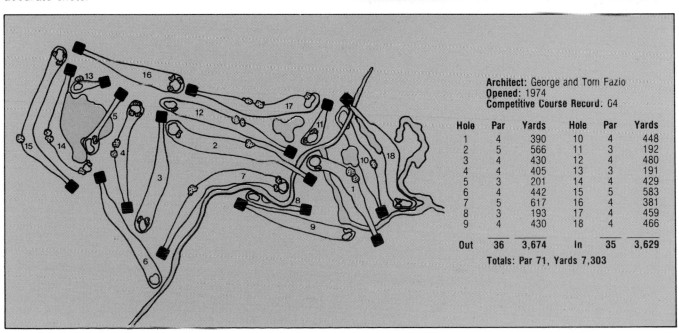

Architect: George and Tom Fazio
Opened: 1974
Competitive Course Record: 64

Hole	Par	Yards	Hole	Par	Yards
1	4	390	10	4	448
2	5	566	11	3	192
3	4	430	12	4	480
4	4	405	13	3	191
5	3	201	14	4	429
6	4	442	15	5	583
7	5	617	16	4	381
8	3	193	17	4	459
9	4	430	18	4	466
Out	**36**	**3,674**	**In**	**35**	**3,629**

Totals: Par 71, Yards 7,303

Cleveland, Ohio

CANTERBURY

Small greens and severe rough make up for a lack of length

Canterbury has small, elevated greens and tees that are exposed to the winds off Lake Erie, and the rough is punishing. In short, it is a demanding test, which explains why the club, founded in 1921, has played host to many championships over the years. The first significant one was the 1932 Western Open, won by Walter Hagen with a score of 287, one under par, and in 1937 the Western was won by Ralph Guldahl in a playoff.

Lawson Little won the Open in 1940 by defeating Gene Sarazen in a playoff that could have involved three players. In one of the most bizarre developments in Open history, six players teed off ahead of schedule in order to get in ahead of an approaching storm. The six were promptly disqualified even though one of them, Porky Oliver, had come in with a 287 that tied Little and Sarazen. Years later, Sarazen said he wished Oliver had been allowed to compete in the playoff. "With those two big-hitters trying to out-drive each other," he said, "I might have managed to sneak in and win the tournament."

The 1942 Open had been assigned to Interlachen in Minneapolis, but it was canceled because of World War II. When the championship was scheduled to resume in 1946, Interlachen declined and the tournament returned to Canterbury. Lloyd Mangrum, Byron Nelson and Vic Ghezzi tied after 72 holes with 284, and each shot 72 in the playoff the next day. In the second playoff Mangrum shot 72 again to beat the others by a stroke.

Lawson Little, one of the game's longest hitters, won the 1940 U.S. Open at Canterbury in a playoff with veteran Gene Sarazen. It was the last of Little's five major titles.

One of the most demanding holes at Canterbury is the 201-yard seventh, which calls for a long iron from an elevated tee to an elevated green. Three bunkers and out-of-bounds on the right can complicate matters.

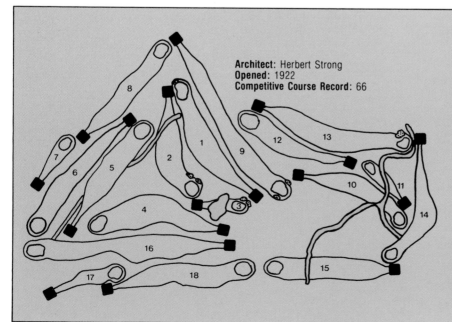

Architect: Herbert Strong
Opened: 1922
Competitive Course Record: 66

U.S. OPEN WINNERS
1940	Lawson Little*	287
1946	Lloyd Mangrum**	284

*Won playoff against Gene Sarazen, 70-73.
**Won 36-hole playoff (72-72) against Byron Nelson (72-73) and Vic Ghezzi (72-73).

PGA CHAMPIONSHIP WINNER
1973	Jack Nicklaus	277

Hole	Par	Yards	Hole	Par	Yards
1	4	430	10	4	360
2	4	372	11	3	165
3	3	180	12	4	372
4	4	439	13	5	490
5	4	405	14	4	385
6	5	500	15	4	358
7	3	201	16	5	605
8	4	410	17	3	232
9	5	535	18	4	438
Out	**36**	**3,472**	**In**	**36**	**3,405**

Totals: Par 72, Yards 6,877

*In tournament play, the 13th hole measures 465 yards, par 4, reducing total yardage to 6,852 and par to 71.

40

CASCADES–UPPER

A hilly and demanding layout that requires a variety of shots

"There isn't any kind of hill you don't have to play from, or any kind of shot you won't hit there," says Sam Snead of the Cascades Course at The Homestead. "If you could train a youngster to play on that course, he'll play anywhere." Snead grew up just down the road from Hot Springs in Virginia's mountain region and has been playing the Cascades course almost from its inception in 1923, the second of Homestead's three layouts. The first dates from 1892, while the third opened in 1962.

The Homestead was founded by Melville Ezra Ingalls and has occupied an elegant and opulent place among America's spas.

It was at the Cascades that Catherine Lacoste, the French amateur star, surprised and dismayed a field of American professionals in winning the 1967 U.S. Open. She led from the start and her margin had increased to seven strokes early in the final round before trouble struck. Louise Suggs, starting nine shots behind, made up eight of them, but double-bogeyed the 16th. Lacoste steadied her game and finished birdie-par for a one-stroke triumph over Susie Maxwell and Beth Stone.

The Cascades has always been ranked among America's greatest courses, and there are many who feel it is *the* best mountain course. Designed by William Flynn, it's even more demanding because of the beautiful surroundings that distract the golfer from the business at hand.

A meandering stream adds difficulty to the 17th hole (center) and 18th (left) on the Cascades Course at The Homestead, a lovely and demanding layout that was the spawning ground of Sam Snead. It also is where Catherine Lacoste became the only amateur to win the U.S. Women's Open in 1967.

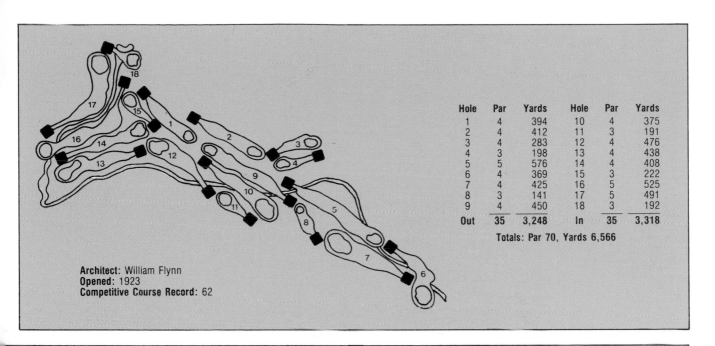

Hole	Par	Yards	Hole	Par	Yards
1	4	394	10	4	375
2	4	412	11	3	191
3	4	283	12	4	476
4	3	198	13	4	438
5	5	576	14	4	408
6	4	369	15	3	222
7	4	425	16	5	525
8	3	141	17	5	491
9	4	450	18	3	192
Out	35	3,248	In	35	3,318

Totals: Par 70, Yards 6,566

Architect: William Flynn
Opened: 1923
Competitive Course Record: 62

CHAMPIONS – CYPRESS CREEK

Trees, trees, trees and no need for bunkers

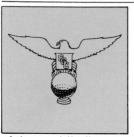

"We wanted a club right in our hometown that would be to Houston what Augusta National is to Georgia, what Pinehurst is to North Carolina and what Pebble Beach is to the California coastline," says Jimmy Demaret of the Champions Golf Club. "Jackie and I have played most of the world's finest courses and we modeled the holes at Champions after the great ones we have seen." Demaret and his partner, Jack Burke Jr., launched their project back in 1957 on 500 heavily wooded acres about 20 miles north of downtown Houston. The area was not particularly affluent, but it soon became so after members bought an additional 1,500 acres for homesites.

Ralph Plummer designed Champions' first course—Cypress Creek—and he had the benefit of the vast knowledge of the owners: Demaret, winner of three Masters titles, and Burke, winner of a Masters and a PGA Championship. Their "advice" consisted of hitting countless shots to the projected sites of greens to make certain they played as planned.

Because of the abundant trees, Plummer didn't feel the need to build any bunkers, and, in fact, there were none in the beginning. Even today, they are scarce.

Cypress, with its 70,000 trees, was opened in 1959 and its companion Jackrabbit Course, designed by George Fazio, opened in 1964. They are presided over by an ample, if not lavish, clubhouse and the whole enterprise is run by Demaret and Burke. As Jack once put it: "Jimmy and I decided we would run the club our way. You can't run a club smoothly through a board of directors, however brilliant each member may be in his own field. One wants a swimming pool, one wants some tennis courts and another wants to fix up a couple of holes. So everything suffers."

The Champions Club achieved prominence in 1969 when Orville Moody, a 35-year-old former Army sergeant, won the U.S. Open by a stroke from Deane Beman, Al Geiberger and Bob Rosburg. Moody, who had failed to make the cut in his only other Open appearance, seven years earlier, had a 72-hole score of 281. Bob Murphy and Miller Barber dominated the first three rounds of the tournament, but Moody outsteadied them and moved ahead to stay on the 12th hole of the final round. Geiberger three-putted the 16th and Rosburg missed a three-footer on the 18th. Moody, who left the Army after 14 years to try his luck on the golf tour, has never won another major tournament.

Another who played a role—although a tragic one—at Champions was Ben Hogan, who entered the 1971 Champions International as a favor to his old partner, Demaret. Hogan shot a 67 and a 65 in practice, but there was no magic once the tournament began. On the fourth hole, a 228-yard par 3, Hogan hit a ball into the ravine, strained his knee trying to climb down after the ball, then limped back to the tee, from where he hit two more into the gulch before finally holing out in 9. He continued to play until the group reached the 12th tee, then he sent for a golf car and rode back to the clubhouse and out of tournament golf forever. "Don't ever get old," he said to a friend as he rode away.

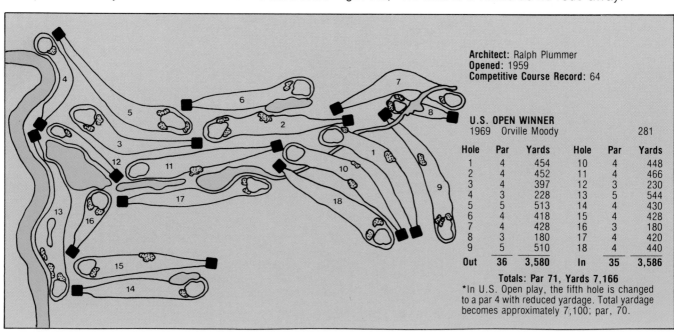

Architect: Ralph Plummer
Opened: 1959
Competitive Course Record: 64

U.S. OPEN WINNER
1969   Orville Moody   281

Hole	Par	Yards	Hole	Par	Yards
1	4	454	10	4	448
2	4	452	11	4	466
3	4	397	12	3	230
4	3	228	13	5	544
5	5	513	14	4	430
6	4	418	15	4	428
7	4	428	16	3	180
8	3	180	17	4	420
9	5	510	18	4	440
Out	**36**	**3,580**	**In**	**35**	**3,586**

Totals: Par 71, Yards 7,166
*In U.S. Open play, the fifth hole is changed to a par 4 with reduced yardage. Total yardage becomes approximately 7,100; par, 70.

From the back tees the 228-yard, par-3 fourth at Champions is literally a dogleg for all but low-handicappers. It was here that Ben Hogan, in his final tournament appearance, hit three drives into the gulch and wound up taking nine strokes.

The owners and operators of the Champions Club and its 36 holes are two of Houston's favorite sons: Jimmy Demaret (left) and Jack Burke Jr. The club is now the hub of an affluent residential area north of Houston.

CHERRY HILLS
Memories of Palmer, Hogan, Guldahl and other great players

The most dramatic shot ever struck at Cherry Hills was in the final round of the 1960 U.S. Open when Arnold Palmer, his river of adrenalin flowing bank full, drove the first green, 355 yards away. Palmer two-putted for his birdie 3 and went on to shoot a 65, win the tournament and send Arnie's Army charging into battle.

Although the 1960 Open was Cherry Hills' most notable occasion, it was not by any means the club's first brush with championship golf. Back in 1938 Ralph Guldahl, then in the middle of a notable championship streak, won his second straight U.S. Open with a 284. And in 1941 Vic Ghezzi reached a career Rocky Mountain high when he beat Byron Nelson on the 38th hole of their PGA final. In the 1938 Open, Ray Ainsley set a tournament record for futility when he took 19 strokes on the 16th hole in the second round.

Designed by William Flynn in 1922, Cherry Hills is both demanding and pivotally historical. While Palmer

was winning the 1960 Open, two of his challengers—paired together—were 47-year-old Ben Hogan and 20-year-old Jack Nicklaus. Jack finished second at 282, still the lowest score ever posted by an amateur in the Open, and gave clear notice of things to come. Hogan, seeking a fifth Open title, saw his precise little pitch to the 71st green spin back into the water. He also drove into the water on the 18th and finished four strokes back, never again to be a genuine threat in the championship.

The Age of Palmer was firmly launched when Arnie (left) won the 1960 U.S. Open at Cherry Hills. Jack Nicklaus, who finished second—as an amateur—was almost simultaneously setting the stage for an "era" of his own.

On the formidable 18th hole, the golfer bites off as much of the lake with his tee shot as he thinks he can handle.

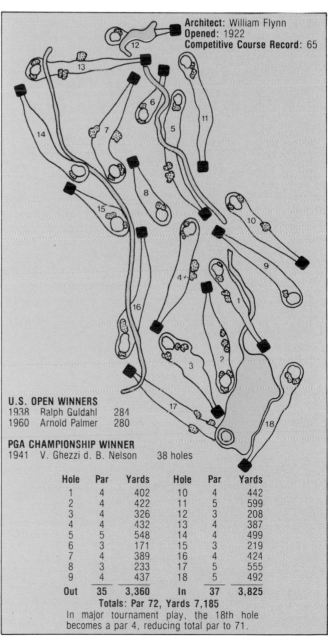

Architect: William Flynn
Opened: 1922
Competitive Course Record: 65

U.S. OPEN WINNERS
1938 Ralph Guldahl   284
1960 Arnold Palmer   280

PGA CHAMPIONSHIP WINNER
1941 V. Ghezzi d. B. Nelson   38 holes

Hole	Par	Yards	Hole	Par	Yards
1	4	402	10	4	442
2	4	422	11	5	599
3	4	326	12	3	208
4	4	432	13	4	387
5	5	548	14	4	499
6	3	171	15	3	219
7	4	389	16	4	424
8	3	233	17	5	555
9	4	437	18	5	492
Out	**35**	**3,360**	**In**	**37**	**3,825**

Totals: Par 72, Yards 7,185
In major tournament play, the 18th hole becomes a par 4, reducing total par to 71.

COG HILL—4
A man named Jemsek creates a publinx haven

Although Cog Hill's four-course complex is synonymous around Chicago with Joe Jemsek, the owner, the place actually was named for the original owners, the Coghill brothers. Jemsek, who used to caddie at Cog Hill, had told the brothers he would own the place someday, and in 1951 he made good on his promise by purchasing the then 36 holes from Marty Coghill, the surviving brother. The No. 1 and No. 2 courses had been designed by Bert Coghill. In 1962 Jemsek hired the celebrated Dick Wilson to design two more courses, one of which—No. 4—became the well-known "Dubsdread," one of the nation's outstanding public courses. Wilson abandoned the project at one point following a disagreement with Jemsek, but subsequently returned to finish the job. Joe Lee, Wilson's associate, did much of the work on No. 4

But the soul of Cog Hill is Jemsek, of whom John Husar wrote: "When he reached the point where he could afford to do nice things for people, Jemsek became known as everyone's 'first touch.' He filled out the raffle books that came in the mail. He dumped thousands of dollars into church and school program ads. Whenever a worthy group needed help, he cut his own prices to the bone. The Illinois PGA might never have developed a tournament schedule if Jemsek had not let it play his courses for free. And he usually added a purse. And afterward, he fed the guys who ran the tourneys. Jemsek sacrificed untold income by closing his courses to paying customers so qualifying rounds could be held for national events. His heart is forever with public links players."

Cog Hill No. 4, whose 11th green is in the foreground, is an obvious combination of challenge and beauty typical of Dick Wilson courses. No less highly regarded is its owner, Joe Jemsek, long-time PGA professional who regularly makes Cog Hill available for important area events, such as U.S. Open qualifying rounds.

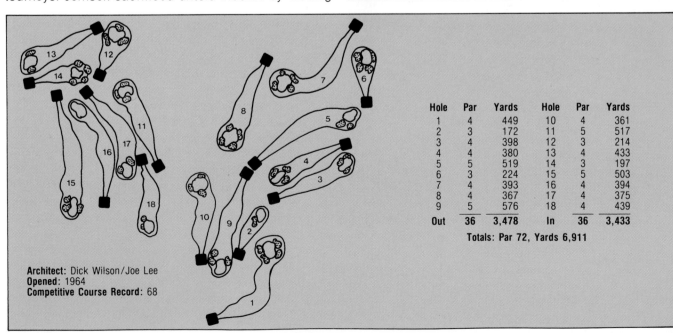

Hole	Par	Yards	Hole	Par	Yards
1	4	449	10	4	361
2	3	172	11	5	517
3	4	398	12	3	214
4	4	380	13	4	433
5	5	519	14	3	197
6	3	224	15	5	503
7	4	393	16	4	394
8	4	367	17	4	375
9	5	576	18	4	439
Out	36	3,478	In	36	3,433

Totals: Par 72, Yards 6,911

Architect: Dick Wilson/Joe Lee
Opened: 1964
Competitive Course Record: 68

Fort Worth, Texas

COLONIAL
There are no "catch-up" holes here

In 1940, when the prize fund for the U.S. Open was only $6,000, it is said that Fort Worth millionaire Marvin Leonard went to the U.S. Golf Association with a check for $25,000 and said, "We want next year's Open." By "we" he meant Colonial Country Club, and Colonial got the 1941 Open, becoming the first southern club ever to host the championship.

Craig Wood won it, despite playing in a corset to support his ailing back, and the event was such a success that Leonard and the other Colonials decided they would like tournament golf on a regular basis. The result was the Colonial National Invitation, which began in 1946 and has been won by some of golf's greatest, including five times by Ben Hogan, a lifelong friend of Leonard.

Perry Maxwell lost a bid to design the course back in 1936 (John Bredemus got the assignment), but Leonard retained Maxwell to build three new holes for the 1941 Open. These were the third, fourth and par-4 fifth, the latter being—at 466 yards—one of the toughest holes in the country. In fact, the entire course—collectively—falls into that category.

Colonial has suffered its share of misfortune. The clubhouse has twice burned down, and a flooding Trinity River in 1949 did so much damage to some of the holes that it's common to hear the line: "If you think the course is tough now, you should have seen it before the river tore it up."

A noted touring pro once remarked that "there are no catch-up holes" at Colonial. Certainly, anyone with a birdie in mind wouldn't be likely to find it on the eighth, a 209-yard par 3 whose destination is a sand-locked green.

Ben Crenshaw has had his ups and downs at Colonial. Everything came together in 1977 when he won the Colonial National Invitational PGA Tour event with a 272, which was a record for 72 holes. The following year he didn't make the cut.

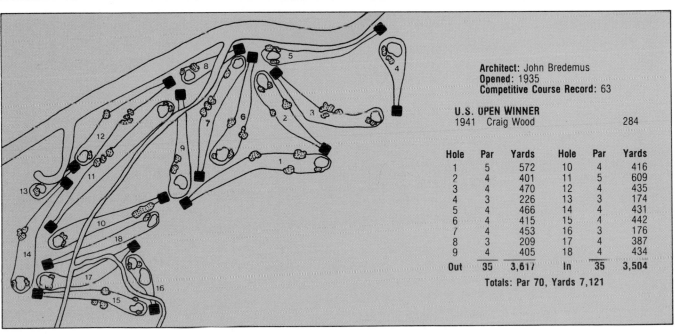

Architect: John Bredemus
Opened: 1935
Competitive Course Record: 63

U.S. OPEN WINNER
1941   Craig Wood   284

Hole	Par	Yards	Hole	Par	Yards
1	5	572	10	4	416
2	4	401	11	5	609
3	4	470	12	4	435
4	3	226	13	3	174
5	4	466	14	4	431
6	4	415	15	4	442
7	4	453	16	3	176
8	3	209	17	4	387
9	4	405	18	4	434
Out	**35**	**3,617**	**In**	**35**	**3,504**

Totals: Par 70, Yards 7,121

CONCORD

Even the best players can't "chop it up"

When architect Joe Finger began work on a new course at the Concord Hotel in 1960, he got unequivocal instructions from Ray Parker, the general manager. "I want a golf course that Arnold Palmer and Jack Nicklaus can't chop up," he said. "Just build us the greatest golf course in the world." The result in 1964, was The Monster, a course that may not be the best in the world, but ranks as one of the toughest to score on.

The Monster, one of three courses at the Concord Hotel, in the heart of New York's Catskill Mountains, not only is difficult, it can be set up to play even tougher. In response to Parker's original instructions, Finger designed the course with an optimum length of almost 7,700 yards. It's never been extended to that extreme—the normal tournament length is 7,200 yards and the regular yardage is a stern 6,800.

The big 18 holes at the Concord provide a rolling, parkland course with dense woods, plenty of water, a modest number of fiendishly placed bunkers and—on top of everything else—great beauty. Jimmy Demaret

Ed Furgol, winner of the 1954 U.S. Open, was the club's professional for several years.

Although the Concord can be stretched to impossible lengths, its difficulty doesn't depend on sheer yardage, as can be seen from the abundance of trees and other obstacles in this aerial view of the great Catskills course.

and Jack Burke, directors of golf at the Concord in the early 1960s, put together a 36-hole pro competition in 1965, and Tommy Bolt won with rounds of 71 and 74. Frank Wharton and Bolt share the course record with 68.

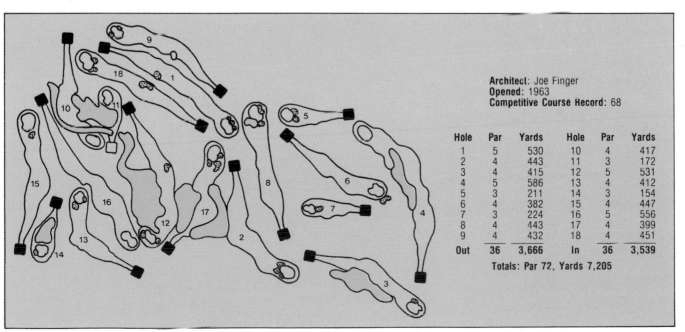

Architect: Joe Finger
Opened: 1963
Competitive Course Record: 68

Hole	Par	Yards	Hole	Par	Yards
1	5	530	10	4	417
2	4	443	11	3	172
3	4	415	12	5	531
4	5	586	13	4	412
5	3	211	14	3	154
6	4	382	15	4	447
7	3	224	16	5	556
8	4	443	17	4	399
9	4	432	18	4	451
Out	36	3,666	In	36	3,539

Totals: Par 72, Yards 7,205

CONGRESSIONAL
A championship course in more ways than one

"How does a championship course acquire such a rank? The ways are various. A few are born that way. Others are worked over and refined through a succession of major events. Still others must undergo the painful process of wholesale face-lifting. This last had been the experience of the Congressional Country Club near Washington before the U.S. Open was played there in 1964." That's how Joseph C. Dey described the evolution of Congressional from a testing but not spectacular suburban country club course into the inferno through which Ken Venturi struggled to a memorable victory in that 1964 Open.

Congressional had been angling for a U.S. Open for several years before 1964, but the USGA—as Dey recalls—felt the course wasn't strong enough. The next move was to bring in Robert Trent Jones, who already had gained fame through his face-lifting at Oakland Hills and Baltusrol. Jones designed a new nine at Congressional, and the club was able to land the 1959 U.S. Women's Amateur, won by Barbara McIntire. After Jones came back and renovated nine holes of the original course, the club got the Open again.

When the USGA decided to make the 465-yard, downhill 17th the finishing hole instead of the regular par-3 18th, the ingredients were there for a memorable championship.

Tommy Jacobs shot a 64 in the second round, and as the field prepared to play 36 holes on Saturday—the last time this has been done—he led Arnold Palmer by one stroke and Venturi by six. The weather was brutally hot and humid and although Venturi shot a 30 on the front nine, he came in with a 36 with bogeys on the last two holes and was in such a state of exhaustion that a physician had to be summoned. There was doubt that he could continue over the long, rolling course with elevated greens, but, with the doctor in attendance and fortified by a thermos of iced tea, Venturi went back out for the afternoon round and shot a 70 to win by four strokes with 278, despite being in a state of imminent collapse. The dramatic victory indelibly impressed Congressional in the minds of golfers everywhere as the scene of one of the game's great moments.

The PGA Championship was held at Congressional in 1976, and Dave Stockton won for the second time when he holed a 12-foot putt on the final green.

Actually, the club at Congressional was championship-caliber from the beginning, even though it took another four decades for the course itself to reach that level. Herbert Hoover was head of the Founders Club, and when the clubhouse opened in 1924, President Calvin Coolidge presided. For many years Congressional was the playground of senators, judges and assorted captains of industry, yet it was never totally solvent.

The facility was turned over to the government during World War II and was used as an OSS training ground. But in 1946 the club was reopened and within five years had reached its membership ceiling of 1,000. Then came Trent Jones, followed by Ken Venturi and the permanent label: championship course.

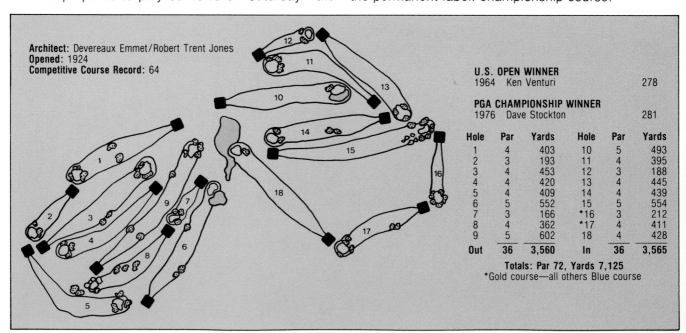

Architect: Devereaux Emmet/Robert Trent Jones
Opened: 1924
Competitive Course Record: 64

U.S. OPEN WINNER
1964   Ken Venturi   278

PGA CHAMPIONSHIP WINNER
1976   Dave Stockton   281

Hole	Par	Yards	Hole	Par	Yards
1	4	403	10	5	493
2	3	193	11	4	395
3	4	453	12	3	188
4	4	420	13	4	445
5	4	409	14	4	439
6	5	552	15	5	554
7	3	166	*16	3	212
8	4	362	*17	4	411
9	5	602	18	4	428
Out	**36**	**3,560**	**In**	**36**	**3,565**

Totals: Par 72, Yards 7,125
*Gold course—all others Blue course

There could hardly be a more majestic setting for the finish of a championship than the 18th at Congressional with the clubhouse looming in the background. Here, in scenes from the club's shining hour, Ken Venturi selects a club for his approach to the par-4 18th (below), and then, after holing his final putt (right), his expression is a mixture of elation, relief and exhaustion.

C.C. OF NORTH CAROLINA
Tall pines, rolling fairways and an island green

Probably no golf course was conceived under more adverse conditions than the Country Club of North Carolina.

When Richard Urquhart Jr. of Raleigh heard that an ideal piece of golf course property was available in the Carolina Sandhills, near Pinehurst, he and his friend Skipper Bowles drove 70 miles through a sleet storm and walked the property for several hours in miserable conditions. "We didn't have a nickel's worth of sense between us," Urquhart said. They took an option to buy, however, formed an investment group and engaged William Byrd and Ellis Maples to lay out the course, which weaves around tall pines and abundant lakes. Ground was broken in January, 1963, and the course was opened for play 11 months later. A third nine was built in 1970 and Trent Jones later altered all three before designing a fourth nine himself. The two nines that make up the Dogwood course constitute the 100 Greatest layout.

Hal Sutton, who later turned professional, won the 1980 U.S. Amateur here by trouncing Bob Lewis, 9 and 8.

There are a number of water shots at the Country Club of North Carolina, but none is more demanding than at the 16th, a 204-yard par 3 that, from the back tees, is almost all carry.

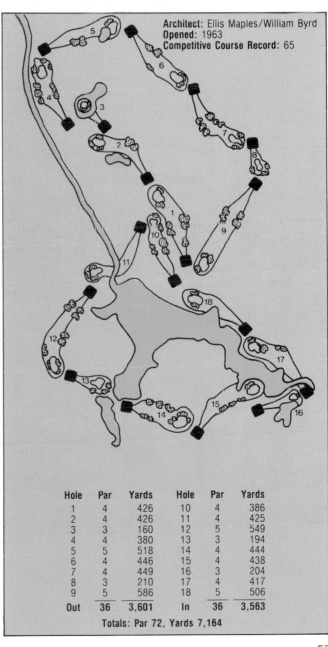

Architect: Ellis Maples/William Byrd
Opened: 1963
Competitive Course Record: 65

Hole	Par	Yards	Hole	Par	Yards
1	4	426	10	4	386
2	4	426	11	4	425
3	3	160	12	5	549
4	4	380	13	3	194
5	5	518	14	4	444
6	4	446	15	4	438
7	4	449	16	3	204
8	3	210	17	4	417
9	5	586	18	5	506
Out	36	3,601	In	36	3,563

Totals: Par 72, Yards 7,164

CYPRESS POINT
The "Sistine Chapel of golf"

More than one noted golfer has confessed that, if forced to play a single course for the rest of his life, he would choose Cypress Point, the masterpiece created by Alister Mackenzie on the Monterey Peninsula. Why? Well, as British golf writer and historian Pat Ward-Thomas once explained: "No golf architect was more richly endowed with natural features for his work than Alister Mackenzie at Cypress Point. Majestic woodland, a hint of links and heathland here and there and the savage nobility of the coast made for unforgettable holes."

The holes are indeed memorable, particularly the 16th and 17th, those spectacular ocean holes that are

The intangible qualities that make Cypress Point unique are readily apparent on the 355-yard par-4 eighth hole, a fascinating amalgam of Scotland, Pine Valley and the Monterey Peninsula.

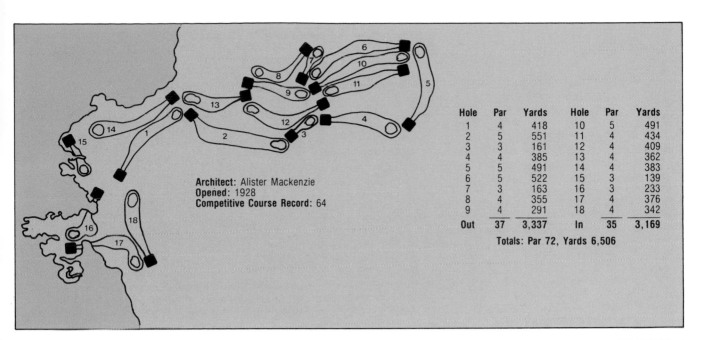

Architect: Alister Mackenzie
Opened: 1928
Competitive Course Record: 64

Hole	Par	Yards	Hole	Par	Yards
1	4	418	10	5	491
2	5	551	11	4	434
3	3	161	12	4	409
4	4	385	13	4	362
5	5	491	14	4	383
6	5	522	15	3	139
7	3	163	16	3	233
8	4	355	17	4	376
9	4	291	18	4	342
Out	**37**	**3,337**	**In**	**35**	**3,169**

Totals: Par 72, Yards 6,506

Properly awed by Cypress Point, but not intimidated by it, was Craig Stadler, who shot a 64 here during the 1982 Bing Crosby National Pro-Am.

One of the most captivating vistas in golf is the panorama of the 376-yard par-4 17th at Cypress, with its gnarled trees, rocks, surf and tantalizingly situated green in the distance.

so often photographed they have become familiar to golfers who haven't been within miles of the course. But there is much more to Cypress Point than just the heroic 233-yard drive over the ocean that tempts pro and duffer alike on the 16th tee. As Cal Brown has written about the peninsula: "There cannot be another place on earth quite like it. It is as though every thundering emotion, every subtle line, had been withheld from the rest of creation and then dumped in this one place to test our understanding of the superlative."

The Crosby tournament, which had begun at Rancho Santa Fe a decade earlier, came to the Monterey Peninsula in 1947, and immediately the world began to hear about Cypress Point and its awesome 16th hole.

The 17th is another magnificent hole, a picturesque 376-yard par 4 on which the golfer must place his drive carefully to avoid being stymied by a cluster of cypress trees in the fairway. It is the rare golfer who, after having come this far, can dispute past USGA president Sandy Tatum's devout observation that Cypress Point "is the Sistine Chapel of golf."

DORAL–BLUE
Long and watery: a Blue Monster

One of the most successful challengers to the Blue Monster has been Raymond Floyd, who won the Doral-Eastern Open in 1980 and 1981. In the latter year he followed with a victory in the Tournament Players Championship to win a $200,000 bonus.

If any one place epitomizes the modern golf resort, that place is the Doral Country Club, a 2,400-acre expanse that includes five golf courses, 660 guest rooms, a convention center and virtually anything else a vacationer might require. The centerpiece of the complex is the celebrated "Blue Monster," a 7,065-yard toughie that is the site of the annual Doral-Eastern Open on the PGA Tour. The Dick Wilson course's famed 18th hole has provided some of golf's most stirring moments.

They called it "Kaskel's Folly" when Alfred Kaskel decided to create his resort on ugly swampland not far from Miami's airport. Even after the job was done, Kaskel was accused of spending his money foolishly, but the popularity of the place soon silenced the critics. The finished product was called Doral, an acronym for Doris (his wife's name) and Alfred. The Doral Open began in 1962 and Billy Casper was the first winner. Subsequent champions have included the likes of Doug Sanders, Jack Nicklaus, and Raymond Floyd.

Tom Weiskopf was involved in two of the most exciting finishes in the tournament's history. In 1968 he overshot the final green and made a double-bogey 6, losing by a stroke to Gardner Dickinson, who hit his second in the water and also took 6. Ten years later, Weiskopf held on to win by a stroke over Nicklaus, who shot 30 on the back nine.

Such hair-raising finishes have become commonplace at Kaskel's Folly.

Sand and water are staples of the golfer's diet at Doral. Shown here are the eighth and 17th holes in the foreground and, beyond them, the par-3 ninth and the famed 18th, where the gallery is packed behind the green.

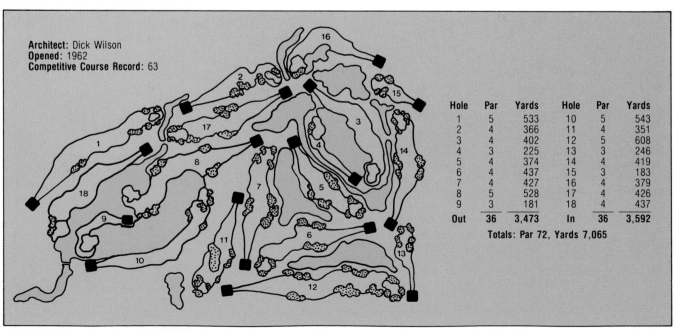

Architect: Dick Wilson
Opened: 1962
Competitive Course Record: 63

Hole	Par	Yards	Hole	Par	Yards
1	5	533	10	5	543
2	4	366	11	4	351
3	4	402	12	5	608
4	3	225	13	3	246
5	4	374	14	4	419
6	4	437	15	3	183
7	4	427	16	4	379
8	5	528	17	4	426
9	3	181	18	4	437
Out	**36**	**3,473**	**In**	**36**	**3,592**

Totals: Par 72, Yards 7,065

Akron, Ohio

FIRESTONE–SOUTH
A difficult test that produces great champions

The story of Firestone Country Club, known to millions of golfers through the televising each year of the World Series of Golf, is divided into two distinct historical periods.

The first began in 1928 when Harvey Firestone built the course principally for the use of his employees at the Firestone Tire and Rubber Co. The course was designed by W.H. (Bert) Way and existed in virtual anonymity for decades until the Rubber City Open was staged there in the 1950s. Then the course was named site of the 1960 PGA Championship, was redesigned by Robert Trent Jones and moved into the second, or modern, stage in its history.

The most successful player at Firestone, Jack Nicklaus has won the American Golf Classic (the tournament that succeeded the Rubber City Open), the 1975 PGA Championship, and five World Series of Golf tournaments.

And for an illustration, there is no better example than the bizarre way Jack played the 16th in winning the 1975 PGA. He drove the ball far into the left rough and it was unplayable behind a large clump of trees. Taking a penalty stroke, Jack went back some 50 yards

until he had some sort of chance to advance the ball past the trees. His third was a long blast across the fairway and behind more trees in the right rough. His fourth was a colossal 9-iron shot over the trees, across the water and all the way to the back of the green, from where he holed a cross-country putt for his par 5.

Al Geiberger, a consistent money-winner on the PGA Tour for two decades, won the 1966 PGA Championship at Firestone, his only major title.

One of many tough holes at Firestone, the 442-yard, par-4 third calls for a demanding second shot over a pond, one of only two on the course.

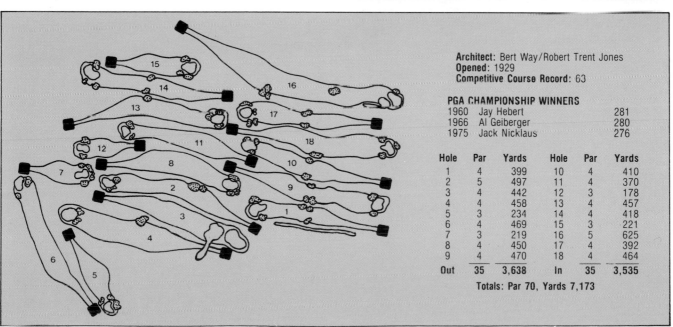

Architect: Bert Way/Robert Trent Jones
Opened: 1929
Competitive Course Record: 63

PGA CHAMPIONSHIP WINNERS
1960	Jay Hebert	281
1966	Al Geiberger	280
1975	Jack Nicklaus	276

Hole	Par	Yards	Hole	Par	Yards
1	4	399	10	4	410
2	5	497	11	4	370
3	4	442	12	3	178
4	4	458	13	4	457
5	3	234	14	4	418
6	4	469	15	3	221
7	3	219	16	5	625
8	4	450	17	4	392
9	4	470	18	4	464
Out	35	3,638	In	35	3,535

Totals: Par 70, Yards 7,173

HARBOUR TOWN LINKS
Railroad ties, 80-yard bunkers and exacting shot requirements

Pete Dye had designed some fine courses before coming to Hilton Head Island, but after he created Harbour Town Golf Links here, he became a recognized celebrity. It helped that Arnold Palmer won the Heritage Classic at Harbour Town right after it was opened, but the course itself was enough to make an architect famous.

Here for the first time, the golfing public saw the vast sandy areas and liberal use of railroad ties that are the Dye trademarks. Here also, it shouldn't be forgotten, the golfing public saw an excellent golf course, one in which Jack Nicklaus had a hand as well.

The par 3s at Harbour Town are superb, but the best-known hole is the fierce 18th, a 458-yard adventure over the marsh that comes as a jolt after the golfer has fought his way through trees for most of 17 holes. It is especially unnerving, coming as it does right after the 169-yard 17th, which requires a carry over water and a menacing, 80-yard-long bunker.

A placid pond and manicured bunkers give a deceptively benign look to the 439-yard eighth hole at Harbour Town. In contrast is the famed finishing hole (right) with its familiar lighthouse behind the green. The 458-yard test calls for a big drive over marshland and a strong approach to a sloping, well-protected green.

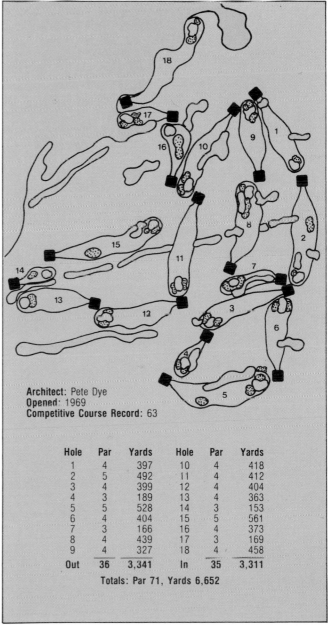

Architect: Pete Dye
Opened: 1969
Competitive Course Record: 63

Hole	Par	Yards	Hole	Par	Yards
1	4	397	10	4	418
2	5	492	11	4	412
3	4	399	12	4	404
4	3	189	13	4	363
5	5	528	14	3	153
6	4	404	15	5	561
7	3	166	16	4	373
8	4	439	17	3	169
9	4	327	18	4	458
Out	36	3,341	In	35	3,311

Totals: Par 71, Yards 6,652

Toledo, Ohio

INVERNESS
Four noted architects had a hand in its design

If a golf course is measured by the number of great people and events that have been associated with it, then Inverness Club, in Toledo, Ohio, has to rank near the top. No fewer than four of the game's most famous architects have left their mark on the course, and some of golf's most notable championships have been played here. The original course was opened in 1903 on 78 acres of land purchased for $12,000. It was designed by Bernard Nicholls, one of the many Scottish pros who migrated to the U.S. at the turn of the century. In 1919 more land was acquired and Donald Ross was brought in to revise the existing nine holes and add nine more. Ted Ray, the long-driving Englishman, won the U.S. Open here the next year. Harry Vardon almost won it—at the age of 50—and the contestants included two 18-year-olds, Bobby Jones and Gene Sarazen. A.W. Tillinghast made some modifications in the course in 1930, and the following year the ''144-hole'' U.S. Open was played. Billy Burke and George Von Elm tied after 72 holes, then played 72 more in a double playoff before Burke won by a stroke.

Dick Wilson was called in for course revisions in 1956, and in 1957 Dick Mayer won the Open in a playoff with Cary Middlecoff. The process was repeated when George Fazio created four new holes in preparation for the 1979 Open, won by Hale Irwin. The rolling course, with its trees, brooks, 110 sand traps and undulating greens, also was the site of the Inverness Fourball.

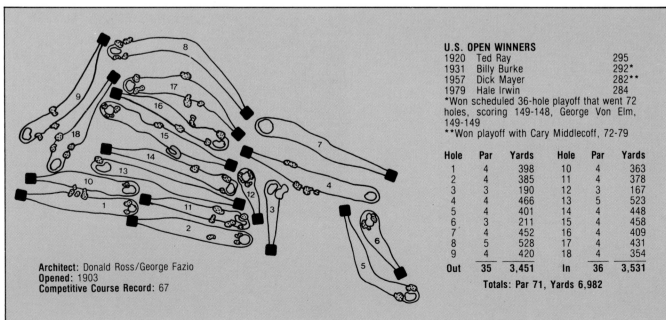

Architect: Donald Ross/George Fazio
Opened: 1903
Competitive Course Record: 67

U.S. OPEN WINNERS
1920	Ted Ray	295
1931	Billy Burke	292*
1957	Dick Mayer	282**
1979	Hale Irwin	284

*Won scheduled 36-hole playoff that went 72 holes, scoring 149-148, George Von Elm, 149-149
**Won playoff with Cary Middlecoff, 72-79

Hole	Par	Yards	Hole	Par	Yards
1	4	398	10	4	363
2	4	385	11	4	378
3	3	190	12	3	167
4	4	466	13	5	523
5	4	401	14	4	448
6	3	211	15	4	458
7	4	452	16	4	409
8	5	528	17	4	431
9	4	420	18	4	354
Out	35	3,451	In	36	3,531

Totals: Par 71, Yards 6,982

One of the shortest finishing holes in championship golf is the 18th at Inverness, a 327-yard par 4 that has withstood the game's best shots during four U.S. Opens.

Among these memorable Opens was the marathon of 1931 in which two 36-hole playoffs were required before Billy Burke won by a stroke. Here, Burke (holding the trophy) is the only one smiling. Herbert Ramsay (left), president of the USGA, and runnerup George Von Elm, are just glad it's over.

The first thought that crosses the golfer's mind when he faces the 388-yard 13th at JDM Country Club is: "You can't get there from here." The liberally trapped, watery course is tough, but not impossible. Sam Snead holds the 72-hole record with a 268 and Jacky Cupit (right) once shot a 63.

JDM-EAST
Dick Wilson's swan song of hazards

If one subscribes to the theory that there are horses for courses, then Jack Nicklaus must have a soft spot in his heart for the JDM Country Club, which by coincidence is just down the road from his home in North Palm Beach, Fla. Back in the days when it was known as the PGA National Golf Club, the East Course at JDM played host to four big tournaments—and Nicklaus won or shared the title in three of them. He and Arnold Palmer won the National Team Championship there in 1966. Then in 1971 Nicklaus scored a double of sorts by capturing both the PGA Championship and the individual title in the World Cup. He and Lee Trevino also won the team title in the latter event.

Those were the glory days for JDM, which was built by multi-millionaire John D. MacArthur and designed by the eminent Dick Wilson. In 1974, following relocation of PGA national headquarters, the club became fully private and has operated since then as JDM.

Every driving area at JDM is threatened by strategic fairway bunkering, lines of tall pine trees or lateral water hazards—and sometimes by all three. There is an angle woven into every one of the full tee-shot holes, ranging from a slight bend near the green, to a full, 90-degree turn on the par-4 13th.

Sam Snead won the 1972 PGA Senior with a 268 total, but the course wasn't at maximum difficulty. When Nicklaus won the PGA Championship, it was with 281, which gives a much clearer indication of its worth.

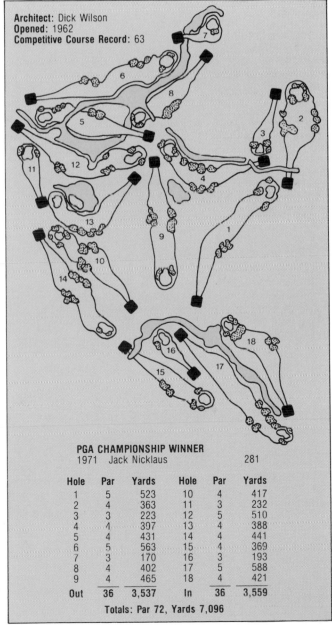

Architect: Dick Wilson
Opened: 1962
Competitive Course Record: 63

PGA CHAMPIONSHIP WINNER
1971   Jack Nicklaus   281

Hole	Par	Yards	Hole	Par	Yards
1	5	523	10	4	417
2	4	363	11	3	232
3	3	223	12	5	510
4	4	397	13	4	388
5	4	431	14	4	441
6	5	563	15	4	369
7	3	170	16	3	193
8	4	402	17	5	588
9	4	465	18	4	421
Out	**36**	**3,537**	**In**	**36**	**3,559**

Totals: Par 72, Yards 7,096

JUPITER HILLS

A south Florida course with a Northern look

Jupiter Hills

Jupiter Hills is the definitive statement by George Fazio, the one-time touring pro who became an outstanding course designer. As if to reemphasize his statement, he incorporated three new holes into the course a few years ago, and he is constantly making subtle improvements. Despite the changes—or because of them—Jupiter Hills is a marvelous course, somewhat reminis-cent of Pine Valley (which also requires strategic shot placement and where Fazio once was the pro), and quite unlike the standard flat Florida courses to be found in abudance only minutes away, Jupiter Hills has a maximum elevation of 70 feet, an almost unheard-of condition in south Florida.

The club was started in 1968 by Fazio, Bob Hope, William Clay Ford and William Elliott. It is an ultra-exclusive place, and Fazio made a special effort to give it a Northern look. About 10,000 trees line the fairways and another 20,000 are grown in a nursery on the

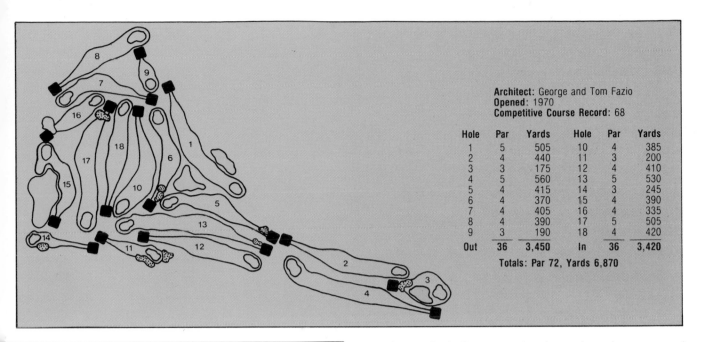

Architect: George and Tom Fazio
Opened: 1970
Competitive Course Record: 68

Hole	Par	Yards	Hole	Par	Yards
1	5	505	10	4	385
2	4	440	11	3	200
3	3	175	12	4	410
4	5	560	13	5	530
5	4	415	14	3	245
6	4	370	15	4	390
7	4	405	16	4	335
8	4	390	17	5	505
9	3	190	18	4	420
Out	36	3,450	In	36	3,420

Totals: Par 72, Yards 6,870

premises. And these are oak and mahogany, not tropical trees.

The par 3s are especially distinctive: the 11th and 14th, which go in opposite directions from adjoining elevated tees, and the ninth, which, from the back tee, rivals anything at Pine Valley. The only thing to equal it is the view from the clubhouse dining room.

Who says all Florida courses are flat? The uphill 18th (left), a 420-yard par 4, and the downhill 11th (below), a 200-yard par 3, are evidence of the changes in elevation at Jupiter Hills.

LANCASTER
A course of continual changes

Like many turn-of-the-century golf clubs, Lancaster today bears little resemblance to the rough layout on which the hazards—besides cow dung—consisted of earthen mounds called chocolate drops. The land was rented and the membership was augmented by leafing through the city directory in search of likely candidates. A milestone was reached in 1911 when the club got an option to buy 150 acres on the site it presently occupies. Nine holes were laid out and work was begun on a new clubhouse, completed in 1914. Additional acreage was purchased in 1919 and William Flynn was hired to design a new course.

Flynn gave the club a lot of advice at low cost, but it was some years before the members realized just how good Flynn was. In the beginning they had little faith in architects and were reluctant to take what he said at face value.

The club's professional in the early 1920s was Cyril Hughes, who weighed only 110 pounds and had one leg shorter than the other. He was, however, a good player and once finished as high as 11th while representing the club in the U.S. Open. He remained with the club until 1934. In 1940 Lancaster bought another 20 acres and the father-son architectural team of William and David Gordon were later retained to build six new holes—four of them on the new land across Conestoga Creek—and revise the others. Finally, in 1948, the club agreed to host the Pennsylvania Amateur, its first important tournament.

The golfer who fails to stay well to the right off the tee of the 16th at Lancaster will have literally nothing but sand between himself and the green on the approach.

Lancaster's professional for many years, 110-pound Cyril Hughes (left), is seen here during a 1927 exhibition match with John Hiemenz, Don Brown and the great Walter Hagen.

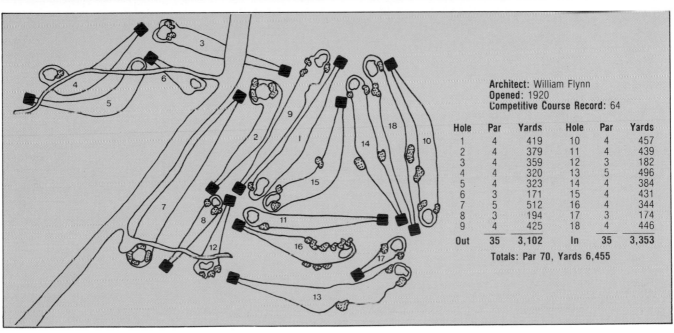

Architect: William Flynn
Opened: 1920
Competitive Course Record: 64

Hole	Par	Yards	Hole	Par	Yards
1	4	419	10	4	457
2	4	379	11	4	439
3	4	359	12	3	182
4	4	320	13	5	496
5	4	323	14	4	384
6	3	171	15	4	431
7	5	512	16	4	344
8	3	194	17	3	174
9	4	425	18	4	446
Out	**35**	**3,102**	**In**	**35**	**3,353**

Totals: Par 70, Yards 6,455

LAUREL VALLEY

A former pheasant farm yields tough birdies

The Laurel Valley Golf Club was founded because, quite simply, a group of Pittsburgh businessmen were looking for a place where they could play golf anytime they felt like it. As Frederick Gwinner, one of the founders, explains it: "We were all members of other area clubs, but as golf grew, so did the demand for golf parties. As time went by, it became a problem; parties tied up the courses. So a group of us decided to build a golf course. Just as a matter of pride, we wanted a good one."

The founders wanted a men-only club with a national membership on the lines of Augusta National or Pine Valley, and they found the land some 50 miles east of Pittsburgh on a gently rolling 260-acre pheasant-shooting preserve owned by the late Richard K. Mellon. They engaged Dick Wilson to design the course. It was opened in 1959, and the members saw a layout with seven lakes, quick greens and a premium on accuracy. The chief change over the years has been the addition of several thousand trees.

Laurel Valley gained national attention in 1965 when Arnold Palmer suggested the members apply for the PGA Championship. They did—and got it. Dave Marr

won by two strokes from Jack Nicklaus and Billy Casper with 280. Palmer and Nicklaus won the National Team title here in 1970 and 1971, and the club hosted the Ryder Cup matches in 1975.

Dave Marr enjoyed the biggest moment of his career at Laurel Valley when he won the PGA Championship here in 1965.

Fairway bunkers give definition to the landing area for the tee shot on the par-4 12th at Laurel Valley.

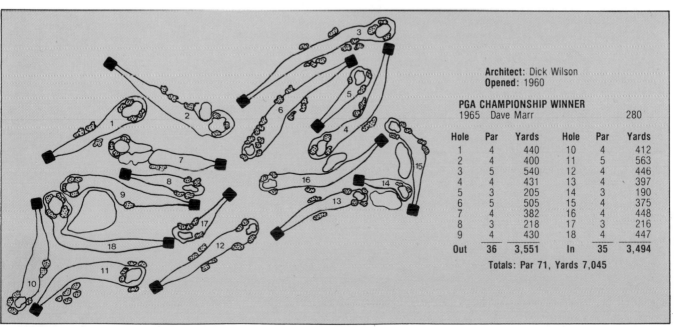

Architect: Dick Wilson
Opened: 1960

PGA CHAMPIONSHIP WINNER

1965   Dave Marr   280

Hole	Par	Yards	Hole	Par	Yards
1	4	440	10	4	412
2	4	400	11	5	563
3	5	540	12	4	446
4	4	431	13	4	397
5	3	205	14	3	190
6	5	505	15	4	375
7	4	382	16	4	448
8	3	218	17	3	216
9	4	430	18	4	447
Out	36	3,551	In	35	3,494

Totals: Par 71, Yards 7,045

LOS ANGELES-NORTH

Transforming a garbage dump into a championship venue

Many of the pioneer golf clubs in the United States had primitive beginnings, but few can match the origins of the Los Angeles Country Club, whose members in 1897 set out nine tomato cans for holes on a rented, 16-acre plot that once had been a garbage dump. The clubhouse was the ruin of an old windmill and the course naturally became known as The Windmill. Despite the makeshift nature of the layout, more than 100 members were playing in less than a year, necessitating a move to a somewhat larger piece of ground. This was followed in 1899 by yet another move, this time to 107 acres that the club purchased and on which was laid out its first 18-hole course.

The prime movers of the club then—and for years thereafter—were Ed Tufts and Joseph Sartori. Tufts, who had been a tennis buff, fell in love with golf and devoted the remaining 30 years of his life to the game. He has been called the father of Southern California golf. Sartori, a banker, handled the club's land and financial problems from the beginning. He then served as club president from 1912 until his death in 1946.

Tufts was involved in one of the favorite anecdotes about the club's primitive beginnings. As the story goes, Tufts sliced a ball near a grazing cow and the beast gobbled up the strange morsel. Tufts untethered the cow, administered many whacks and drove it to the green, where it dropped the ball. Tufts then neatly rolled in his putt and claimed he had holed out in two

strokes. "No you didn't," said his opponent. "You made it in 39. You hit that cow 37 times, for I counted every stroke." Tufts conceded the hole.

Sartori soon found the property that was to become the club's permanent site and prepared to move once again. Although what is the present South Course was laid out in 1907, it wasn't dedicated until 1911, after the previous property had been sold. All the club's courses to this point had been laid out by Tufts and Sartori, plus other members. It wasn't until the club decided to build a second course (the present highly regarded North Course) that an architect was called in. This was George Thomas, whose credits also include Bel-Air, Riviera and Whitemarsh Valley.

The North, at 6,445 yards, par 71, opened in August of 1921 and soon became recognized as one of the area's most demanding. Harry Cooper won the Los Angeles Open there in 1926, Glenna Collett beat Virginia Van Wie for the U.S. Women's Amateur title in 1930, Macdonald Smith won the 1934 Los Angeles Open and Vic Ghezzi won it in 1935.

The combination of distant skyline and menacing bunkers can easily distract the golfer from the task at hand on the 235-yard par-3 11th at Los Angeles Country Club.

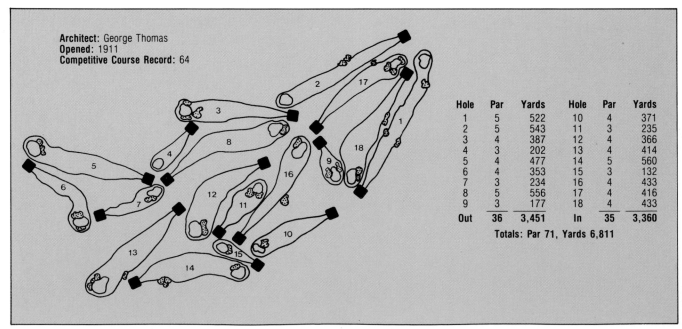

Architect: George Thomas
Opened: 1911
Competitive Course Record: 64

Hole	Par	Yards	Hole	Par	Yards
1	5	522	10	4	371
2	5	543	11	3	235
3	4	387	12	4	366
4	3	202	13	4	414
5	4	477	14	5	560
6	4	353	15	3	132
7	3	234	16	4	433
8	5	556	17	4	416
9	3	177	18	4	433
Out	**36**	**3,451**	**In**	**35**	**3,360**

Totals: Par 71, Yards 6,811

Medinah, Illinois

MEDINAH–3
Low scores are scarce on this tough, tough course

The United States Golf Association, which is known for ribbon-like fairways on its U.S. Open courses, doesn't have to change much when it holds the Open at Medinah No. 3. In 1975, for example, only two fairways had to be narrowed and one actually had to be widened in preparation for the Open, won by Lou Graham in a playoff with John Mahaffey.

Medinah, you see, is trees, trees and more trees, hemming in a collection of dogleg par 4s and demanding par 3s that make the Chicago-area layout one of the toughest tests in the country. In 1949, when Dr. Cary Middlecoff won the first U.S. Open played at Medinah, his winning score of 286 was two over par. Graham and Mahaffey tied at 287 in 1975.

Difficult as it is, Medinah didn't start out that way. Originated by the Shriners (Medinah's clubhouse wouldn't look out of place in Mecca), the club opened in the late 1920s with a course designed by Tom Bendelow. It staged the Medinah Open in 1929, and Harry Cooper won with a score that included a 63 in one

The eminent player and architect George Fazio drives from the tee of the 220-yard 17th at Medinah No. 3, a hole that has ruined the chances of more than one golfer in tournament competition. One who survived was Cary Middlecoff (below), receiving a kiss from his wife, Edie, after winning the 1949 U.S. Open at Medinah.

80

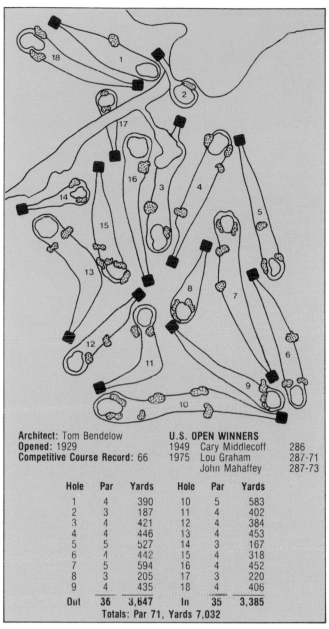

Architect: Tom Bendelow			U.S. OPEN WINNERS		
Opened: 1929			1949 Cary Middlecoff		286
Competitive Course Record: 66			1975 Lou Graham		287-71
			John Mahaffey		287-73

Hole	Par	Yards	Hole	Par	Yards
1	4	390	10	5	583
2	3	187	11	4	402
3	4	421	12	4	384
4	4	446	13	4	453
5	5	527	14	3	167
6	4	442	15	4	318
7	5	594	16	4	452
8	3	205	17	3	220
9	4	435	18	4	406
Out	36	3,647	In	35	3,385

Totals: Par 71, Yards 7,032

round. The members quickly announced a redesign program that would preclude such unwelcome scores in the future—and five new holes were constructed. A Shriners' Open was played at Medinah in 1935 and Cooper won again. This time he shot 289—with no 63s. The club also played host to three Western Opens, and nobody has ever broken 280 for 72 holes.

Medinah has several demanding holes, the best known probably being the 17th, the 220-yard par 3 that calls for a shot over Lake Kadijah. The toughest, however, might be the seventh, a par 5 of almost 600 yards that legend says has never been reached in two shots. Originally small and flat, the green of the seventh now is deeper and has two levels. The change had little effect on the hole's overall difficulty, though; it still can't be reached even by the big hitters.

So Medinah, with its course rating of 74.8 from the championship tees, remains undefeated after half a century. Tommy Armour, once the club's professional, held the course record at 67 for years and even today the 66 shot by Eddie Merrins in 1966 still stands. In a word, Medinah is *tough*.

MERION–EAST

A complex course—rich in history, yet ahead of its time

Some courses are famed because of superb design, others because they have been host to great championships. Merion qualifies on both counts. This classic course, in the lovely, rolling Mainline countryside west of Philadelphia, is relatively short by modern standards, but has such inifinite variety that it has kept the game's best players at bay since its beginning in 1912.

Critics say Merion is an outmoded course that has to be tricked up to be fit to host a U.S. Open. Others say it's so complex that, far from being an anachronism, Merion is a course ahead of its time. Whatever the differences of opinion, the United States Golf Association has held 15 championships at Merion, including four Opens.

Thus the course is rich in history. It was at Merion in 1916 that the 14-year-old Bobby Jones played in his first national championship, the U.S. Amateur, and it was there in 1930 that he won the Amateur to complete golf's fabled Grand Slam. Merion is where Ben Hogan scored perhaps his most memorable triumph, winning the 1950 U.S. Open in a playoff only a year after an automobile crash almost cost him his life. In the 1960

On this hole, the historic 11th, Bobby Jones wrapped up the Grand Slam in 1930. It is also where, in 1934, Bobby Cruickshank tossed his club in the air in elation over carrying the creek after hitting a mediocre shot. The club came down and hit him on the head, bringing him to his knees.

The most recent in Merion's pantheon of champions is David Graham, who set a tournament record of 273 in winning the 1981 U.S. Open by three shots from Bill Rogers and George Burns.

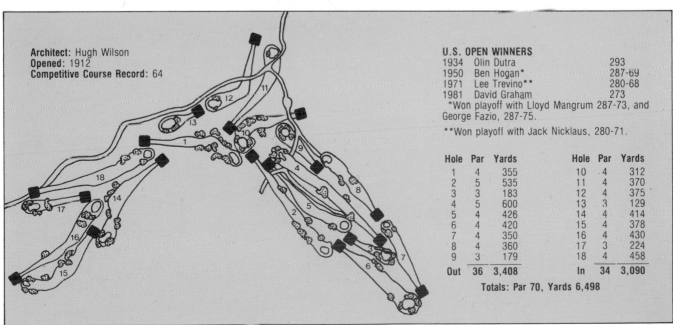

Architect: Hugh Wilson
Opened: 1912
Competitive Course Record: 64

U.S. OPEN WINNERS

1934	Olin Dutra	293
1950	Ben Hogan*	287-69
1971	Lee Trevino**	280-68
1981	David Graham	273

*Won playoff with Lloyd Mangrum 287-73, and George Fazio, 287-75.

**Won playoff with Jack Nicklaus, 280-71.

Hole	Par	Yards		Hole	Par	Yards
1	4	355		10	4	312
2	5	535		11	4	370
3	3	183		12	4	375
4	5	600		13	3	129
5	4	426		14	4	414
6	4	420		15	4	378
7	4	350		16	4	430
8	4	360		17	3	224
9	3	179		18	4	458
Out	**36**	**3,408**		**In**	**34**	**3,090**

Totals: Par 70, Yards 6,498

World Amateur Team Championship, a 20-year-old Jack Nicklaus shot a startling 269 for four rounds.

Merion was designed by Hugh Wilson, a club member who never before dabbled in course architecture. To prepare for the task, Wilson spent several months in Britain and Europe, studying the famed courses there. He must have learned something, because he produced an artful mixture of long and short holes that gives Merion a pace—or change of pace—unmatched among the great courses.

From the first tee, which is only a few feet from the clubhouse veranda and appears to be straight out of an Edwardian garden party, to the stern closing stretch, Merion offers variety. The first six holes, which include the only two par 5s on the course, are the first act of what noted golf writer and editor Jerry Tarde has called Merion's three-act play. Then comes a stretch of seven holes that average only 300 yards each and on which scores invariably exceed expectations. Then one reaches the long finish, the last three of which Gene Sarazen calls the toughest three-hole stretch in the world.

One of the most demanding finishing holes in golf is the 18th at Merion, a 458-yard par 4. It was here that Ben Hogan drilled a 1-iron to the green, setting up the par that tied him for the lead in the 1950 U.S. Open. He won the playoff the next day.

The 16th, the ''quarry'' hole, starts what many believe to be the toughest three-hole finishing stretch in golf. The second shot on the 430-yard hole must carry all the way to the green.

MUIRFIELD VILLAGE

The demanding test that Jack built

The concept for the Muirfield Village Golf Club was born on the veranda of the Augusta National during the 1966 Masters. Jack Nicklaus, gazing in admiration at the scene around him, turned to his longtime friend Ivor Young and said, ''Wouldn't it be great to have something like this in Columbus?'' The golf course that has evolved in the rolling woodland of Dublin, Ohio, on the outskirts of Columbus, now rivals the Augusta National, both as a test for championship play and as a course that members and their guests from around the world can enjoy.

It was named after Muirfield in Scotland, where Jack won his first British Open in 1966. He designed the course, first in collaboration with Desmond Muirhead, but then taking over the entire project himself. It was ready by the summer of 1974, and it was put to its first major test in 1976 when the inaugural Memorial Tournament was played.

The examination proved so difficult it drew some-

what deserved cries of protest from the touring professionals, who are quick to affix the "unfair" label anywhere a ball takes odd and penal bounces. It had taken Roger Maltbie and Hale Irwin 288 strokes of regulation play to earn a playoff in the first event, won by Maltbie. From the onset, Jack had said there would be changes, and he quickly acknowledged the need for them, refining bunkering and green contours, and even substituting a stream for a lake in front of the 538-yard par-5 11th hole.

While the scores at the Memorial are still among the highest on tour, they have come down considerably, and the course has succumbed to some superlative competitive rounds—including 66s by Maltbie and Fuzzy Zoeller in 1982. However, Jack is not about to compromise his beliefs about what makes a great course or a great hole. Until 1980 the par-3 16th had been variously played from three tees, ranging from 173 to 204 yards. Jack feels the hole plays best from the back tees. When Gordon Glenz, the tour's advance man, arrived to set up the 1980 event, Jack told him, "I want to

play from the back, Gordon. Don't make me go out and bulldoze that front tee, because I'll do it if I have to." They played it from the back tees.

What always makes Muirfield a contender for the top 10 among *Golf Digest*'s 100 Greatest is not its resistance to low scores, but the variety of shots it demands from golfers who want to score well. You need, as they say, all the clubs in your bag. The course

One demanding hole after another greets the golfer at Muirfield Village, and one of the most exacting is the ninth, with water in front of both tee and green. It's a 410-yard par 4 that presents a small target for the second shot.

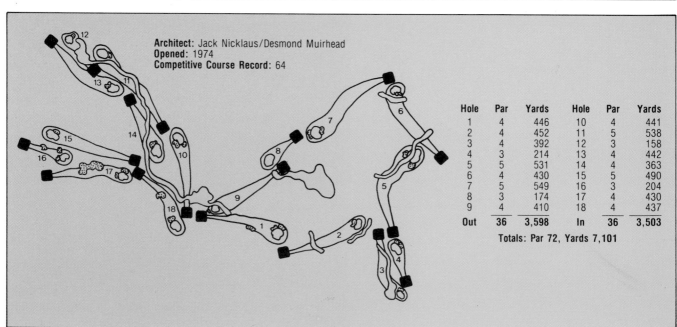

Architect: Jack Nicklaus/Desmond Muirhead
Opened: 1974
Competitive Course Record: 64

Hole	Par	Yards	Hole	Par	Yards
1	4	446	10	4	441
2	4	452	11	5	538
3	4	392	12	3	158
4	3	214	13	4	442
5	5	531	14	4	363
6	4	430	15	5	490
7	5	549	16	3	204
8	3	174	17	4	430
9	4	410	18	4	437
Out	**36**	**3,598**	**In**	**36**	**3,503**

Totals: Par 72, Yards 7,101

plays at 7,101 yards from the tournament tees, with water coming into play on 11 holes.

All par 5s can be reached in two shots, but if this is the goal, either the drive or the approach will be made in peril. Streams of water guard three of the four greens. The only par 5 without such a layout is the seventh, measuring 549 yards. The pitches and rolls in the fairways, the contouring of the elevated greens, and the sculpturing of the traps all contribute to the infinite variety of required shot-making.

This view of the 11th hole (left) is ample proof for the claim that Muirfield Village is second to none in the matter of conditioning. It's a 538-yard par 5 whose elevated, water-protected green is reachable in two only by the biggest hitters.

Sunset softens the harshness of the finishing hole, a par 4 of 437 yards. The well-guarded undulating green provides pin placements requiring well-struck, accurate approaches.

Rochester, New York

OAK HILL– EAST

Great championships, but controversial changes

Members of Oak Hill Country Club understandably give credit for their fine course to Donald Ross, the man who designed it. But an assist should go to Dr. John R. Williams and to the University of Rochester. The club began in 1901 and flourished for more than 20 years before the University showed an interest in acquiring the club as part of a much-needed expansion.

In exchange for the land, the university offered 355 acres several miles away and agreed to meet the cost of designing two 18-hole courses and the construction of a clubhouse. Oak Hill members agreed, then engaged Ross to design the courses. After the East Course was completed in 1926, Dr. Williams then planted thousands of trees and transformed an open, featureless piece of ground into the tree-lined test the world knows today.

In 1934 the course was first tested by top professionals in an event called the Walter Hagen Centennial Open, which honored favorite-son Hagen and observed Rochester's 100th birthday. Leo Diegel won the event, becoming the first in a series of distinguished players to win at Oak Hill. The local newspaper sponsored the Times-Union Open there in 1941 and 1942, the winners being Sam Snead and Ben Hogan. The club moved into the championship rotation in 1949 as host of the U.S. Amateur, won by Charlie Coe. Cary Middlecoff won the U.S. Open at Oak Hill in 1956, but after Lee Trevino won the 1968 Open—with all four rounds under 70—there

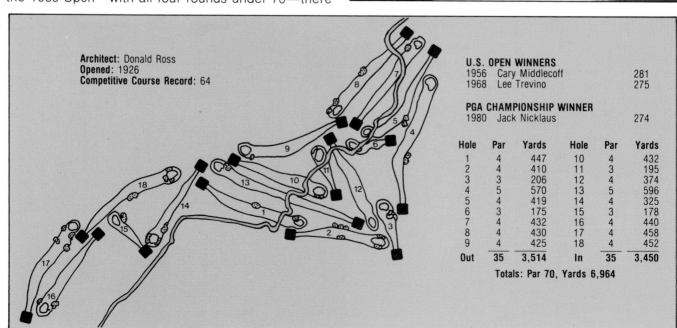

Architect: Donald Ross
Opened: 1926
Competitive Course Record: 64

U.S. OPEN WINNERS

1956	Cary Middlecoff	281
1968	Lee Trevino	275

PGA CHAMPIONSHIP WINNER

1980	Jack Nicklaus	274

Hole	Par	Yards	Hole	Par	Yards
1	4	447	10	4	432
2	4	410	11	3	195
3	3	206	12	4	374
4	5	570	13	5	596
5	4	419	14	4	325
6	3	175	15	3	178
7	4	432	16	4	440
8	4	430	17	4	458
9	4	425	18	4	452
Out	**35**	**3,514**	**In**	**35**	**3,450**

Totals: Par 70, Yards 6,964

90

It is said that nobody has ever reached the 596-yard 13th hole at Oak Hill in two strokes. It's easy to understand why when viewing the hole (above) from behind the green. The tee is far in the distance, beyond the fairway sprinklers.

Lee Trevino, who captured the public's fancy at Baltusrol in 1967, came into his own a year later when he won the U.S. Open at Oak Hill with 275, tying the record set by Jack Nicklaus.

was the feeling the course was no longer difficult enough for the premier players. George and Tom Fazio were then engaged to strengthen the layout and in the process they made some controversial changes, namely revamping the fifth and sixth holes. The 1980 PGA Championship was played at Oak Hill and won by no less than Jack Nicklaus, whose score of 274 was a stroke less than Trevino's 1968 total.

OAKLAND HILLS–SOUTH

A perfect blend of fairness and difficulty

At Oakland Hills Country Club in suburban Detroit, members feel they have a course that offers the best of two worlds: a Donald Ross design brought up to date by Robert Trent Jones.

Ross first saw the stretch of rolling Michigan farmland in 1916 and is said to have remarked, "The Lord intended this for a golf course." He completed the South Course two years later, and it quickly became recognized as a layout of championship quality. Darkhorse Cyril Walker won the U.S. Open there in 1924, and Ralph Guldahl overtook Sam Snead to win the Open on the same course in 1937. Then, in 1951, Jones was called in to modernize the place.

Jones filled in obsolete fairway bunkers and created new ones 50 yards farther from the tees, just the distance a professional golfer's drives were likely to carry. Then he enlarged the greens to provide more pin positions and made certain each position was defended by a bunker or other obstacle—one of his bedrock principles. The result of Jones' efforts was a golf course so tough and unyielding that it sent shock waves through the field that gathered there for the 1951 U.S. Open.

That was the event in which a tight-lipped Ben Hogan shot a masterful 67—some call it the best round ever played—and then said, "I'm glad I brought this monster to its knees."

The well-guarded par-3 ninth (left) is typical of Trent Jones' bunkering at Oakland Hills. Three mainstays of the immediate pre-World War II era gathered (below) at Oakland Hills in 1940 are Jimmy Demaret, Ben Hogan and Ralph Guldahl. Overleaf: The historic 16th hole, where Gary Player won the 1972 PGA.

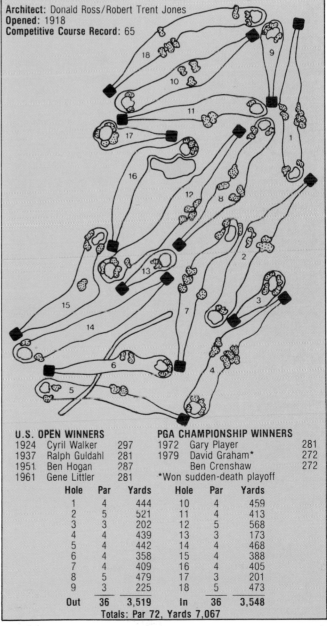

Architect: Donald Ross/Robert Trent Jones
Opened: 1918
Competitive Course Record: 65

U.S. OPEN WINNERS			PGA CHAMPIONSHIP WINNERS		
1924	Cyril Walker	297	1972	Gary Player	281
1937	Ralph Guldahl	281	1979	David Graham*	272
1951	Ben Hogan	287		Ben Crenshaw	272
1961	Gene Littler	281	*Won sudden-death playoff		

Hole	Par	Yards	Hole	Par	Yards
1	4	444	10	4	459
2	5	521	11	4	413
3	3	202	12	5	568
4	4	439	13	3	173
5	4	442	14	4	468
6	4	358	15	4	388
7	4	409	16	4	405
8	5	479	17	3	201
9	3	225	18	5	473
Out	36	3,519	In	36	3,548
Totals: Par 72, Yards 7,067					

OAKMONT
Lightning-fast greens and church-pew bunkers

When asked what characteristic they associate with Oakmont, golfers invariably reply "fast greens" or "huge bunkers." Both answers are correct, yet they fail to give a complete picture of this western Pennsylvania giant. It is indeed difficult—scary, even—but it is fair. Well aware of its qualities, the U.S. Golf Association has staged five U.S. Opens at Oakmont, and the sixth is scheduled for 1983.

The most striking feature of the course is the bunkers. There are lots of them (about 220 at one time; perhaps 30 fewer now) and some are incredibly large. The most famous are the Church Pews, a series of sandy rows lying between the third and fourth fairways. The size and number of the bunkers was compounded in the early days by a rake that left grooves, or furrows, in the sand. In a humane gesture, the furrows were eliminated in the 1960s.

But even at their most diabolical, the bunkers were never cursed as roundly as the greens. As Cal Brown once wrote: "The tiny greens and tricky rolls of Merion, the slick, wind-baked surfaces of Pebble Beach, pale before the terrors of Oakmont's greens. With few exceptions they are large. From a distance they appear rather flat and plain, almost innocent. This is a deception. Oakmont's greens are like polished glass. They are dynamite."

Says Lew Worsham, the club's long-time professional: "This is a course where good putters worry about their second putt before they hit the first one." One favorite story has it that a player marked his ball with a dime, then the dime slid off the green.

Oakmont was created originally by Henry C. Fownes, son of a Pittsburgh steel tycoon. His original version, opened in 1904, had eight par 5s and a par 6. Soon his son William took over and began a lifetime project of revising the course with the avowed intention of creating the toughest in the world. It is said that if a long driver happened to carry the fairway bunkers on a certain hole, Fownes would have a new bunker constructed the next day. No course could have been more penal, and that's just the way Fownes wanted it.

One of the most remarkable rounds in golf history was the closing 63 by Johnny Miller to win the 1973 U.S. Open at Oakmont. Hard rains had slowed the course's lightning-fast greens, but did little to diminish the brilliance of Miller's performance.

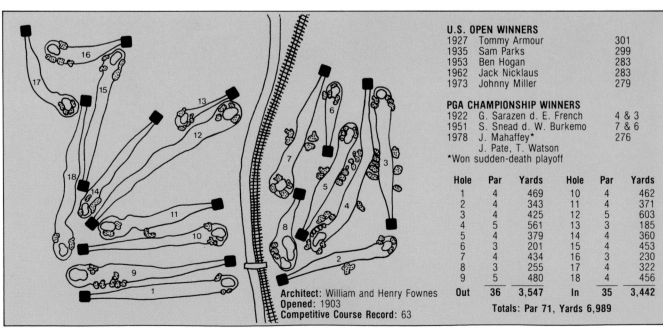

U.S. OPEN WINNERS

Year	Winner	Score
1927	Tommy Armour	301
1935	Sam Parks	299
1953	Ben Hogan	283
1962	Jack Nicklaus	283
1973	Johnny Miller	279

PGA CHAMPIONSHIP WINNERS

Year	Winner	
1922	G. Sarazen d. E. French	4 & 3
1951	S. Snead d. W. Burkemo	7 & 6
1978	J. Mahaffey*	276
	J. Pate, T. Watson	

*Won sudden-death playoff

Hole	Par	Yards	Hole	Par	Yards
1	4	469	10	4	462
2	4	343	11	4	371
3	4	425	12	5	603
4	5	561	13	3	185
5	4	379	14	4	360
6	3	201	15	4	453
7	4	434	16	3	230
8	3	255	17	4	322
9	5	480	18	4	456
Out	**36**	**3,547**	**In**	**35**	**3,442**

Architect: William and Henry Fownes
Opened: 1903
Competitive Course Record: 63

Totals: Par 71, Yards 6,989

Oakmont is famous for huge, swift greens, such as the 10th (above), and abundant bunkers. The most spectacular of these bunkers are the Church Pews (left), which lie between the third and fourth fairways and menace the golfer who pulls or hooks.

OAK TREE
An elegant group of 3s, 4s and 5s

Oak Tree has a couple of distinctions, aside from being what some consider Pete Dye's best course. First, it has five members who are regulars on the PGA Tour: Dr. Gil Morgan, Mark Hayes, Danny Edwards, David Edwards and Doug Tewell. Second, one doesn't have to sign up for a golf car; when ready to play, a member simply goes downstairs to the car storage room, hops in and drives to the first tee without even a minute's delay.

As to the course itself, here's what Herbert Warren Wind said about the undulations and moguls that Dye created to give the flat Oklahoma land a Scottish flavor: "Along with its ample length, Oak Tree is loaded with great golf . . . in his insistence on avoiding banal holes, Dye moved some 450,000 square yards of earth, and, along with some elegant par 3s and par 5s, came up with what, in my opinion, may be the most interestingly variegated collection of par 4s since Pine Valley was unveiled over half a century ago."

Here are the start (below) and finish (opposite page) of the 16th hole at Oak Tree, a par 5 that offers rocks, trees and Pete Dye's ever-present railroad ties. For those who feel they've had enough, a hangman's noose, a bit of Dye's humor, dangles permanently from a tree to the left of the green.

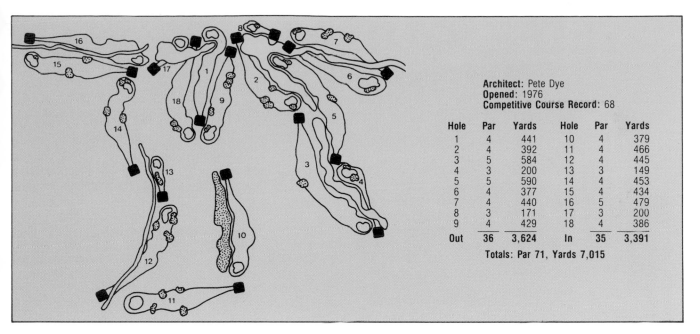

Architect: Pete Dye
Opened: 1976
Competitive Course Record: 68

Hole	Par	Yards	Hole	Par	Yards
1	4	441	10	4	379
2	4	392	11	4	466
3	5	584	12	4	445
4	3	200	13	3	149
5	5	590	14	4	453
6	4	377	15	4	434
7	4	440	16	5	479
8	3	171	17	3	200
9	4	429	18	4	386
Out	**36**	**3,624**	**In**	**35**	**3,391**

Totals: Par 71, Yards 7,015

OLYMPIC CLUB–LAKE

Tight, tree-lined fairways and small greens, but few hazards

In the truest meaning of the word, it is proper to say that the Lakeside Course at the Olympic Club is "unique." Although the greens are well-guarded by sand bunkers, there is only one fairway bunker on the entire course. Furthermore, there are no water hazards. These apparent lapses on the part of architect Wilfrid Reid were actually premeditated strokes of genius; uneven lies combined with countless trees that have since been planted, more than compensate. Olympic has another distinction as well. It has been the site of two of the most stunning finishes in the history of the U.S. Open. These were in 1955, when an unknown Jack Fleck came out of nowhere to catch Ben Hogan, then beat him in a playoff, and in 1966, when Bill Casper made up seven strokes in nine holes to tie Arnold Palmer, then did virtually the same thing to win a playoff the next day. Olympic's tight, tree-lined fairways and small greens are conducive to such unforseen disasters.

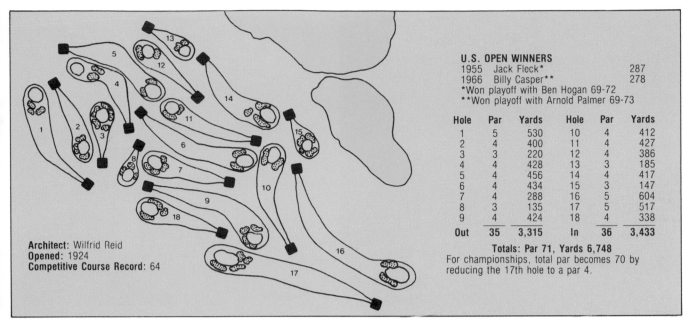

U.S. OPEN WINNERS

1955	Jack Fleck*		287
1966	Billy Casper**		278

*Won playoff with Ben Hogan 69-72
**Won playoff with Arnold Palmer 69-73

Hole	Par	Yards	Hole	Par	Yards
1	5	530	10	4	412
2	4	400	11	4	427
3	3	220	12	4	386
4	4	428	13	3	185
5	4	456	14	4	417
6	4	434	15	3	147
7	4	288	16	5	604
8	3	135	17	5	517
9	4	424	18	4	338
Out	35	3,315	In	36	3,433

Totals: Par 71, Yards 6,748
For championships, total par becomes 70 by reducing the 17th hole to a par 4.

Architect: Wilfrid Reid
Opened: 1924
Competitive Course Record: 64

Ben Hogan (right) was in the clubhouse at Olympic, accepting congratulations for winning a record fifth U.S. Open when the unknown Jack Fleck (left) birdied two of the last four holes to tie. Fleck went on to win the 18-hole playoff the next day.

Although a par 4 of only 338 yards, the 18th hole at Olympic Club is deceptively difficult. Its amphitheater-like setting just below the clubhouse helps to make it one of the finest viewing holes anywhere.

PEACHTREE

The classic Trent Jones style, with the Bobby Jones touch

When Robert Trent Jones was designing the Peachtree Golf Club course just after World War II, he was doing so in association with Bobby Jones, the famed player. As the architect puts it: "While we were doing Peachtree I realized that there could be only one Bobby Jones, so I became Trent." Trent's critics claim that Bobby Jones deserves more of the credit for Peachtree than Trent Jones, but knowledgeable observers disagree. Geoff Cornish and Ron Whitten, in their definitive work, *The Golf Course*, wrote: "While it (Peachtree) was perhaps intended to be another expression of Robert Tyre Jones's design philosophy, it in fact became an expression of Robert Trent Jones's philosophy. Its features were unprecedented. Its tees were huge . . . and its greens were also enormous."

However the credit is distributed, the result was a course with broad, gently sloping fairways, a handful of doglegs, a substantial amount of water and plenty of trees. And in what was to become the classic Trent Jones style, the long tees offered great flexibility and the big greens provided five or six different pin positions.

But it was Bobby Jones who brought together the founding group in 1946, who served as the club's first president and whose exemplary demeanor set the tone that pervades the club to this day.

Of the group of prime movers (below),
Bobby Jones, left, and Trent Jones, right,
were the key figures.

A classic example of a parkland course is Peachtree, and the 12th hole (opposite page) is typical, a 423-yard par 4 dogleg right that requires an accurate drive to set up the approach.

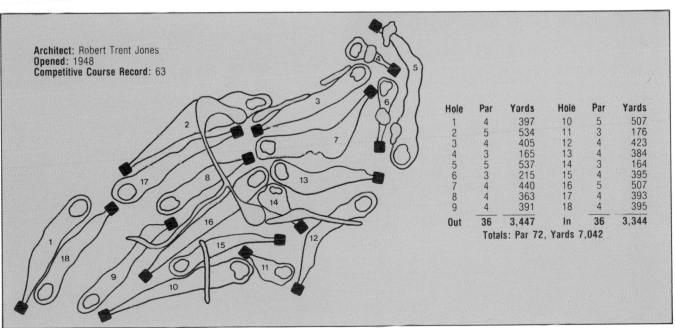

Architect: Robert Trent Jones
Opened: 1948
Competitive Course Record: 63

Hole	Par	Yards	Hole	Par	Yards
1	4	397	10	5	507
2	5	534	11	3	176
3	4	405	12	4	423
4	3	165	13	4	384
5	5	537	14	3	164
6	3	215	15	4	395
7	4	440	16	5	507
8	4	363	17	4	393
9	4	391	18	4	395
Out	36	3,447	In	36	3,344

Totals: Par 72, Yards 7,042

PEBBLE BEACH
Breathtaking cliffs, spectacular views and open to the public

There is little argument that Pebble Beach is one of the world's most spectacular golf courses. Situated on the Monterey Peninsula 120 miles south of San Francisco, Pebble Beach offers an array of breathtaking holes that cling to the cliffs bordering Carmel Bay. And it is the great good fortune of American golf fans that this public course is the site of the annual Bing Crosby Pro-Am and two recent U.S. Opens, and thus available on television to all those millions who will never play it.

There are those carpers who say Pebble has too many indifferent holes to be classed among the great courses. Certainly it is true that the course, unlike March, comes in like a lamb before turning leonine at about the sixth hole. But once it hits its stride, Pebble is magnificent.

The sixth, a 515-yard par 5 that Byron Nelson has called the toughest on the course, begins a stretch of holes that must be the equal of any in golf. The seventh is a 120-yard downhill gem that can be anything from a wedge to a long iron, depending on the wind. Then there's the eighth, an awesome par 4 that requires an approach from the edge of a cliff over a 180-yard chasm to a small green surrounded by bunkers. The ninth is a 450-yarder that can't be reached in two shots if the wind is against. This hole runs right along the cliffs and has been called the hardest par 4 in golf. The 10th is almost as demanding, and if it seems easier, it's only in relation to the ninth, which is 15 yards longer.

The inland holes that follow aren't pushovers, they just seem that way after what the golfer has just been through. Then, just as sanity seems to have reappeared, the golfer returns to the ocean for the last two holes. The green of the par-3 17th sits on the precipice and invites heroism or disaster. In the 1972 U.S. Open Jack Nicklaus struck a 1-iron shot that hit the pin and stopped only inches from the cup, sealing his victory. In the 1982 Open, television viewers got a dramatic picture of Tom Watson holing a seemingly impossible chip shot from heavy rough to gain the lead by a shot, then birdie 18 for a two-stroke triumph, his first Open win.

Because of its television exposure, the 18th also is one of the most familiar holes in America. It, too, hugs the edge of the cliff, and in a high wind is a tough customer.

Like many of America's great courses, Pebble Beach, opened in 1919, was designed by amateurs. Jack Neville, a California Amateur champion, was hired to lay out the course, and, in collaboration with Douglas Grant, another state champion, Neville produced a masterpiece.

In the opinion of many, the first five holes at Pebble Beach are just a warmup for the "real" course, which starts at the 516-yard uphill sixth (right), whose green brings the golfer to the rocky coast. The 464-yard par-4 ninth and 426-yard par-4 10th (above) also run along the shoreline.
Nathaniel Crosby, shown here with his father, continues the annual Bing Crosby-Pebble Beach Clambake tradition.

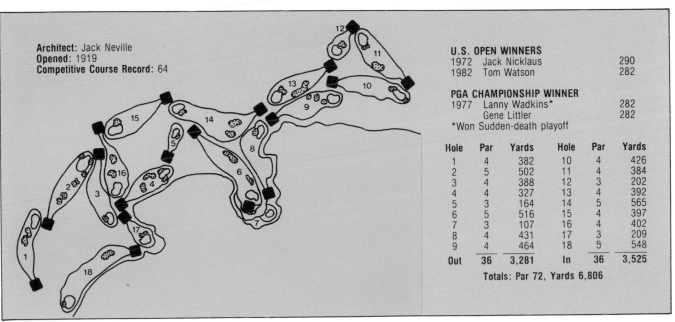

Architect: Jack Neville
Opened: 1919
Competitive Course Record: 64

Hole	Par	Yards	Hole	Par	Yards
1	4	382	10	4	426
2	5	502	11	4	384
3	4	388	12	3	202
4	4	327	13	4	392
5	3	164	14	5	565
6	5	516	15	4	397
7	3	107	16	4	402
8	4	431	17	3	209
9	4	464	18	5	548
Out	36	3,281	In	36	3,525

Totals: Par 72, Yards 6,806

Greens whose edges slope off toward waiting bunkers, as on the 13th hole (below), are typical of the way Donald Ross designed his No. 2 course at Pinehurst.

PINEHURST–2
Ross' subtle design provides an enduring challenge

In the minds of many Americans, Pinehurst is synonymous with golf. Even those who have never been there are likely to pick it first when asked to name the ideal golfing resort. Such is the spell cast by the North Carolina sandhills spa since its inception at the turn of the century. The place has abundant charm—six golf courses in all—but its reputation is primarily based on the one

called, simply, No. 2. Yet all this isn't readily apparent to the visitor because, like the Old Course at St. Andrews, Pinehurst No. 2 tends to grow on you.

As Cal Brown once put it: "Of all the famous golf courses in the United States, the least obvious gem is the No. 2 course at Pinehurst. It is not as dramatic as Pine Valley or Pebble Beach, not as elegant as Augusta National or Merion. It appears quiet, unassuming, almost drab in comparison with those American classics. Its individual holes are seldom discussed when golfers list the great golf holes of America. Some who

play it for the first time are puzzled at its high ranking.''

That this is so is a tribute to the subtle design of Donald Ross, the creator of Pinehurst's courses and one of the game's greatest architects. Ross was noted for contoured greens and mounded approaches, which, as he explained: ''makes possible an infinite variety of nasty short shots that no other form of hazard can call for. Competitors whose second shots have wandered a bit will be disturbed by these innocent-appearing slopes and by the shots they will have to invent to recover.''

Pinehurst was developed by the Tufts family in the

Dick Tufts, left, and his son Peter are shown preparing the No. 2 course for the 1962 U.S. Amateur. The Tufts family founded the Pinehurst resort around the turn of the century.

late 1890s as a place for New Englanders to get away from Northern winters. It might have become a popular spot anyhow, but that success was hastened by the arrival in 1900 of Donald Ross as resident professional. Ross was raised in Dornoch, Scotland, and had the added advantage of an apprenticeship under Old Tom Morris at St. Andrews. With such a background, and given a sandy turf not unlike his native linksland, it's no wonder Ross thrived in his new environment. By the time he finished, he had designed five courses at Pinehurst. Thirty years after his death in 1948, George and Tom Fazio created a sixth course.

Ross completed work on No. 2 in 1907; that is, he completed 18 holes—he never actually stopped changing the course. It didn't achieve its present form until 1925 and the greens weren't changed from sand to grass until 1935.

Ross built the fairways wide, recognizing that the margin for error should be greatest on tee shots, but he clearly intended that golfers look beyond the landing area before driving. He considered the ability to play the longer irons the supreme test of the great player and therefore shaped his greens so they fade away to the sides and back. This created a much smaller effective target than the golfer might at first think.

The courses—especially No. 2—were an immediate hit, and great players beat a path to Pinehurst from the beginning. The North and South Amateur began in 1901, and the North and South Open started in 1903, lasting until 1951. The most famous names in golf grace the winners' list of both events. Ben Hogan, for example, won the North and South Open in 1940 for his first victory as a professional.

Some changes were made in the course after the Diamondhead Corp. bought Pinehurst from the Tufts family in the early 1970s, but efforts have been made to put it back the way Donald Ross left it.

Pinehurst has now been taken over by a group of banks who have installed a vigorous management that is working to restore the charm and elegance—and the quality of the courses—that existed in its pre-1970 days.

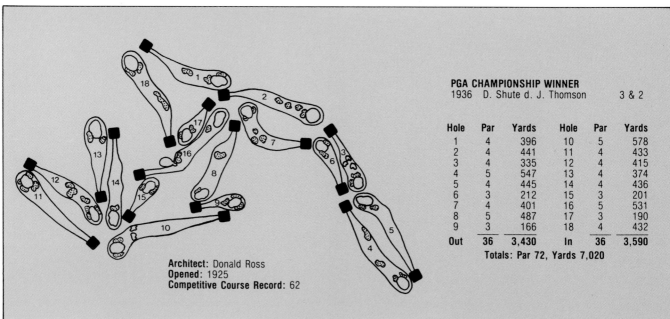

Architect: Donald Ross
Opened: 1925
Competitive Course Record: 62

PGA CHAMPIONSHIP WINNER
1936   D. Shute d. J. Thomson   3 & 2

Hole	Par	Yards	Hole	Par	Yards
1	4	396	10	5	578
2	4	441	11	4	433
3	4	335	12	4	415
4	5	547	13	4	374
5	4	445	14	4	436
6	3	212	15	3	201
7	4	401	16	5	531
8	5	487	17	3	190
9	3	166	18	4	432
Out	**36**	**3,430**	**In**	**36**	**3,590**

Totals: Par 72, Yards 7,020

The natural look of the rough at
Pinehurst is seen in these two views of
the third hole on the No. 2 course. The
wire grass and hardpan at the left and
the pine needles at the right illustrate
the effect sought by Donald Ross.

PINE TREE

An abundance of sound holes that appeal to the better player

In 1962 Ben Hogan drove from Palm Beach to Delray Beach to see if Dick Wilson's Pine Tree course was as good as he had heard it was. Accompanied by his three playing partners, a gallery of 15 people and a very anxious Wilson, Hogan, obviously relishing many of the finesse shots he was required to play, was around in 73, one over par. He promptly told Wilson in so many words that Pine Tree was the best course he ever played. The fact that some persons question whether it is even Wilson's best course is no reflection on Hogan's judgment—or on Pine Tree—but rather indicates how good an architect Wilson was. At Pine Tree he designed a layout with one sound hole after another, and the only criticism of it usually is that the high-handicap player finds it a bit too demanding. But the good players love it, which may explain why the club's rolls include such noted names as Ed Tutwiler, Dale Morey, Bill Hyndman and even Sam Snead himself,

who holds the course record of 63. The course was opened in 1962, and the only changes have been to extend the 10th to a par 5 and shorten the 12th to a par 4. It was first class right from the start.

The immaculate 18th hole, with no grain of sand or blade of grass out of place, will give you an idea of what to expect at Pine Tree, which many consider to be Dick Wilson's masterpiece of subtle deception.

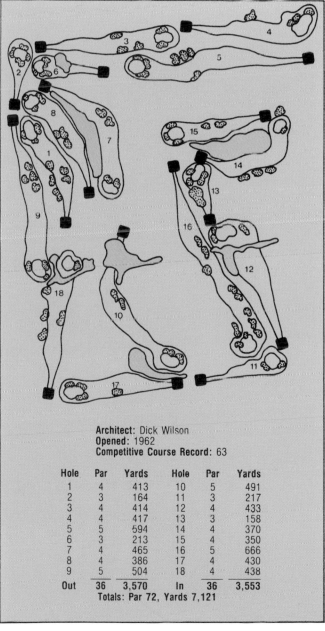

Architect: Dick Wilson
Opened: 1962
Competitive Course Record: 63

Hole	Par	Yards	Hole	Par	Yards
1	4	413	10	5	491
2	3	164	11	3	217
3	4	414	12	4	433
4	4	417	13	3	158
5	5	594	14	4	370
6	3	213	15	4	350
7	4	465	16	5	666
8	4	386	17	4	430
9	5	504	18	4	438
Out	**36**	**3,570**	**In**	**36**	**3,553**

Totals: Par 72, Yards 7,121

PINE VALLEY

Vast wastelands, island fairways and forests terrorize the golfer

When Philadelphia hotel man George Crump first saw the land that now is the Pine Valley Golf Club, he thought it was the perfect terrain on which to build a golf course. He was right. For more than 60 years, golfers—even those who were no match for it—have sought words to describe this magnificent layout in the pine-covered New Jersey sandhills east of Philadelphia. Its effect on its challengers might best be summed up in the title of a book: *Winning Through Intimidation.*

It is widely regarded as the toughest golf course in the world, but that isn't true for the low-handicap player who drives consistently straight. A textbook on course architecture would define it as penal, but, as George Fazio put it, "It's only penal if you are not playing well."

"Pine Valley's full length of 6,765 yards," Cal Brown once wrote, "does not strike fear into anyone's breast—not until one steps to the first tee. There one glimpses the two principal design features that give

Pine Valley its stern, intimidating character—vast, sandy wilderness and thick forest. There is no 'rough' at Pine Valley. Instead desert-like scrub surrounds every fairway and most of the greens, which are immaculately conditioned and appear, in contrast, as islands of green velvet.

"One must play to these 'islands' from start to finish. Tee shots must carry expanses of up to 175 yards of unkempt dune on most holes to reach safe ground. The careless, wild or indifferent shot is dealt with severely."

But Pine Valley offers much more than rugged terrain. It also has an impressive lineup of outstanding golf holes. Its two par 5s are memorable. Although both are long, length isn't what distinguishes them. The seventh calls for a carry over Hell's Half Acre, a mammoth sand trap, while the 15th fairway steadily narrows as it runs uphill toward the green, until, ultimately, there is no margin for error.

The par 3s, collectively, may be unmatched. All of them call for a shot over sand, water or wilderness—or a combination of the three—yet they vary widely in length, and each has a distinct character of its own.

Although Bernard Darwin called Pine Valley "an examination in golf," it was, figuratively, only a blank piece of paper when Crump first beheld the land back in 1912. He was so enthralled by the property that he moved there and spent almost six years on the site, personally directing the felling of trees, removal of stumps, damming of natural springs to form lakes. He had secured the services of H.S. Colt to help with the original route plan, and in 1914 began construction. Fourteen holes were completed by the end of 1917, then Crump died in January, 1918, with holes 12 through 15 still incomplete. Hugh Wilson, who had designed Merion, and his brother Alan were called in to finish the course, which opened in 1919.

Geoffrey Cornish and Ronald Whitten summed it up in their fine book on architecture, *The Golf Course:* "Because it required such precise placement of each golf shot, Pine Valley was punishing to even the finest of players. Its introduction marked the zenith of the penal school of golf course architecture in America. No course quite like it has been built since, and no course has ever been as demanding of every stroke."

A fitting finish at Pine Valley is the 18th, a 424-yard par 4 on which the golfer must drive over a 175-yard expanse of sand, then face an approach over water and more sand to an elevated green.

One of the most beautiful—and most difficult—par-3 holes anywhere is Pine Valley's 14th: 185 yards from an elevated tee, over a bunker that runs the width of the green, and a lake that protects the front and rear left.

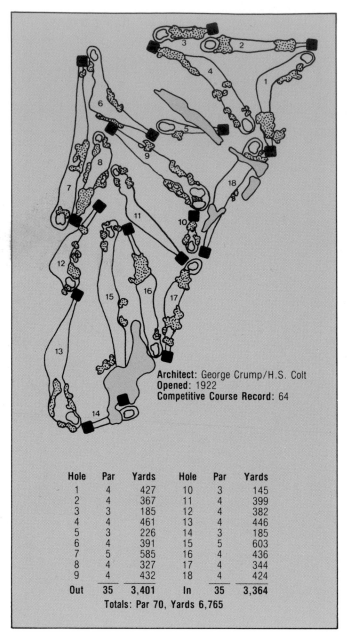

Architect: George Crump/H.S. Colt
Opened: 1922
Competitive Course Record: 64

Hole	Par	Yards	Hole	Par	Yards
1	4	427	10	3	145
2	4	367	11	4	399
3	3	185	12	4	382
4	4	461	13	4	446
5	3	226	14	3	185
6	4	391	15	5	603
7	5	585	16	4	436
8	4	327	17	4	344
9	4	432	18	4	424
Out	**35**	**3,401**	**In**	**35**	**3,364**

Totals: Par 70, Yards 6,765

The 603-yard 15th is the longest hole at Pine Valley—so long that it's never been reached in two shots. After driving over a lake to a wide fairway, the golfer faces a gradually narrowing, uphill target.

POINT O'WOODS
An "ideal location" and a rugged, wooded course

It was a familiar story: five prominent golfers of the St. Joseph-Benton Harbor area of Michigan, feeling courses were getting too crowded, began to explore the possibility of creating a new club. The five, Fred Upton, Richard Merrill, Charles Gore, Malcolm Ross and C.E. Blake, found what they felt to be good ground on a 350-acre plot owned by Ross' brother. Then they got Robert Trent Jones to look at the property, which he pronounced an ideal location. Construction began early in 1957 and the course was opened June 14, 1958. The merits of the new course were apparent from the begin-

ning, and arrangements were made for the club to host the Western Amateur, a hoary championship that had been in existence since 1899. The first event played at "The Point" was the 1963 Western, won by a teen-aged Tom Weiskopf. Bob E. Smith won the title in 1965 at Point O'Woods. Then, beginning in 1971, the club became the tournament's permanent site. The winners have included such future tour stars as Andy North, Ben Crenshaw, Curtis Strange, Andy Bean and Bobby Clampett. Despite the difficulty of the rugged, wooded course, Strange set the record with a 65.

A buttonhook twist to the fairway makes the 523-yard second a difficult hole to reach in two shots. The course is now the regular site of the Western Amateur, which was won 10 times by Chick Evans (bottom, left), founder of the Evans Scholars, the caddie foundation administered by the Western Golf Association.

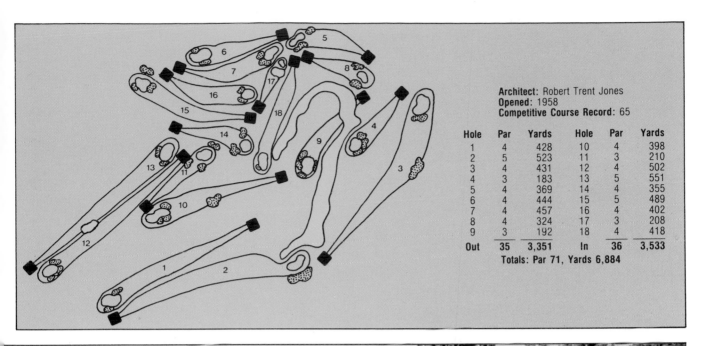

Architect: Robert Trent Jones
Opened: 1958
Competitive Course Record: 65

Hole	Par	Yards	Hole	Par	Yards
1	4	428	10	4	398
2	5	523	11	3	210
3	4	431	12	4	502
4	3	183	13	5	551
5	4	369	14	4	355
6	4	444	15	5	489
7	4	457	16	4	402
8	4	324	17	3	208
9	3	192	18	4	418
Out	**35**	**3,351**	**In**	**36**	**3,533**

Totals: Par 71, Yards 6,884

PRAIRIE DUNES
A touch of Scotland in Kansas

"Prairie Dunes is a feisty little course. If you doubt this, consider that honorary member Jack Nicklaus, who won the Trans-Mississippi title here in 1958, has yet to break par for 18 holes. It is, to use a boxing analogy, a bantamweight rather than a heavyweight, and calls for skill and craftiness rather than brute force." This is the opinion of Peter Macdonald, a club member who also belongs to the Royal and Ancient at St. Andrews. He is particularly qualified to comment because Prairie Dunes, while not so "little," is known as the St. Andrews of the Prairies, a chunk of Scotland that somehow found itself in the middle of Kansas.

The course is the work of the late Perry Maxwell, who designed the original nine holes in the mid-1930s at the behest of William and Emerson Carey Jr., members of a prominent Hutchinson, Kan., family who had played Scottish courses and wanted one for their hometown.

"Prairie Dunes needs only a firth or a bay to look just like a British Open venue," says Nick Seitz. "It has to be this country's most unusual great course. If there were degrees of the word 'uniqueness,' it would be our most unique."

When Perry Maxwell first began the project, he said, "There are 118 golf holes here. All I have to do is eliminate the 100."

Prairie Dunes is a particular favorite of Tom Watson, who is an honorary member of the club.

Rolling sandhills, heavy rough and plentiful bunkers make the 399-yard ninth hole at Prairie Dunes— in fact the whole golf course—look like a piece of Scottish real estate misplaced in the middle of America.

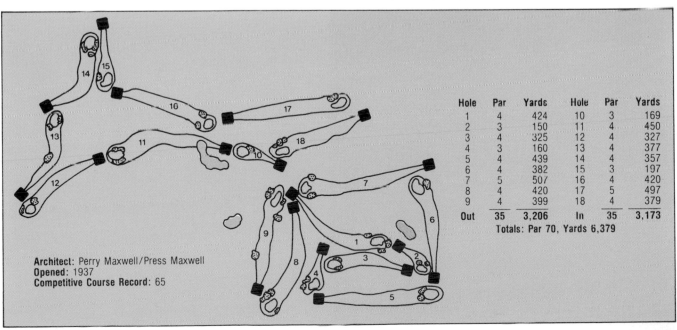

Hole	Par	Yards	Hole	Par	Yards
1	4	424	10	3	169
2	3	150	11	4	450
3	4	325	12	4	327
4	3	160	13	4	377
5	4	439	14	4	357
6	4	382	15	3	197
7	5	507	16	4	420
8	4	420	17	5	497
9	4	399	18	4	379
Out	35	3,206	In	35	3,173

Totals: Par 70, Yards 6,379

Architect: Perry Maxwell/Press Maxwell
Opened: 1937
Competitive Course Record: 65

QUAKER RIDGE

An outstanding course living in anonymity

In a sense Quaker Ridge can be called one of the nation's best unknown golf courses. The outstanding A.W. Tillinghast layout, which bears comparison with its celebrated Winged Foot neighbors, hasn't held a significant tournament since 1936, when Byron Nelson made the Metropolitan Open his first big victory. Johnny Farrell represented the club when he won the U.S. Open in 1928. Otherwise, Quaker Ridge has dwelled in anonymity. It isn't that the members planned it that way, they just made no effort to court fame.

Back in colonial days, the Quakers built a meeting house at the corner of Griffen Ave. and Weaver St.; hence the club's name. Its history begins in 1915 when a small group of men led by Otto Elsass bought a nine-hole course that was in financial difficulties. Then they raised money to purchase another 120 acres and hired Tillinghast to alter the old nine and add a new one. Except for the building of new tees and some re-bunkering

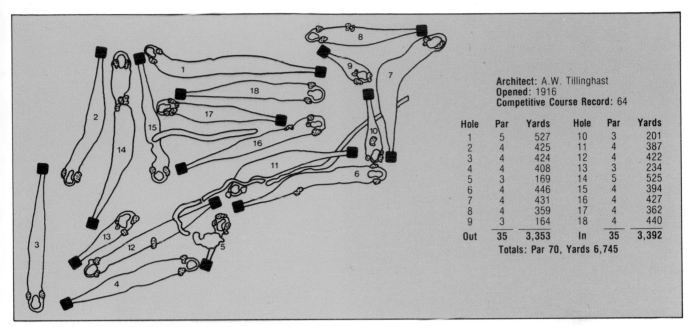

Architect: A.W. Tillinghast
Opened: 1916
Competitive Course Record: 64

Hole	Par	Yards	Hole	Par	Yards
1	5	527	10	3	201
2	4	425	11	4	387
3	4	424	12	4	422
4	4	408	13	3	234
5	3	169	14	5	525
6	4	446	15	4	394
7	4	431	16	4	427
8	4	359	17	4	362
9	3	164	18	4	440
Out	35	3,353	In	35	3,392

Totals: Par 70, Yards 6,745

One of the more successful performers at Quaker Ridge has been Dick Siderowf, the former British Amateur champion, who has won four Hochster Memorial titles over the A.W. Tillinghast layout.

A creek in front of the green leaves no margin for error on the 11th hole at Quaker Ridge. The 387-yard par 4, viewed here from behind the green, crosses the same creek in front of the tee.

by Trent Jones and Francis Duane in the 1960s, the course is the same type of rolling, wooded layout with pear-shaped greens that Tillinghast created at Winged Foot and elsewhere.

Pacific Palisades, California

RIVIERA
A glamourous place called Hogan's Alley

Douglas Fairbanks was an enthusiastic early member; Will Rogers played polo on the club's field; Ben Hogan's life story was filmed there. Where? The Riviera Country Club, a glamorous spot from the start in 1927 and one that has always insisted on going first class. Riviera is an arm of the Los Angeles Athletic Club, whose members had long sought a place where they could engage in golf and other outdoor pursuits. The club bought 290 acres in Santa Monica in 1925 and cajoled architect George Thomas Jr. into coming out of retirement to design the course. They also employed young designer William P. Bell as "superintending architect."

The quality of the course was quickly apparent and in less than two years it became the site of the Los Angeles Open, won by Macdonald Smith. The club hosted the L.A. Open again in 1930, 1941 and from 1945 through 1953, then resumed in 1973. While golf was a principal activity, Riviera was the center of the polo boom in the 1920s and 1930s. The club also was the site of the equestrian events for the 1932 Olympic Games, held in Los Angeles.

Riviera's great golfing moments were centered around Ben Hogan, who won two Los Angeles Opens and a United States Open in the space of 18 months in 1947 and 1948. Understandably, the course became known as Hogan's Alley. Riviera was also the scene of Hogan's comeback in 1950, less than a year after his

A familiar sight to television viewers is the approach to the 18th green at Riviera, annual home of the Los Angeles Open. The 454-yard par 4 requires a straight drive and a long, accurate approach.

A figure on the tour in the 1940s and 1950s was the late Lloyd Mangrum, who counted four Los Angeles Opens among his 34 tournament titles.

automobile crash. He tied for first, and the subsequent loss to Sam Snead in a playoff did nothing to diminish his achievement. Riviera's pro shop for many years has been the domain of the Hunter family. Willie, winner of the 1921 British Amateur, was professional at the club from 1936 to 1964, then was succeeded by his son Macdonald.

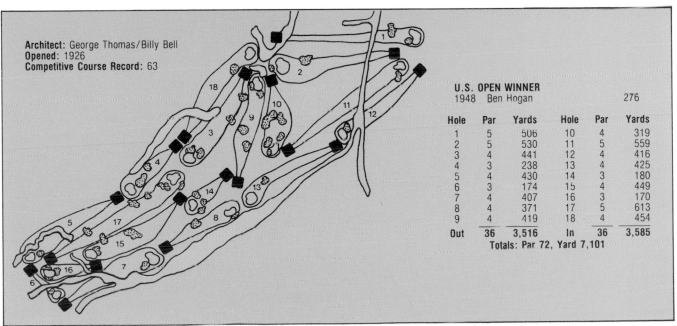

Architect: George Thomas/Billy Bell
Opened: 1926
Competitive Course Record: 63

U.S. OPEN WINNER
1948   Ben Hogan   276

Hole	Par	Yards	Hole	Par	Yards
1	5	506	10	4	319
2	5	530	11	5	559
3	4	441	12	4	416
4	3	238	13	4	425
5	4	430	14	3	180
6	3	174	15	4	449
7	4	407	16	3	170
8	4	371	17	5	613
9	4	419	18	4	454
Out	**36**	**3,516**	**In**	**36**	**3,585**

Totals: Par 72, Yard 7,101

SAN FRANCISCO

From tragic duels in the beginning to a stellar membership today

In 1859 two staunch California Democrats, U.S. Senator David Broderick and State Supreme court Justice David Terry, fought a duel near the site of the present seventh green at San Francisco Golf Club. Broderick was killed in the tragic confrontation and as a result dueling was made illegal in California. Nevertheless, golfing confrontations have been waged on the site ever since

A.W. Tillinghast designed the course in 1918.

The club was begun by homesick Scotsmen in 1895 with a nine-hole layout at The Presidio that existed until a move to Ingleside in 1905. The final move was made after the club lost its lease. Although it hosted the San Francisco Match Play Championship in 1938 (won by Jimmy Demaret) and the Curtis Cup in 1974, the club traditionally has kept a low profile and takes quiet pride in having such golf-minded members as Douglas Grant (designer of Pebble Beach), Bing Crosby, Harvie Ward, Alistair Cooke and Frank (Sandy) Tatum.

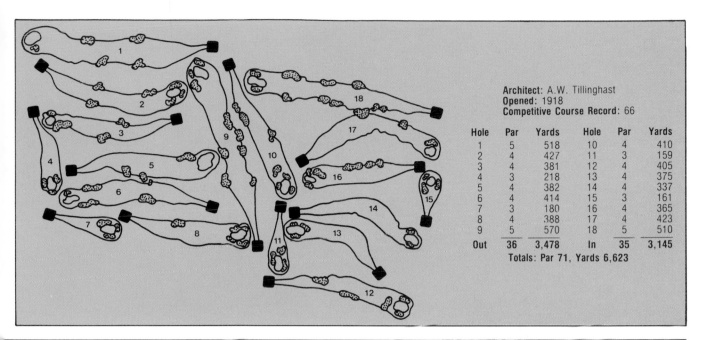

Architect: A.W. Tillinghast
Opened: 1918
Competitive Course Record: 66

Hole	Par	Yards	Hole	Par	Yards
1	5	518	10	4	410
2	4	427	11	3	159
3	4	381	12	4	405
4	3	218	13	4	375
5	4	382	14	4	337
6	4	414	15	3	161
7	3	180	16	4	365
8	4	388	17	4	423
9	5	570	18	5	510
Out	**36**	**3,478**	**In**	**35**	**3,145**

Totals: Par 71, Yards 6,623

A zig-zag route among the bunkers is the prudent course on the 410-yard 10th hole at San Francisco.

SAUCON VALLEY—GRACE

Where par is usually beyond reach

A member at Saucon Valley once hit a high hook from the first tee of the Grace Course and the ball went into the cup of the 18th, enabling him to go to the 19th with the boast that he had played the course in one stroke. That feat notwithstanding, par on the Grace Course has generally been beyond reach. The course record is only 69, and in the lone tournament played totally over the Grace—the 1977 Philadelphia PGA—Dick Smith won with a five-over-par 221. The course was named for Eugene Grace, long-time president of Bethlehem Steel, on whose estate the club's first course was opened in 1922. This was called the Old Course, and hosted the 1951 U.S. Amateur, won by Billy Maxwell. The club now has 60 holes, the jewel being the Grace, designed by William Gordon and completed in 1955. The Grace isn't hilly, but is tight, with lots of water and bunkers. A stream comes into play on seven holes, including the first four, which, along with the closing four, are rated the most difficult. The club's pro for many years has been Jerry Pittman, who occupies the same post at Seminole during the winter.

Capping an outstanding amateur career, the diminutive Billy Maxwell beat Joe Gagliardi, 4 and 3, to win the 1951 U.S. Amateur at Saucon Valley.

Despite its pastoral setting, the 173-yard 14th hole is fraught with trouble.

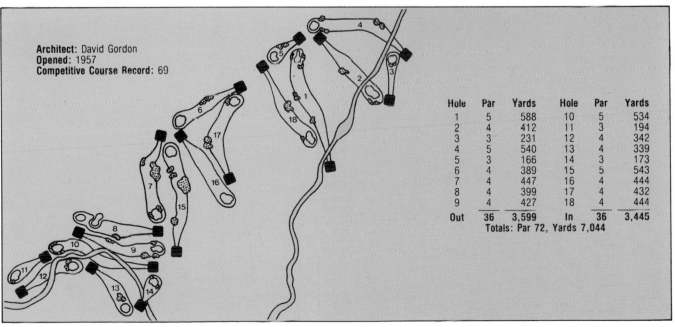

Architect: David Gordon
Opened: 1957
Competitive Course Record: 69

Hole	Par	Yards	Hole	Par	Yards
1	5	588	10	5	534
2	4	412	11	3	194
3	3	231	12	4	342
4	5	540	13	4	339
5	3	166	14	3	173
6	4	389	15	5	543
7	4	447	16	4	444
8	4	399	17	4	432
9	4	427	18	4	444
Out	36	3,599	In	36	3,445

Totals: Par 72, Yards 7,044

SCIOTO
Where Nicklaus learned the game

Scioto Country Club in Columbus, Ohio, has carved fame as the place where Jack Nicklaus learned the game under the tutelage of club professional Jack Grout. Its history of golfing significance, however, dates to 1916, when it was designed by Donald Ross, the most popular architect of the day. It went on to become the scene of notable tournaments, including the U.S. Open, the Ryder Cup, the PGA Championship and the U.S. Amateur. And because one of those events—the 1926 U.S. Open—was won by Bobby Jones, Nicklaus was to grow up using the Georgian as his role model in golf.

Jones first went to Scioto in 1918 when, as a 16-year-old phenomenon, he played there in an exhibition for the Red Cross. Eight years later he won his second of four Opens, finishing with 293 to edge Joe Turnesa by a stroke. In 1931 the United States stopped Britain, 9-3, in the Ryder Cup matches as Gene Sarazen, Denny Shute and Walter Hagen scored notable victories. In the 1950 PGA, most of the famous players lost in early matches and Chandler Harper beat Henry Williams Jr., 4 and 3, in the final. In the 1968 U.S. Amateur, Bruce Fleisher shot 284 and came home a stroke in front.

Dick Wilson was called in to make some alterations in the course in 1963, but essentially it remains a Donald Ross creation that uses the natural contours of the land, has subtle sloping around the greens and, above all, requires considerable thought as well as distance to score well.

There's no such thing as a lucky bounce on the eighth hole at Scioto. The green of the 505-yard par 5 is surrounded by water—in effect, a moat.

Scioto was where Jack Nicklaus began playing golf under the watchful eye of Jack Grout. Here, Jack hits practice shots in an all-weather cage designed by Grout.

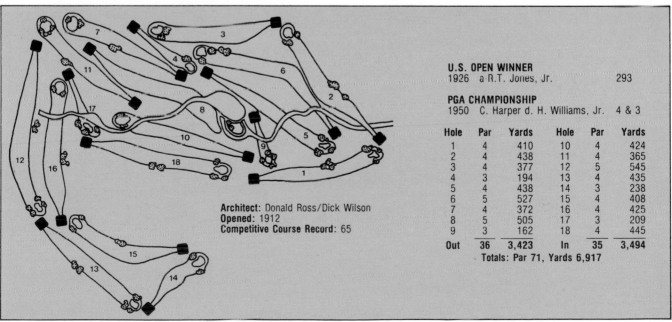

Architect: Donald Ross/Dick Wilson
Opened: 1912
Competitive Course Record: 65

U.S. OPEN WINNER
1926   a R.T. Jones, Jr.   293

PGA CHAMPIONSHIP
1950   C. Harper d. H. Williams, Jr.   4 & 3

Hole	Par	Yards	Hole	Par	Yards
1	4	410	10	4	424
2	4	438	11	4	365
3	4	377	12	5	545
4	3	194	13	4	435
5	4	438	14	3	238
6	5	527	15	4	408
7	4	372	16	4	425
8	5	505	17	3	209
9	3	162	18	4	445
Out	**36**	**3,423**	**In**	**35**	**3,494**

Totals: Par 71, Yards 6,917

The 438-yard fifth hole at Scioto: it looks like a wide-open avenue to the green, but a stream crossing the fairway menaces long hitters.

SEMINOLE
A "placement" course that tests players of all abilities

It is said that of the 600 or so courses designed and remodeled by Donald Ross, Seminole is the only one he actively campaigned to do. That is, the other commissions came to him, but he went after Seminole's. The results certainly justify whatever it took for him to get the assignment, because Seminole is a marvelous course—some say Ross' finest.

As Herbert Warren Wind once described it: "Appearances can be deceiving. Seminole, along with Pinehurst No. 2, is the quintessential Ross course. It may look mild and manageable—the fairways are wide, the rough is civilized, the undulations restrained, the greens large and candid—and because of its reasonable length from the standard tees the average player can sometimes salvage a par after a poorish drive. Nonetheless, when all is said and done, the course demands golf of the first order. Unless a player positions his tee shots carefully, he will not be able to regularly hit and hold the splendid variety of stiffly bunkered greens, and strokes will inevitably start to slip away fast."

Ben Hogan, a member and staunch admirer of Seminole, has said: "The wind is different nearly every day, and that changes all the shots. I used to play Seminole for 30 straight days when I was preparing for the Masters, and I was just as eager to play it on the 30th morning as I was on the first.

"Seminole is a placement course," he continued. "Most of the holes bend one way or the other slightly, and you must place your tee shot on the right side or left side of the fairway to have the best angle to the green on your approach shot. If I were a young man going on the pro tour, I'd try to make arrangements to get on Seminole. If you can play Seminole, you can play any course in the world."

Hogan's favorite hole—and the favorite of many others as well—is the sixth, a 390-yard par 4 that dramatically illustrates his remarks on placement. Four large bunkers on the left almost compel the prudent golfer to drive to the right, yet that isn't the ideal route. A line of bunkers extending diagonally from mid-fairway to, and along, the right side of the green means that the farther right one goes, the harder the green is to hit.

No less memorable than the sixth are the holes along the ocean—the 13th, 16th, 17th and 18th—the last three a difficult stretch in the prevailing southeast winds. These four greens are set on a sandy ridge just above the beach and separated from it by thick seagrape bushes. Of the 17th, a 175-yarder, Dave Marr, a former assistant pro at Seminole, says: "Try standing

The epitome of strategic bunkering, the sixth at Seminole, a 390-yard par 4, is often rated among the great golf holes of the world.

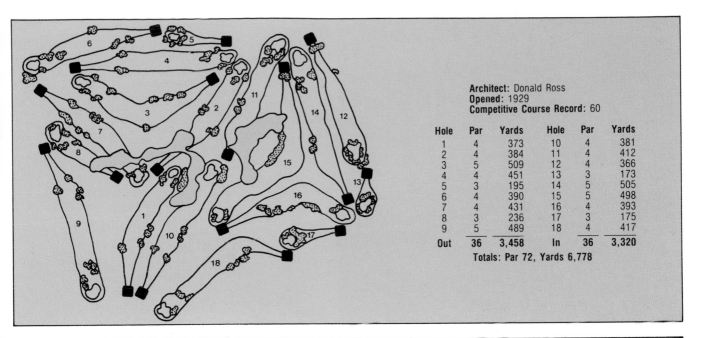

Architect: Donald Ross
Opened: 1929
Competitive Course Record: 60

Hole	Par	Yards	Hole	Par	Yards
1	4	373	10	4	381
2	4	384	11	4	412
3	5	509	12	4	366
4	4	451	13	3	173
5	3	195	14	5	505
6	4	390	15	5	498
7	4	431	16	4	393
8	3	236	17	3	175
9	5	489	18	4	417
Out	**36**	**3,458**	**In**	**36**	**3,320**

Totals: Par 72, Yards 6,778

The comfortable, Spanish-style clubhouse is tasteful, but not pretentious. The large locker room is second to none.

Sand and a persistent stiff breeze off the ocean make this a demanding stretch of holes. The greens shown here, separated from the beach only by sea-grape bushes, are the 13th, 16th and 17th.

there in a high wind with a 2-iron in your hand, knowing you have to make 3.''

Seminole is situated on the Atlantic, about 15 miles up the Florida coast from Palm Beach, that poshest of winter playgrounds. It has an exclusive membership, and is only open about half the year—roughly from November through April. Yet there is nothing stuffy or pretentious about the place. Its Spanish-style clubhouse is comfortable, but not showy, and its large, warm locker room is a hospitable place that many have envied, but few have successfully copied.

The club was opened in 1929, just in time for the market crash and subsequent Depression, but it weathered those storms and eventually began to prosper under the guidance of Chris Dunphy, who, while not as dictatorial perhaps as John Arthur Brown at Pine Valley and Clifford Roberts at Augusta National, was no less concerned with the welfare of the club.

Seminole is a course with alternate tees and, often, alternate routes to the green. It was designed to test players of all handicaps, and, along with only a handful of courses in the world, it succeeds in doing just that.

SHINNECOCK HILLS

A links-style course with an Indian heritage

The founding of the Shinnecock Hills Golf Club proved to be one of the most significant events in the history of American golf, yet it came about almost by accident. William K. Vanderbilt, Duncan Cryder and Edward Mead, all prominent New Yorkers, were in Biarritz, France, in the winter of 1890-91 when they happened to see the Scottish professional Willie Dunn hitting some shots as he was laying out a course there. They were so impressed they wrote home about it, and Dunn subsequently was engaged to design Shinnecock Hills, which was near the Shinnecock Indian reservation on Long Island.

Previous to watching Dunn in action, none of the members had ever seen the game played. Dunn constructed the course with the help of 150 Indians from the reservation and soon had completed 12 holes. The club also engaged the eminent Stanford White to design the clubhouse (which still stands).

The club, which opened late in 1891, was the first to be incorporated, the first with its own clubhouse and the first with a waiting list. A nine-hole course was constructed for the exclusive use of women, but the two

Not technically a linksland course, but with all the atmosphere of one, Shinnecock Hills sits in splendor at the end of Long Island. The course was built by Indians from the nearby Shinnecock reservation, and one of them, John Shippen (right), who was half Negro and half Indian, became the first black to play in the U.S. Open, in 1896.

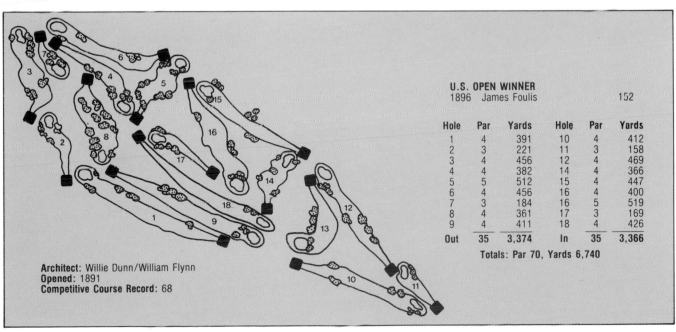

U.S. OPEN WINNER
1896   James Foulis   152

Hole	Par	Yards	Hole	Par	Yards
1	4	391	10	4	412
2	3	221	11	3	158
3	4	456	12	4	469
4	4	382	14	4	366
5	5	512	15	4	447
6	4	456	16	4	400
7	3	184	16	5	519
8	4	361	17	3	169
9	4	411	18	4	426
Out	**35**	**3,374**	**In**	**35**	**3,366**

Totals: Par 70, Yards 6,740

Architect: Willie Dunn/William Flynn
Opened: 1891
Competitive Course Record: 68

were quickly combined into a single 18-hole layout.

The U.S. Open and Amateur championships, first played at Newport, R.I., in 1895, were staged at Shinnecock in 1896. H.J. Whigham replaced his father-in-law, C.B. Macdonald, as Amateur champion and James Foulis won the Open. The latter event included John Shippen, the 21-year-old son of a black Presbyterian minister and a Shinnecock mother.

Shinnecock's best player doubtless was Beatrix Hoyt, only 17 years old when she won in 1896 the first of three straight U.S. Women's titles. After the event was played at Shinnecock in 1900, Hoyt, who lost in the semifinals, retired from golf at age 21.

Highway construction threatened the club property in the late 1920s and new land was bought to give the club room to rearrange the course. The design was directed by Dick Wilson, who was working for the firm of Toomey and Flynn, of Philadelphia. The new layout was opened in 1931 and immediately began to be known as the nearest thing in America to a British linksland course. Actually, it lies two miles from the ocean, but it has the feel of a seaside course with the Atlantic in view on one side and Long Island Sound on the other.

At 6,697 yards, Shinnecock isn't long by modern standards, but it requires precise driving, inspired iron play and an ability to control the ball in the wind. The course was always respected by insiders, but not until the Walker Cup matches of 1977 did it gain widespread acceptance—so much so, in fact, that it was chosen as the site of the 1986 U.S. Open.

There's nothing concealed about the 366-yard 14th; all its numerous bunkers and undulations are in plain view of the golfer. A long drive of extreme accuracy is suggested.

Lurking behind an array of bunkers, the 16th green is watched over by the imposing clubhouse, which looks much as it did when it opened in 1891, the handiwork of Stanford White.

SOUTHERN HILLS

Accuracy off the tee is a distinct requirement for its champions

When approached about providing land for Southern Hills back in 1935, oil millionaire Waite Phillips agreed to donate 300 acres, but only if the club members came up with $150,000 and agreed to spend half that amount the first year as a guarantee of their intentions. He gave them 18 days to raise the money. This was in the depths of the Depression, and even relatively wealthy men had little ready cash. Nevertheless, three men were persuaded to put up $1,000 each, and 71 others signed up for $250 down and agreed to pay $250 every four months until the $1,000 figure was reached. Encouraged by this response, the club's prime movers redoubled their fund-raising efforts and collected a total of $140,000 in pledges with only one day remaining before the deadline imposed by Phillips, who then deeded the land. The club engaged Perry Maxwell to design the course, and it was opened for play in May of 1936.

Dave Stockton drove expertly in winning the 1970 PGA Championship at Southern Hills. So did Hubert Green who won the 1977 U.S. Open there. And Green's victory was all the more impressive because he had other things on his mind. He had learned of a death threat with four holes to play, and it wasn't until after his narrow, one-stroke win over Lou Graham that the gallery knew the strain Green had been under.

Members at Southern Hills have an unparalleled view of the action on the 18th green, which sits directly below the handsome clubhouse. The 430-yard par 4 has been the scene of stirring championship finishes.

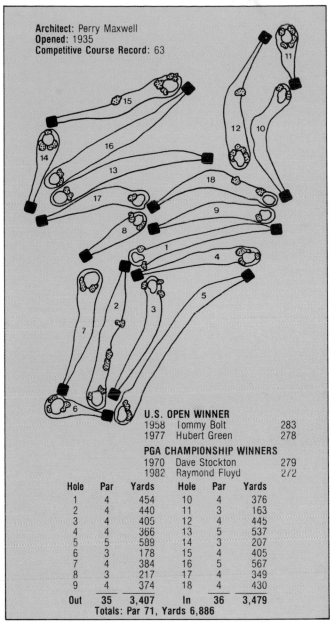

Architect: Perry Maxwell
Opened: 1935
Competitive Course Record: 63

U.S. OPEN WINNER

1958	Tommy Bolt	283
1977	Hubert Green	278

PGA CHAMPIONSHIP WINNERS

1970	Dave Stockton	279
1982	Raymond Floyd	272

Hole	Par	Yards	Hole	Par	Yards
1	4	454	10	4	376
2	4	440	11	3	163
3	4	405	12	4	445
4	4	366	13	5	537
5	5	589	14	3	207
6	3	178	15	4	405
7	4	384	16	5	567
8	3	217	17	4	349
9	4	374	18	4	430
Out	**35**	**3,407**	**In**	**36**	**3,479**

Totals: Par 71, Yards 6,886

Tommy Bolt, long recognized as one of golf's great strikers of the ball, harnessed all his talent for one memorable week in 1958 and won the U.S. Open at Southern Hills.

THE GOLF CLUB
No parallel fairways, plus the "Pete Dye look"

A number of America's golf clubs have been benevolent dictatorships, the best examples being the Pine Valley of John Arthur Brown and the Augusta National of Clifford Roberts. Another is The Golf Club in New Albany, Ohio, just outside Columbus. It was conceived, founded and administered by the late Frederick E. Jones, an insurance man who wanted a place where he and his friends could play without crowded conditions.

The story goes that Jones, a member of Columbus Country Club, got tired of coping with ladies' days, juniors and commercial outings, and decided to build his own course. He began looking for a suitable site in 1963, and the course was opened four years later.

Jones also spent considerable time in selecting a man to design the course, and his final choice—Pete Dye—surprised many because at the time Dye's modest credentials were far from those of more celebrated architects.

The Golf Club was launched with 49 charter members, all friends of Jones. He stipulated that there be no parallel fairways because, as he put it, he wanted to recognize his friends but didn't want to be close enough to stop and talk to them. When work began, Jones asked Dye how many acres he needed to build the kind of course required. A hundred and fifty, Dye replied. "Well," Jones said, "that's no problem. I've got 400." Dye then asked Jones what sections of the property he planned to reserve for housing lots. "Young man," Jones told him briskly, "you almost lost the job with that statement. I don't want any homes out here."

Dye produced a course that looked like it had always been there, by his skillful use of native grasses and by cutting away the soil in front of greens and utilizing the natural ground level of the greens to create the illusion that a relatively level course was on rolling terrain. The Golf Club also gave Dye the opportunity to further develop his use of railroad ties, a variation on the wooden pilings in Scotland. He had first tried this at Crooked Stick and by the time he finished The Golf Club, people began to talk about the "Pete Dye look" and began to seek him for their own courses.

Dye's own favorite hole is the par-4 12th, possibly because its construction posed additional problems. Despite having 400 acres to work with, Dye told Jones he had run out of ground and needed another 10 acres in order to put the 12th tee where he wanted it. Jones then went out and bought the additional land and the 12th was done properly, a clear demonstration of the advantages of dictatorship over a committee.

At The Golf Club, Pete Dye produced a course as natural looking as a Scottish seaside links. Nowhere is that more apparent than at the 15th, a 448-yard par 4 on which the bunkers look as if they had always been there.

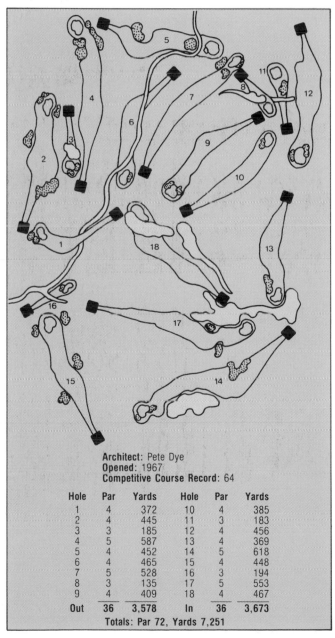

Architect: Pete Dye
Opened: 1967
Competitive Course Record: 64

Hole	Par	Yards	Hole	Par	Yards
1	4	372	10	4	385
2	4	445	11	3	183
3	3	185	12	4	456
4	5	587	13	4	369
5	4	452	14	5	618
6	4	465	15	4	448
7	5	528	16	3	194
8	3	135	17	5	553
9	4	409	18	4	467
Out	36	3,578	In	36	3,673

Totals: Par 72, Yards 7,251

Mamaroneck, New York

WINGED FOOT–WEST
Tillinghast masterpiece stands test of time

In the nearly 60 years since Albert W. Tillinghast cut down 6,800 trees to create Winged Foot's two great golf courses, the East and the West, relatively little has been done architecturally to alter the original designs. As one of the last and finest of Tillie's works, Winged Foot West has withstood the test of longer play with remarkable endurance.

Essentially, the course puts the player to the same exam Tillinghast had in mind when he designed it. In preparation for the 1974 Open, some length was added to a few holes, the entrances to some greens were narrowed, and the 10th green, which Tillinghast regarded as the finest he ever designed, was propped up. Prior to the 1929 Open he said, "The contouring of the greens places great premium on the placement of the drives, but never is there the necessity of facing a prodigious carry of sink or swim sort. If shots home are wide of the green centers, the boys will be using niblicks rather than putters."

The first six holes give Winged Foot West a challenging versatility that lets you know you're playing a golf course requiring not only power but accuracy and restraint. Perhaps the key to its greatness is the same as any work of art. It seems to get better the more you get to know it.

This photo of the 18th hole illustrates the undulations on the greens and the deep bunkers around them that are Winged Foot's marks of great distinction. This is the green on which Bobby Jones made his most famous putt—a curving 12-footer on the 72nd hole of the 1929 Open to tie Al Espinosa, whom he overwhelmed in a 36-hole playoff. Billy Casper, getting a playful pat here from Sam Snead after the third round, won the 1959 U.S. Open with a two-over-par 282.

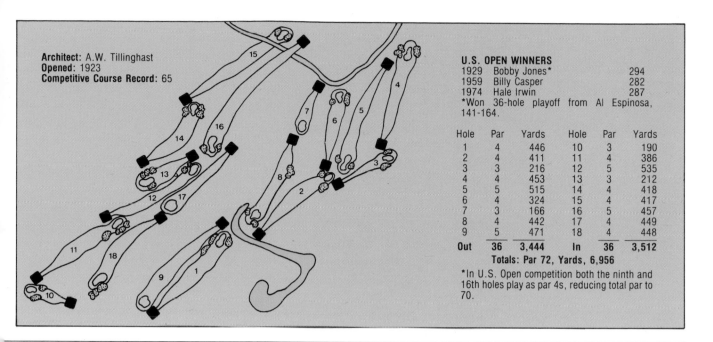

Architect: A.W. Tillinghast
Opened: 1923
Competitive Course Record: 65

U.S. OPEN WINNERS
1929 Bobby Jones*   294
1959 Billy Casper   282
1974 Hale Irwin   287
*Won 36-hole playoff from Al Espinosa, 141-164.

Hole	Par	Yards	Hole	Par	Yards
1	4	446	10	3	190
2	4	411	11	4	386
3	3	216	12	5	535
4	4	453	13	3	212
5	5	515	14	4	418
6	4	324	15	4	417
7	3	166	16	5	457
8	4	442	17	4	449
9	5	471	18	4	448
Out	**36**	**3,444**	**In**	**36**	**3,512**

Totals: Par 72, Yards, 6,956

*In U.S. Open competition both the ninth and 16th holes play as par 4s, reducing total par to 70.

AMERICA'S SECOND 50 COURSES

by John P. May

As more great courses are built and others mature and are redesigned, it becomes a significant achievement simply to qualify for a place among the 100 Greatest. The difference between courses in the top 50 and the second 50 shrinks with each new ranking, and the competition becomes increasingly fierce.

Making the list is no guarantee a course will remain there forever, but it is a fact that turnover is slow. Only after long and serious reflection do the panelists downgrade a course. They agree, however, that no course should remain on the list solely by dint of its reputation.

Because the panelists are determined to weigh carefully the merits of new candidates and courses that have been improved, the result has been remarkable continuity over the years. But because the makeup of the panel undergoes changes and because subjectivity is part of the judging process, each listing inevitably is different. Which means that while it may be slow motion, there is always movement in the second 50.

SECOND FIFTY
In alphabetical order

	YARDS	PAR	YEAR
ARCADIAN SHORES G.C.	6,960	72	1974
Myrtle Beach, S.C.—Rees Jones			
ARONIMINK G.C.	6,958	70	1926
Newtown Square, Pa.—Donald Ross			

ATLANTA A.C. (HIGHLANDS)	6,980	72	1967
Duluth, Ga.—R.T. Jones/J. Finger/G. & T. Fazio			
ATLANTA C.C.	7,019	72	1965
Atlanta—Joe Finger/Willard Byrd			
BELLERIVE C.C.	7,310	71	1960
Creve Coeur, Mo.—Robert Trent Jones			
BOYNE HIGHLANDS G.C.	7,084	72	1968
Harbor Springs, Mich.—Robert Trent Jones			
CEDAR RIDGE C.C.	7,112	71	1971
Broken Arrow, Okla.—Joe Finger			
CHAMPIONS G.C. (JACKRABBIT)	7,121	72	1964
Houston—George and Tom Fazio			
CHICAGO G.C.	6,553	70	1892
Wheaton, Ill.—C.B. Macdonald/Seth Raynor			
COLDSTREAM C.C.	7,170	71	1960
Cincinnati—Dick Wilson			

	YARDS	PAR	YEAR
COLONIAL C.C. (SOUTH)	7,193	72	1971
Memphis—Joe Finger			
C.C. OF BIRMINGHAM (WEST)	7,000	71	1929
Birmingham, Ala.—Donald Ross/Robert Trent Jones			
C.C. OF DETROIT	6,875	72	1914
Grosse Pointe Farms, Mich.—Colt & Alison/R.T. Jones			
C.C. OF NEW SEABURY (BLUE)	7,175	72	1964
Wequoit, Mass.—William Mitchell			
CROOKED STICK G.C.	7,086	72	1964
Carmel, Ind.—Pete Dye			
DESERT FOREST C.C.	6,831	72	1962
Carefree, Ariz.—Red Lawrence			
DISNEY WORLD G.C. (PALM)	6,951	72	1971
Lake Buena Vista, Fla.—Joe Lee			
DUNES G. & B.C.	7,008	72	1949
Myrtle Beach, S.C.—Robert Trent Jones			
EUGENE C.C.	6,700	72	1924
Eugene, Ore.—Chandler Egan/Robert Trent Jones			
GARDEN CITY G.C.	6,746	73	1899
Garden City, N.Y.—Devereaux Emmet			

	YARDS	PAR	YEAR
GOODYEAR G. & C.C. (GOLD)	7,220	72	1965
Litchfield Park, Ariz.—Robert Trent Jones			
GREENVILLE C.C. (CHANTICLEER)	6,815	72	1970
Greenville, S.C.—Robert Trent Jones			
GRENELEFE G. & R.C. (WEST)	7,325	72	1970
Haines City, Fla.—Dave Wallace			
HAZELTINE NATIONAL G.C.	7,134	72	1961
Chaska, Minn.—Robert Trent Jones			
HERSHEY C.C. (WEST)	6,928	73	1930
Hershey, Pa.—Maurice McCarthy			
INNISBROOK G. & C.C.	6,955	71	1972
(COPPERHEAD) Tarpon Springs, Fla.—Larry Packard			
INTERLACHEN C.C.	6,733	73	1911
Edina, Minn.—Willie Watson/Donald Ross			
KEMPER LAKES	7,092	72	1978
Hawthorn Woods, Ill.—Ken Killian and Dick Nugent			
KITTANSETT CLUB	6,545	17	1922
Marion, Mass.—Fred Hood/William Flynn			
LA COSTA C.C.	6,800	72	1964
Carlsbad, Calif.—Dick Wilson			

	YARDS	PAR	YEAR
MAIDSTONE G.C.	6,510	72	1891
East Hampton, N.Y.—Willie and John Park			
MAYACOO LAKES C.C.	6,822	71	1972
West Palm Beach, Fla.—Desmond Muirhead/J. Nicklaus			

	YARDS	PAR	YEAR
MEADOW BROOK CLUB	7,101	72	1954
Jericho, N.Y.—Dick Wilson			
MOSELEM SPRINGS C.C.	7,003	70	1965
Fleetwood, Pa.—George and Tom Fazio			
NATIONAL CASH REGISTER G.C.	6,910	71	1953
(SOUTH) Dayton, Ohio—Dick Wilson			
NORTH SHORE C.C.	7,009	72	1924
Glenview, Ill.—Colt/Mackenzie/Alison			
OLD WARSON C.C.	7,292	71	1955
Ladue, Mo.—Robert Trent Jones			
OLYMPIA FIELDS C.C. (NORTH)	6,750	71	1922
Olympia Fields, Ill.—Willie Park			
PAUMA VALLEY C.C.	7,003	71	1960
Pauma Valley, Calif.—Robert Trent Jones			
PLAINFIELD C.C.	7,086	72	1921
Plainfield, N.J.—Donald Ross			

	YARDS	PAR	YEAR
PRINCEVILLE G.C.	6,948	72	1972
Kauai, Hawaii—Robert Trent Jones Jr.			
SAHALEE C.C.	6,948	72	1972
Redmond, Wash.—Ted Robinson			
SALEM C.C.	6,796	72	1926
Peabody, Mass.—Donald Ross			
SAWGRASS G.C.	7,111	72	1974
Ponte Vedra Beach, Fla.—Ed Seay/Gardner Dickinson			
SEA ISLAND G.C.	6,692	71	1929
St. Simons Island, Ga.—Colt/Alison/Dick Wilson			
SHOAL CREEK	7,029	72	1977
Shoal Creek, Ala.—Jack Nicklaus			
SPYGLASS HILL G.C.	6,810	72	1966
Pebble Beach, Calif.—Robert Trent Jones			
THE COUNTRY CLUB	6,464	72	1927
Brookline, Mass.—F. Hood/L. Curtis/W. Flynn			
WANNAMOISETT C.C.	6,630	69	1898
Rumford, R.I.—Donald Ross			
WILMINGTON C.C. (SOUTH)	6,912	71	1960
Wilmington, Del.—Robert Trent Jones			

ARCADIAN SHORES
Myrtle Beach, South Carolina

Building challenges into courses hugging Myrtle Beach's seaside flatlands is a stern test of the golf course architect's creativeness. At Arcadian Shores, Rees Jones had an additional caveat—that of producing a course not so back-breaking as to discourage the resort golfer. That was because Arcadian Shores is affiliated with a 390-room hotel.

What resulted here is a marvelous combination of sandy and watery problems blended into a course that can go from 6,960 yards to 5,721. On five of the holes the last full shot must clear green-fronting water. Most fairways glide between stands of tall pines and leafy oaks. This creates a certain nervousness in all golfers, including club professionals from the Carolinas PGA section who every other year play in the Winston Classic at Arcadian Shores.

ARONIMINK
Newtown Square, Pennsylvania

Although Aronimink's present course dates from 1926, the club itself has been in existence since 1896. The membership twice outgrew its surroundings before settling on today's 300 acres of rolling countryside in the Radnor Hunt country at Newtown Square west of Philadelphia. One of golf's foremost architects, Donald Ross, designed a course that fits warmly into the tumbling terrain. Fairways burrow through stands of pines and oaks to greens that are on the small side, from 7,200 to 9,000 square feet.

Shortly before Ross died in 1948, he came by to visit Aronimink. Obviously he had a warm spot in his heart for this course.

"I intended to make this (Aronimink) my masterpiece," he said, "but not until today did I realize that I built better than I knew."

Most of Aronimink's greens are at least slightly elevated, so that high, soft shots are the type of approaches you want to hit. The greens on shorter holes are guarded by deep bunkers directly in front and to the sides. Most of the greens are wider than they are deep, so there is not excessive room for maneuvering shots onto the putting surfaces.

Maintaining an Indian heritage, each of Aronimink's holes has an Indian name.

Twice the course has hosted national championships: the 1962 PGA Championship, won by Gary Player, and the 1977 U.S. Amateur, captured by John Fought.

A 250-yard drive on the 420-yard, par-4 13th at Arcadian Shores leaves a 170-yard approach that must clear this pond, covering the last 95 yards. A Rees Jones design, Arcadian Shores features five holes on which the last full shot must clear water. The course often hosts competitions for area club professionals.

Deep bunkers challenge approaches on the par-4, 437-yard 10th at Aronimink (below), to a green of some 7,400 square feet. Most of the greens at this course are elevated and somewhat shallow. This Philadelphia suburban 18 has hosted the 1962 PGA Championship and the 1977 U.S. Amateur.

ATLANTA A.C.-HIGHLANDS

Duluth, Georgia

Some clubs jealously retain the original designs of their courses, but not the Atlanta Athletic Club. The home club of Bobby Jones, AAC abandoned its East Lake location in 1967 in favor of a new 27-hole Robert Trent Jones layout in suburban Duluth. A few years later Joe Finger added a fourth nine, which now plays as the Highlands' front nine. The

championship course features extraordinarily large sand bunkers, many situated along the edges of fairways to discourage shortcuts around doglegs, or to dictate accurate drives. Most greens on par 4s are guarded by bunkers that minimize roll-on approaches.

Because of its Bobby Jones connection, AAC sought, and was awarded, the 1976 U.S. Open. Architects George and Tom Fazio were then called in to alter the Finger and Jones nines into the present Highlands Course. The remaining 18, hard by the Chattahoochee River, was dubbed the Riverside Course.

Jerry Pate won that 1976 Open with a dramatic 5-iron shot to two feet on the final hole. In 1981, the Highlands Course, further refined by the Fazios, hosted the PGA Championship, won by local choice Larry Nelson.

ATLANTA C.C.
Atlanta, Georgia

It has plenty of lakes and bunkers and trees, but the Atlanta Country Club has more than its share of hills as well. This Willard Byrd design has more peaks and valleys than the stock market. Yet this fact has not kept PGA players from shooting some low numbers at the annual Atlanta Classic, especially Andy Bean, who scored a record 265, 23 under par for 72 holes, in 1979.

But Atlanta is no pushover. Besides the tour event, Atlanta Country Club has hosted the U.S. Women's Amateur, the USGA Senior Amateur and the inaugural Tournament Players Championship, won by Jack Nicklaus. The Golden Bear, incidentally, supervised some tightening of the course after Bean's onslaught in 1979. His suggested changes worked, and scores in the 1980 Atlanta Classic were higher, hometown favorite Larry Nelson winning with 270.

It was on the Atlanta Athletic Club's 18th (left), a 460-yard par 4, that Jerry Pate scored his dramatic birdie to clinch the 1976 U.S. Open championship. He hit a 5-iron to two feet, then sank the putt for a two-stroke victory.

Contestants at suburban St. Louis' Bellerive course must play very carefully on the 164-yard, par-3 third (below), what with water almost all around the green. Gary Player won the 1965 U.S. Open title here.

One of four exceptional par 3s at the Atlanta Country Club, the 160-yard sixth (above) requires a tee shot over water to an angled green. This long and demanding course was redesigned recently by Jack Nicklaus.

BELLERIVE
Creve Coeur, Missouri

After 50 years at a metropolitan location, Bellerive moved into suburban Creve Coeur in 1960, St. Louis' bicentennial year. Robert Trent Jones was hired to design the new course, and it is a very long layout that can go as much as 7,305 yards. Only five years later Bellerive played host to a national championship, the U.S. Open. It remains the youngest club ever to entertain the tournament. Length is a factor at Bellerive, but so are the elevated greens that demand careful approaches. South African Gary Player won that '65 Open, beating Kel Nagle of Australia in a playoff for the championship. In 1981 the first U.S. Mid-Amateur (for golfers 25 and over) was played at Bellerive and won by Jim Holtgrieve of St. Louis. Bellerive's history goes back to 1897, its first 18-hole course opening in 1910.

BOYNE HIGHLANDS

Harbor Springs, Michigan

Because of its unusually high number of dogleg holes—there are 12—playing Boyne's Heather Course is a strategic confrontation. Every tee and fairway shot must be carefully plotted, keeping in mind the many angles produced by the twists and turns of the fairways. One nine is designed by Robert Trent Jones, the other by William Newcombe, and together total 7,084 yards at its lengthiest, with fairways wide enough to be forgiving at times. The greens are large,

On the 540-yard, par-5 11th hole at Boyne Highlands' original course, fairway sand bunkers limit the target area off the tee, and four deep bunkers surround the two-tiered green. This is a Robert Trent Jones course, with large greens that average 10,000 to 12,000 square feet.

averaging 10,000 to 12,000 square feet. With such expansive surfaces, good approach putting becomes vital to scoring. Because the tees and fairways, as well as the greens, are turfed with bent grass, close mowing is the rule.

Heather is one of five 18-hole regulation courses in Boyne Country, a 10,000-acre recreational complex that includes four resort developments. Located in the northwestern part of Michigan's lower peninsula, Boyne Country golf courses are open from May through October.

CEDAR RIDGE

Broken Arrow, Oklahoma

Fairway bunkers are the most important hazards at Cedar Ridge. Architect Joe Finger has positioned them so they challenge every full drive, and the well-played tee shot away from or around these hazards always pays off; few of these bunkers, however, can be flown. Approaches to the large greens—they average 10,000 square feet—must be carefully planned and executed so first putts are not unusually

The green on Cedar Ridge's 409-yard, par-4 12th is typical of this Oklahoma course's putting surfaces—large, gently contoured and tiered. Sand bunkers protect the greens from off-target approaches, but a straight, low-runner has a chance to get home. Cedar Ridge is the site of the 1983 U.S. Women's Open.

A 220-yard carry over water greets the golfer on the par-3 11th hole at the Champions Jackrabbit course. Add a few trees and a small green, and you have an extremely demanding hole. The Jackrabbit is one of two courses at the Champions, owned and operated by Jimmy Demaret and Jack Burke Jr.

long. Three-putts come easily on these contoured surfaces.

Since Cedar Ridge was opened for play in 1969, more than 4,000 oaks, elms and pines have been planted to provide definition and beauty to the course. Among the important championships played here are the 1974 Trans-Mississippi Amateur and the 1978 Oklahoma State Amateur. It is also the site of the 1983 U.S. Women's Open.

CHAMPIONS-JACKRABBIT
Houston, Texas

This is the second course at Champions, the Jimmy Demaret-Jack Burke Jr. facility in Houston that may have the best 36 holes of any private American club. Although the Cypress Creek 18, designed by Ralph Plummer and opened in 1959, has been the site of all of the Champions' major tournaments, the Jackrabbit is considered only slightly less demanding. Certainly it is different. Demaret and Burke wanted a second course that looked nothing like the first, which has wide fairways and big, rolling greens.

George Fazio produced the Jackrabbit, opened in 1964, and stuck to what has been called the "Eastern" style—narrow fairways, plenty of sand bunkers, small, elevated greens. High, backspinning approaches are the best shots to bring with you to the Jackrabbit. The course is compact, having been built on only 125 acres, but for tournaments it can play up to a monstrous 7,000 yards.

CHICAGO
Wheaton, Illinois

When the Chicago Golf Club course was completed in 1894, it became the first in the United States with 18 holes. Chicago Golf, as the course is known, was designed and constructed under the supervision of Charles Blair Macdonald, one of the giants of early American golf, who had learned the game in Scotland as a teenager. The course was remodeled in

1923 by Macdonald's partner, Seth Raynor. Macdonald was reported to be a slicer and hence many fairways dogleg to the right. In December 1894, Chicago Golf was one of five clubs to organize and sponsor the United States Golf Association, and the next year, 1895, Macdonald won the first U.S. Amateur, played at Newport, R.I. Later he brought the U.S. Open to Chicago Golf three times (1897, 1900, 1911). The Open winners at Chicago were, in chronological order, Joe Lloyd, an English professional who was then working at the Essex Country Club in Manchester, Mass.; Harry Vardon, the great English golfer who eventually won six British Opens, and John McDermott of Philadelphia, the first native-born American to win the Open.

Many features of Scotland's St. Andrews can be seen at Chicago Golf. Most recognizable are the numerous mounds scattered over the fairways. The greens, however, are not as small as might be expected, considering the course's age; most of the bunkers are set well below green level. Today the course is still a sturdy test at par 70, 6,553 yards.

COLDSTREAM
Cincinnati, Ohio

The name of this lengthy course is derived from the Coldstream Guards, the red-coated Scottish regiment founded in 1659 that protects the English royal household in a formal sense. One of the golf club's founders had visited Great Britain and obtained permission from the Guards to use the name and crest.

Opened for play in 1960, the course was designed by Dick Wilson and spotlights his use of unusually large tees, greens and sand bunkers—more than 100 of the latter. Because the greens are quite long, from 54 to 138 feet, pin placement affects play here considerably. All four par 3s play over or past water, and two par 4s show lateral water hazards some 220 yards from the

tees. The course can play up to 7,494 yards, but its usual championship length is near 7,100. The terrain was originally treeless, but 4,500 pines, pin oaks and fruit trees have been planted. Coldstream is a frequent site of sectional qualifying for such important tournaments as the PGA Championship.

The 16th, a 450-yard par 4, is one of the more difficult holes at Coldstream. The course was named after the Coldstream Guards, a regiment that formally protects the English royal household.

You can't see them until you're up close, but the 30 pot bunkers that inhabit the Chicago Golf Club course can be troublesome. There are two on this hole, the 414-yard, par-4 12th, one to the right side of the fairway 225 yards out, the other directly in front of the green.

COLONIAL-SOUTH
Memphis, Tennessee

When land in Memphis proper spectacularly increased in value in the 1960s, members of the Colonial Country Club there sold its original acreage at a handsome profit and moved the club to suburban Cordova. Two Joe Finger-designed courses (North and South) were opened for play in October, 1971.

The South, highest-ranked of the two, can be stretched to 7,193 yards. Water is a major problem for the golfer, with lakes and ponds on eight of the last nine holes. The original Colonial course, which dates from 1915, was the site of a PGA Tour event since 1958. The new South Course has continued as host of the Danny Thomas Memphis Classic. In 1977 Al Geiberger scored an 18-hole tour record 59 on this difficult test in the process of winning, and in 1981 Jerry Pate celebrated his Memphis win with a dive into the lake off the 18th green that became one of the top tour stories of the year.

C.C. OF BIRMINGHAM-WEST
Birmingham, Alabama

Two of the best-known names in golf course architecture had a hand in the framework of Birmingham West. Donald Ross was the original architect. His work was completed in 1929 as a culmination of a relocation of the club. Then in 1959 Robert Trent Jones resculptured the greens, enlarging them slightly and adding contour. Today the course plays at 7,000 yards, a rigid examination that features creeks winding through the landscape.

The club was formed in 1898, and in 1903 combined with the Birmingham Golf Club. That was a tidy move, for the Country Club had had a clubhouse, but no course; the Golf Club had had a course, but no clubhouse. The present course came about after members purchased 300 acres in the heart of Birmingham in 1926.

U.S. Amateur qualifying is often held here, and the Birmingham Invitational is one of the top events in the state. The club also has an East Course.

Colonial South's tough finisher, the par-5, 548-yard 18th (left), features a pond to the left, one of eight water hazards that peril play on the back nine. It is also the pond into which professional Jerry Pate jumped after winning the Danny Thomas Memphis Classic here in 1981.

The Country Club of Detroit is the oldest club in the Detroit area, begun at another location in 1898. The present course, with its demanding par-4 414-yard 18th hole shown here, was renovated by Robert Trent Jones for the 1954 U.S. Amateur.

The green on the seventh hole at Birmingham West (above) offers a large but nevertheless difficult approach target. This course's greens were resculptured by Robert Trent Jones, but the original course design is by Donald Ross.

C.C. OF DETROIT

Grosse Pointe Farms, Michigan

In preparation for the 1954 U.S. Amateur, the Country Club of Detroit authorized Robert Trent Jones to renovate and strengthen its course. Jones responded with his customary antidote of eliminating fairway bunkers close to the tees that today's long-hitters could easily clear, then installing other bunkers some 230-260 yards out. This instantly shrank the target areas. In 1970, 350 trees were planted in a program to replace those lost to disease.

This club, the oldest in metropolitan Detroit, had its first course in 1898 on lakefront property in Grosse Pointe. It was a crude nine-holer replaced in 1912 by an interesting 18-hole course designed by the British architect, Harry Colt. In 1915, Bob Gardner of Chicago won the U.S. Amateur here. By 1927 another 18, utilizing parts of the 1912 layout, was completed and remains the basis for today's 18.

What hasn't changed over the years is the view from the clubhouse veranda, which overlooks play on the 18th green. As you complete your round, you can hear some good-humored razzing (and perhaps cheering) from the observing clubhouse crowd.

Golf at New Seabury's sun- and sea-kissed Blue Course on Cape Cod is often played in bracing ocean winds. The opening nine plays tag with the beach, while the second wends inland. Here is a view of the second (415 yards) and third (425), a pair of sterling par 4s.

As its name implies at Desert Forest (right), cacti and Joshua trees rise near the green on the par-4, 428-yard second hole, the No. 1 handicap test of the course. Soil was imported to elevate many of the greens, adding to their challenge.

Architect Pete Dye's familiar upright pilings reinforce the edge of the water hazard and green on the par-3, 189-yard sixth hole (below) at Crooked Stick. The Indianapolis-area course often hosts state and city competitions and was the site of the 1982 U.S. Boys Junior.

C.C. OF NEW SEABURY-BLUE
Wequoit, Massachusetts

Playing golf at New Seabury is one of the contrasting delights of the game. The Seaside nine of the Blue Course undulates smoothly on treeless, sandy terrain, with Nantucket Sound always in sight. White-sanded bunkers explode from the fairways. Because the terrain is level, distance is more difficult to judge than usual.

The incoming Cedars nine is the exact opposite, trundling over rough, hilly terrain stirred up by the glaciers that once covered the area. The holes curl pleasantly through wooded dells and past manmade water hazards.

New Seabury is a William Mitchell design, which gained instant recognition as one of the best when it was opened in 1964.

CROOKED STICK
Carmel, Indiana

There is a sort of Magna Carta of course maintenance at Crooked Stick that reads in part: "(There shall be) progressively difficult rough away from the fairways and greens... Greens will be consistently true and dry enough to hold a well-struck shot, but not a poor one; pin placements will be so that any putt from under six feet is controllable, and as flat as possible for putts from within three feet." Certainly laudable objectives, and they've been followed.

Crooked Stick, one of Pete Dye's earlier designs, was opened for play in 1964. There are some of his familiar waste bunkers—long, fairway-hugging sand hazards, and also railroad ties supporting the banks of ponds and other hazards. Unlike many of Dye's other creations, however, Crooked Stick has rather large greens, some with pronounced undulations. It was originally built for low-handicappers only, but now the club accepts players of all skills.

Numerous state and city tournaments have been played here, and in 1982 the club hosted its first national championship, the U.S. Boys Junior.

DESERT FOREST
Carefree, Arizona

An important concern of Desert Forest's builders was to leave the desert foliage intact, and golf course architect Red Lawrence was true to the task. Desert shrubbery, cacti and sturdy Joshua trees line the fairways, harassing off-line shots and rewarding accuracy. The terrain is naturally rolling, and this effect was enhanced during construction when soil was imported to elevate some tees and greens and execute bunkers.

The course was opened for play in 1962 as part of a residential community 23 miles from Scottsdale, a Phoenix suburb. At that time the Scottsdale-Carefree road, which takes you to the course, was paved for only three miles—the rest was dirt. But by 1964 the other 20 miles were completed. Even then the course, a testy 6,831-yarder that emphasizes strategy, was beginning to attract attention. Since then the Arizona State Open and Amateur have been played here, and also the Pacific Coast Amateur. Usually only the winner and two or three others break par.

DISNEY WORLD-PALM

Lake Buena Vista, Florida

Walt Disney World's three courses occupy an area that in its original state would not seem a likely place for golf. The low and level terrain was covered with scrub pine and a few palms and was extremely wet. Nevertheless, modern construction technology helped turn the courses into parkland wonders.

Of the three, the Palm is the most demanding. It is cut through an especially wooded area, so the fairways are not usually visible from one to another. Many of the tees are elevated to afford a preview of play. Small mounds have been built here and there and produce a few uneven lies. Water comes into play on eight holes.

Joe Lee designed the Palm and the Magnolia, both of which opened in 1971, plus the Lake Buena Vista, which opened in 1972. All three sites annually host PGA Tour competitions and many other tournaments.

Water is a constant hazard on the 460-yard, par-4 sixth at Disney World's Palm Course, threatening pulled shots at first and then crossing the fairway in front of the green. The Palm, site of a PGA Tour event, is built through a heavily forested, low-lying area.

DUNES

Myrtle Beach, South Carolina

Seaside golf at its most interesting is in store for golfers at the Dunes. Hard against a marshy inlet of the Atlantic, the course will spring a surprise on the unwary. Except for the uphill ninth and downhill 10th, the holes are generally level, but evil lurks to the sides of many fairways in the form of ponds and soggy swampland. The fast-draining soil is sandy, and in the rough shots are often from a thicket of pine needles fallen from the many trees that divide the fairways. Nearly every green is elevated and all are hunkered behind one or more of the Dunes' 60 sand bunkers. Off-target approaches are often disastrous.

A Robert Trent Jones design, the Dunes was opened for play in 1949, and while it has hosted only one national championship, the 1962 U.S. Women's Open, many regional and state competitions are played here. It is also the site of the annual Golf Writers Association of America tournament, played here every spring just before the Masters since 1953.

A nerve-wracking test of skill, the Dunes Golf and Beach Club's 575-yard, par-5 13th challenges golfers to bite off as much of the water as they dare on the second shot. Only one man, Mike Souchak, has reached this green in two. This is regarded as architect Robert Trent Jones' classic heroic hole.

With mountain ranges in the back-ground, Eugene Country Club is surrounded by a lovely setting. The green of the 383-yard, par-4 14th is an undulating putting surface that invites three-putts. Eugene was opened for play in 1924, but the present course is a Robert Trent Jones redesign.

EUGENE
Eugene, Oregon

Chandler Egan, the former U.S. Amateur champion, laid out the Eugene course in 1924, but he'd never recognize it today. In 1967 Robert Trent Jones was summoned to remodel the course and literally turned things completely around. Jones reversed the holes, putting tees where greens had been and vice versa. This placed existing water hazards in front of the greens instead of harmlessly next to the tees.

Jones, in fact, might have difficulty in recognizing Eugene Country Club. Unlike many of his courses, it has tight fairways, multiple tees and smallish greens. Eugene was once a regular stop on the LPGA Tour, and in 1964 Johnny Miller won the U.S. Junior here.

GARDEN CITY
Garden City, New York

Garden City plays much like a Scottish links course, what with its unkempt look—pot bunkers and grassy mounds in the fairways and clumpy grass in the rough. Tournament professional Ben Crenshaw, a noted student of golf history, once observed that Garden City seemed to have been designed by architect Devereaux Emmet with little alteration in the existing terrain.

First opened as a nine-hole public course in 1896, then completed in 1899 and at that time incorporated as a private club, Garden City played an important part in the early days of American golf. Walter Travis, who made major redesigns in the course, was a member and in 1900 won the U.S. Amateur at his home club. Three more Amateurs, plus the 1902 U.S. Open and the 1924 Walker Cup matches, were subsequently played here. The course is the site of the annual Travis Memorial, an important New York metropolitan amateur event.

Deep sand bunkers off elevated greens are part of Garden City's Scottish look (below). This is the 16th, a 401-yard, par-4 dogleg left with swales off both sides of the fairway.

Goodyear's golf course, built over level terrain, is stiffened by water hazards on 14 holes. Trees separate the reasonably wide fairways of this course, which is part of the Wigwam, a resort near Phoenix with three full-sized courses.

GOODYEAR-GOLD
Litchfield Park, Arizona

Those who play at Goodyear Gold usually remember each hole as an entity in itself, a stern test not to be taken lightly. Water makes up much of the challenge, and is present on 14 holes. Although the fairways are reasonably wide, if you go into the rough you'll encounter many large trees, mostly tamarac or willow. The seaside bent greens are large and moderately fast and each is protected by at least one of the 100 sand bunkers on the course. From the championship tees, Goodyear plays to a back-breaking 7,220 yards.

The present blue course was designed in 1965 by Robert Trent Jones, who utilized some of an original 18 at The Wigwam, which opened its first nine in 1930. A second nine was added in 1941. In 1966 Jones built the championship Gold Course at Goodyear, and in 1975 a third 18, the West, a Red Lawrence design, was added. The Wigwam, 12 miles west of Phoenix, is the only resort in the Southwest that offers three full-sized golf courses.

GREENVILLE-CHANTICLEER

Greenville, South Carolina

Golfers playing at Chanticleer are often led to comment about the "naturalness" of the setting. Everything seems to be as nature would have decided. Tree-lined fairways snuggle comfortably over easily walked glens, each hole an entity in itself. Inexact approaches often cause bogeys, for 11 of the greens are guarded by lakes or streams, which existed before the golf course was constructed. Also, the rolling, bent-grass greens test even the best of putters.

Chanticleer was opened for play in 1970, the design of architect Robert Trent Jones, who had studied possible sites for the three previous years. The Greenville club itself dates from 1877, when a group constructed a crude nine-hole course and eventually formed the Greenville Country Club in 1927, with an 18-hole course still being played. Today the club has two 18-hole courses, plus a nine-hole par-3, and often entertains regional and state competitions.

An early-morning 18th hole tableau at the West Course of the Grenelefe Golf and Racquet Club is a common sight, with golf car tracks outlined on the dewy fairways as a foursome prepares to shoot for the well-trapped green at the upper left.

Greenville's Chanticleer Course blends into a completely natural setting. Trees and sand bunkers line most fairways, as on this, the par-4, 368-yard sixth hole that curves sharply right.

GRENELEFE-WEST
Haines City, Florida

Approaches on the par-4, 414-yard 10th at Hazeltine are treacherous, what with the water behind the green and the surrounding sand. This Minneapolis-area course has hosted the U.S. Open, two U.S. Women's Opens and a PGA Tour stop.

Reynaud Grenelefe would have enjoyed this mid-Florida condominium-golf resort; it would provide him with plenty of natural cover. As a "spy" for the legendary Robin Hood, Grenelefe was actually that happy hulk, Little John. Today's Grenelefe filters through groves of slash pines and oak trees, a rolling test that has played host to the Florida Amateur and several collegiate competitions. The West Course was completed in 1970 by Dave Wallace, a Tampa architect who left such flexibility in his design that the yardage can run from a monstrous 7,325 yards down to a puny 5,403. Robert Trent Jones did the original routing.

Since the West's completion, another 18, designed by Ed Seay and Bob Walker, has been added to the Grenelefe complex. Under construction and scheduled to open in January, 1983, is a third course, designed by Andy Bean and Ron Garl.

Grenelefe West's best holes are the ninth and 14th, each a long par 4. The ninth plays 458 yards from the back tees with trees lining both sides of the narrow fairway. The green is protected on three sides by bunkers. The 14th, a slight dogleg left, is 479 yards. Both, however, mellow quite a bit from the middle markers; they're each a more negotiable 360 yards from there.

HAZELTINE NATIONAL
Chaska, Minneapolis

Hazeltine National was built with the express purpose of creating a championship test, and that aim has been fulfilled, partly as a result of early criticism from Dave Hill during the 1970 U.S. Open, won by Tony Jacklin. Hazeltine was extensively remodeled in the late 1970s. Since it was opened in 1961, this Minneapolis-area course has also played host to two U.S. Women's Opens and a PGA Tour stop, besides the men's Open and numerous state competitions.

Nearly all contestants have found Hazeltine to be a difficult case with its imposing and long par 4s and par 5s topped by large, undulating greens averaging 7,500 square feet. Since the course was developed through farmland and forest, the holes alternate between open landscape and threatening trees. The architect was Robert Trent Jones, designated as a Hazeltine co-founder with Totton P. Heffelfinger, a former president of the United States Golf Association.

HERSHEY-WEST
Hershey, Pennsylvania

The names of Ben Hogan and Henry Picard are well-remembered in Hershey. Picard served as the club professional from 1934 until 1941, and during that time he won the PGA Championship and the Masters. Hogan succeeded Picard and was associated with Hershey for the next 10 years, when he won three of his four U.S. Opens. Byron Nelson and Sam Snead also have Hershey connections; Nelson defeated Snead in the final of the 1940 PGA Championship here. For years a PGA Tour event was played at Hershey. One year Nelson was contending when a ball he hit down the center of the fairway on 18 was never found, and he lost the tournament. A few weeks later he received a check for $7,500, equal to the winner's purse, from Milton S. Hershey, the chocolate man himself. The club now hosts an annual LPGA Tour event.

Hershey West is a narrow-fairwayed, heavily wooded test that is a good example of the golf course architecture of an earlier day. Maurice McCarthy was the designer of the course, opened for play in 1930. The Hershey Country Club has another 18, the East, designed by George Fazio and opened in 1969.

INNISBROOK-COPPERHEAD
Tarpon Springs, Florida

Set a golfer unaware of his whereabouts in the middle of any of Innisbrook's three stringent courses and the thought may occur: "This must be North Carolina." Wrong. These courses are in west Florida, north of Tampa, in one of the state's few hilly areas. The towering pines native to the section, along with the rolling terrain, create the North Carolina impression.

Innisbrook's Copperhead can go to 6,955 yards, long and strategically demanding enough for the tournament professional, and indeed it often is the site of state competitions. This course boasts 80-foot elevations, almost unheard of in Florida. When there are no trees to challenge shots, water and sand take over. Golf course architect Larry Packard left no weak holes here.

Hershey West's 18th (left), a 430-yard par 4, rises gently toward a large green with monstrous sand bunkers on either side. There are two courses at Hershey, the West and the East, and both Ben Hogan and Henry Picard have been club professionals here.

INTERLACHEN
Edina, Minnesota

Interlachen's place in golfing history is secure. It was here that Bobby Jones won the 1930 U.S. Open on the way to his still-unmatched Grand Slam (he also won the British Open, British Amateur and U.S. Amateur that year). Willie Watson designed the course on open, rolling terrain in 1911. Donald Ross modified it a bit in 1919, and over the years oak and maple have covered the hills. In 1960 Robert Trent Jones revised the first and third holes, bringing the course to its present maximum length of 6,733 yards and par 73.

Water threatens both the tee shot and the approach on the Copperhead's 450-yard, par-4 16th (below). This course, part of the Innisbrook Golf and Country Club complex, is routed through one of the few hilly areas in west Florida.

Besides Jones' Open, the best-known national championship played here was the 1935 U.S. Women's Amateur, when Interlachen's own Patty Berg, then 17, lost in the final to Glenna Collett Vare. The Western Open and the Trans-Mississippi Amateur have also been played here.

The likes of Bobby Jones and Glenna Collett Vare have walked this fairway, Interlachen's ninth, on the way to winning national championships. A large pond patrols play in front of the green on this 520-yard, par-5 hole where Jones skipped his approach off the water on his way to winning the 1930 U.S. Open.

As the course's name implies, water is prevalent at Kemper Lakes. It makes its point from tee to green on the par-4, 456-yard 16th hole. This course, within the Kemper Group's national headquarters grounds, is open to the public.

KEMPER LAKES
Hawthorn Woods, Illinois

This is an intimidating course, built on 270 acres, with lakes occupying 125 of them. Thus it isn't surprising that water comes into play on 11 holes and must be carried on eight shots. Two of these are on the par-4, 456-yard, 16th—the tee shot *and* the approach. There was room left for 57 sand bunkers.

Kemper Lakes was designed by Ken Killian and Dick Nugent, with input from Jack Tuthill, then the PGA Tour tournament director. It can be played from a minimum of 5,635 to a maximum of 7,092 yards. Opened in 1978, and located 40 miles northwest of Chicago, the public course is within the Kemper Group's national headquarter grounds and is also the home of the Illinois PGA, hosting many sectional events.

Even par always contends and often wins.

KITTANSETT CLUB
Marion, Massachusetts

There was a brisk wind that day during the 1978 Massachusetts Amateur at Marion's redoubtable Kittansett Club, scuffling across the nearby coastline at 20 knots per hour. A young contestant asked a long-time member, ''Is it always like this?'' ''No,'' replied the old-timer, probably hoping for a chance to make this crack, ''usually it's windy.''

Wind is certainly a factor at Kittansett, built along the flat shoreline off Buzzard's Bay, but that's not all that makes this 6,545-yard course a mighty mite. Almost ex-

Kittansett's seaside nature is amply demonstrated in this overview of the Massachusetts course. Brisk winds from Buzzard's Bay often buffet the course. The green isolated on the beach in the foreground is of the 170-yard par-3 third hole.

actly today as it was when Fred Hood and William Flynn laid out the holes in 1922, Kittansett has those Old World ribbon fairways to small greens hunkered between deep sand bunkers. There are even cross roughs—areas of untended grass in the middle of some fairways—an almost-forgotten practice coming back these days as a step toward lower maintenance costs.

Like many Scottish courses, Kittansett takes you straight out on the front nine, then does an about face and heads home to the clubhouse. When the Ryder Cup was played here in 1953, the only concession to the modern golfer was an added bunker directly in front of the par-3 14th's green.

LA COSTA
Carlsbad, California

Some who visit the expensive La Costa resort don't even realize that a superb golf course traverses the 6,000-acre property. That's because of the luxurious accommodations, a widely known health spa and tennis courts. The course, nevertheless, is a splendid one, site of the annual Tournament of Champions on the PGA Tour since 1969. Only winners of tour events over the past year are invited.

The Dick Wilson-designed 18 opened only five years before the first T of C arrived, and the layout became an immediate threat to the professionals' temperaments. Thick, wiry rough makes recoveries difficult, and the fairways are narrower than usual.

There are about 100 bunkers on this 6,800-yard course, along with greens smaller than on most Wilson creations. When the wind blows, as it often does, watch out. The 16th, 17th and 18th are usually into a fierce breeze, so finishes here can be tumultuous.

MAIDSTONE
East Hampton, New York

Maidstone. The very name sounds Neanderthal, as if the great god Golf might have sprung from its back-swing. And that's not too far off the mark. Opened for play in 1891, this Long Island club is the oldest of America's 100 Greatest Courses. The designers were W.H. Tucker Sr., joined by Willie Park Jr. and John Park, a pair of Englishmen whose golfing background goes back to the gutta-percha days, for Pete's sake. Their father, Willie Park Sr., won the very first British Open, in 1860, and subsequently three more. Junior added a pair of British titles himself, in 1887 and 1889.

Their course, near the ocean and barely touched by time, is Scottish from the beachgrass in its sand bunk-

ers to the gorse-type brush in its rough. There are hardly any trees on the wind-swept terrain, but the inland ponds, sand and nasty rough make it a demanding test. You hang onto your bowler at Maidstone, but don't swing hard. It's only 6,510 yards from the championship tees, but if the wind's against you it feels like 7,510.

La Costa's strong course looks like a patch of lush greenery amidst a beautiful Southern California desert. Here sand bunkers frame the green on the par-3, 203-yard 14th hole as a desert hill rises in the background.

There's a definite linksland aura about Maidstone's coastal course on New York's Long Island. As a matter of fact, Maidstone was designed mainly by two Scotsmen, Willie Park Jr. and John Park. Here the par-4, 330-yard ninth doglegs right, past brush-covered dunes.

Water comes into play on 13 holes at Mayacoo Lakes and fills more than half of the fairway on the par-4, 395-yard 12th, shown here. This East Coast course in Florida was considered too difficult when it was first opened, in 1972. But it has been softened to some degree over the years.

MAYACOO LAKES
West Palm Beach, Florida

It is said that no hole at Mayacoo Lakes will penalize a good shot nor force a layup. This is the result of the thinking of Jack Nicklaus, who with Desmond Muirhead designed this course. When it was first opened in 1972, Mayacoo Lakes was considered too difficult, but with Nicklaus periodically making alterations it has become a forceful test of golf for players of all handicaps.

Built on level land and 6,822 yards from the back tees, the course packs much of its punch into the 13 holes that feature water hazards. Stands of melaleuca trees, palmetto bushes and cabbage palms line most fairways. Because of the water and trees, shot placement is always important here.

Mayacoo Lakes has hosted the PGA Club Professional Series, the Eastern Seniors and several state and local events. The best scores are seldom below par 71.

Dangerous fairway bunkers patrol the tee shot on the 527-yard, par-5 first hole at Long Island's Meadow Brook Club. The first U.S. Women's Amateur, in 1895, was played at Meadow Brook's original course, at a different site than the present 18.

Water intrudes into the fairway of the 18th at Moselem Springs. This is a rugged par 4 of 470 yards, a hole not to be trifled with in any event. This lovely hillside course is a favorite of its architect George Fazio. It is known to better golfers in the Philadelphia area as a demanding test.

precise shot-making from start to finish. Beginning in 1979, Meadow Brook hosted an annual LPGA Tour event, and the women pronounced the course one of the most difficult they play.

MOSELEM SPRINGS
Fleetwood, Pennsylvania

MEADOW BROOK CLUB
Jericho, New York

This club's origins date back to the very first U.S. Women's Amateur, in 1895. This was the third national championship conducted by the United States Golf Association, only the U.S. Open and U.S. Amateur preceding it. Mrs. C.S. Brown of nearby Shinnecock won with an 18-hole score of 132 that included an 11, 12, 13 and 14.

That tournament was at Meadow Brook's original course, a nine-holer in Westbury, N.Y. In 1954 the club moved to Jericho, N.Y., and hired Dick Wilson to design a modern and demanding course. Wilson responded by building an expansive test over rolling hills that requires

Tucked into a valley among central Pennsylvania hills, Moselem Springs has earned national recognition despite its remote location and a lack of leading championships played here. Surrounding hills are in sight from everywhere on this course, so it isn't surprising that most fairways slope. Many tees and greens are elevated, each offering a special challenge.

In 1968, only three years after Moselem Springs was opened, Susie Berning won the U.S. Women's Open here with a 289 total, edging Mickey Wright by three strokes. This is the sole U.S. title decided here, and the course has hosted only a limited number of regional competitions.

George Fazio designed the course, and it is one of his favorites. It utilizes streams and ponds formed by a spring on the grounds, which has never frozen over.

NATIONAL CASH REGISTER-SOUTH

Dayton, Ohio

Employees of the National Cash Register Company in Dayton, Ohio who are golfers enjoy a special treat! They have two fine golf courses open exclusively to them.

This was the idea of C.W. Allen, an avid golfer and obviously enlightened chairman of the board of NCR. There are two courses, both dating from 1953. The South is the championship test that took on the world's best professionals when it played host to the 1969 PGA Championship won by Ray Floyd. The North is more gentle, more level and more open than its haughtier cousin. Dick Wilson designed both, and made the South the challenge it is with his large fairway bunkers and some lulus around the green. One of the latter is a 15-foot-deep approach-killer directly in front of the green on the par-5 sixth hole. Be sure to use enough club on that shot.

NORTH SHORE

Glenview, Illinois

North Shore's members have never been content to live in the past, as far as their course is concerned. Originally a social club in 1900, North Shore thrived in two locations before it settled at its present site in 1924. There the architectural firm of Colt, Alison and Mackenzie built an excellent test with narrow fairways and small greens that was demanding enough to host the 1933 U.S. Open (Johnny Goodman

won, the last amateur to win an Open) and the 1939 U.S. Amateur (won by Bud Ward).

As modern equipment and swing techniques lengthened golfers' games, North Shore fought back by narrowing the target areas with new lakes on the front nine in 1964 and on the back nine in 1979. Also, when disease killed many of the course's stately elms, a program that added from 50 to 75 sturdy maples and honey locusts a year was instituted. Competitors in future national championships here won't find this course any more of a pigeon than did Goodman and the other competitors in 1933.

A wildly rolling fairway leads to an elevated green on the par-5, 548-yard sixth hole at the National Cash Register Country Club's South Course. Large fairway bunkers threaten golfers all the way on this Dick Wilson-designed layout, which hosted the 1969 PGA Championship.

OLD WARSON
Ladue, Missouri

Golfers prone to pull or hook do not always enjoy Old Warson. Of the 10 holes showing out-of-bounds, the problem is to the left on seven. Water is to the left on five holes, to the right on two. Get the idea?

Otherwise, this suburban St. Louis course treats golfers even-handedly. It can play long—7,292 yards from the tips. The eight par-4 doglegs are egalitarian—four turn to the left, four to the right. There are only 69 bunkers, but they're large, as are the undulating greens.

Discerning players might recognize the design work of Robert Trent Jones, for he was the architect of the course, which opened in 1955. It often hosts area competitions and in 1971 the Ryder Cup was played here.

It's a straight but narrow path from tee to green on the 443-yard par-4 18th hole at North Shore. As are most of the greens at this Glenview, Ill., course, the 18th's is small. It was here in 1933 that Johnny Goodman became the last amateur to win the U.S. Open.

Golfers play from a large teeing area to a substantial green on the 208-yard, par-3 third hole at the Old Warson Country Club. This course, in a suburb of St. Louis, is a Robert Trent Jones design that played host to the 1971 Ryder Cup.

OLYMPIA FIELDS-NORTH
Olympia Fields, Illinois

Olympia Fields North was one of the last assignments of Willie Park Jr., a Scottish professional and architect with two British Open Championships in his background. Three years after the course opened in 1922, Park died at age 61. What he produced was an extremely testing layout in a sylvan, rolling setting that over the years has proven a very effective tournament site. Here in 1928, Johnny Farrell defeated Bob Jones in a playoff for the U.S. Open title. It has also been the site of five Western Opens and two PGA Championships.

The first three holes are fairly open, but from the fourth on it plunges deep into heavy woods. For competition, the rough is grown thick and wiry.

Olympia Fields' first course (there are 36 holes here) was completed in 1916, and for a time the club had four 18-hole courses. Two were given up during World War II to residential developments.

Thick stands of oak and maple are close to the fairways at the North Course of the Olympia Fields Country Club, in a Chicago suburb. This is the 415-yard, par-4 third hole, with a fairway that starts in the open, but tightens as the green is approached.

California's Pauma Valley course is nestled in an especially attractive setting, in a mountain valley with a great variety of trees and shrubs off the fairways. This is the 461-yard, par-4 18th, with a rolling fairway and interceding bunkers, typical of the rest of the layout.

PAUMA VALLEY
Pauma Valley, California

Variety is the by-word at Pauma Valley—every hole is sharply different from all the others, the doglegs are equally divided between those that turn left and those that turn right, and the golfer who can hit all kinds of shots is the one who scores well. Oak, cottonwood, pine and amber trees line the generous fairways, which also feature many sidelining sand bunkers. This is a Robert Trent Jones course, with long tees and large greens.

Established in 1959, Pauma Valley's operations have undergone several changes. Originally planned by Jimmy Hines and John Dawson, famed as Palm Springs developers, the course has been a residential community, a resort with a lodge, a retreat owned by a mining company and finally a private club (in 1975). It is located near the foot of Mt. Palomar, 50 miles northeast of San Diego.

PLAINFIELD
Plainfield, New Jersey

Plainfield's first course, completed in 1896, was only 5,707 yards long, occupying land just north of the present course. A Donald Ross design was finished in 1921, and 10 years later he did a final revision. The result is a flexible test of golf that can go up to 7,086 yards. Distinctive Ross features include nine fairway-crossing bunkers and grass-covered knolls near many greens that can frustrate even the best chippers. In preparation for the 1978 U.S. Amateur, 20 sand bunkers were added and on four holes major water hazards were created. John Cook defeated Scott Hoch in this Amateur final; today both are successful tournament professionals.

An additional nine holes across the Raritan Road from the championship (and private) 18 has been open to the public since the mid-1930s.

Golfers approach the green on the par-4, 368-yard 18th at Plainfield warily to avoid the heavily lipped, deep sand bunkers that are typical of this New Jersey course. The Donald Ross design retains many of its original features, which date from 1921.

The green at Princeville's 180-yard, par-3 third hole (Ocean nine) is an island among lush Hawaiian foliage, and the tee shot had better land on the putting surface. Princeville, on the north shore of Kauai, is set high above the ocean on a bluff, with craggy mountains on the other side.

PRINCEVILLE
Kauai, Hawaii

Not many golf courses in the world equal the scenery at Princeville. Its 27 holes are set high above a peaceful Pacific surf and inviting beach, and craggy blue mountains complete with jungles and waterfalls can be seen in the other direction. The red-flowered Plumeria tree is everywhere, lining the fairways and even providing an occasional hazard to the wayward golfer. Even the 150-yard markers carry the flower motif—they are hyacinth plants.

Any two of the Lake, Woods and Ocean nines can be combined for a championship test of some 6,900 yards from the back tees. Ravines, manmade ponds and numerous sand bunkers serve to keep golfers alert. It isn't just all beauty here. The course is the work of architect Robert Trent Jones Jr., and in 1978 hosted the World Cup.

SAHALEE
Redmond, Washington

In the language of the Chinook Indian, Sahalee means "high, heavenly ground," and that is an accurate description of this golf course. Its fairways run through mildly undulating ground covered with heavy stands of fir, cedar and hemlock. Sahalee gained respect immediately after its first 18 was completed in 1969 under the supervision of architect Ted Robinson. A third nine was added the next year. Sahalee's three nines, each about 3,800 yards from the back, are used interchangeably for tournament competition. All combinations for 18 holes are equally strong. Par-5 greens are reachable in three shots by the average golfer, but if the long-hitter goes for any in two, that second shot is chancey. Accuracy is generally more rewarding here than distance.

Sahalee is the home course for the Seattle University and Redmond High School golf teams and hosts a number of area and regional competitions.

A typically rough-hewn New England landscape greets golfers at the Salem Country Club in Massachusetts, as this view of the 344-yard, par-4 13th hole shows. Hilly lies are common on this Donald Ross-designed course, where Virginia Van Wie won the 1932 U.S. Women's Amateur and Babe Didrikson Zaharias captured the 1954 Women's Open.

SALEM
Peabody, Massachusetts

Although the Salem Country Club dates from 1895, and indeed was one of the first clubs to join the United States Golf Association (in 1896), its major golfing history began in 1926. That was the year the present 18 was opened, with a bang—a small cannon was obtained and fired as part of the ceremonies. Donald Ross, the Scottish architect, designed a course with tight fairways that furrow through groves of oak, maple and pine. Maine lumberjacks cut 1,000 cords of wood and used 10 tons of dynamite to clear the area. Hilly lies are common because of the area's many dips and swales.

Salem's first course was an impromptu nine in North

There are three nines at the Sahalee Country Club in Washington, and any combination forms a championship 18-hole test. This is a view of the 426-yard, par-4 third hole of the North nine, with towering evergreens covering the course's rolling terrain.

Literally dredged out of seaside marshland, the Sawgrass course in Florida is a low-lying, hard-knuckle case that is a match for the best from the back tees. The par-5, 527-yard fourth is typical, with watery hazards off the fairway and a green nestled among tall palms.

Salem, and in 1912 the club built a tricky nine that is now the site of another course. In 1932, Virginia Van Wie defeated Glenna Collett Vare in the final of the U.S. Women's Amateur here.

SAWGRASS
Ponte Vedra Beach, Florida

The tournament professionals never did figure out Sawgrass. From 1977 through 1981 they competed for the Tournament Players Championship here and Sawgrass never took a backward step. The lowest score was 278, with the other four winners well over 280. Because it's near the Atlantic coast, Sawgrass is naturally level. Many hazards are formed by the marsh areas, and water comes into play on 12 holes. When the wind blows—and it does often—scores skyrocket as shots fly into these hazards. Architect Ed Seay moved a million yards of dirt in building the course. Later, tournament professional Gardner Dickinson added 21 new fairway "links bunkers."

The resort itself is comfortably low key, with rental units scattered in residential fashion. Management does not encourage large conventions—it has no facility for this—and thus the grounds are always quiet. Except when you can hear groans from the golf course.

Shoal Creek's 385-yard, par-4 14th creates a handsome panorama as it tumbles downward to the distant green. This Alabama course, designed by Jack Nicklaus, gained esteem soon after its opening in 1977.

greens and deep bunkers. While they were there, the Englishmen altered Travis' Plantation a bit. In 1960 the Retreat nine was established by Dick Wilson, with his typically longer yardage and bigger greens. Finally Joe Lee produced Marshside in 1973; water and marshes are everywhere.

When a tournament is played at Sea Island, usually the Seaside (3,371 yards) and Retreat (3,506 yards) are combined for the competition.

Large, deep sand bunkers and threatening marshland occupy the attention of golfers playing at Sea Island, off the Georgia coast. This is the seventh hole of the Seaside nine, a 425-yard par 4. Sea Island has four nines, each designed by a different architect.

SHOAL CREEK
Shoal Creek, Alabama

SEA ISLAND
St. Simons Island, Georgia

The Sea Island Golf Club came into existence in the late 1920s and has never lost its Southern charm and style. At the hotel, gentlemen wear jackets for dinner. The silver service shines brightly and fresh flowers greet guests daily.

There are four nines at Sea Island, each designed by a different architect. The first was the Plantation, built by Walter Travis, the naturalized American born in Australia who in 1904 became the first foreigner to win the British Amateur. In 1929 the English team of Colt and Alison came up with the magnificent Seaside, constructed over filled marshland with sharply elevated

Completed only in 1977, Shoal Creek has moved quickly into the upper strata of American golf courses. Its designer is Jack Nicklaus, arguably the best golfer ever and certainly the best of his time. Nicklaus has several Masters championships among his major victories and is an admirer of Augusta National, so it shouldn't be surprising that any course he designs has Augusta overtones. Shoal Creek is no exception.

The course is highlighted with large pines and many azaleas and rests on relatively level terrain with hills in the background. There is a creek that runs through the grounds with water rushing past stones set in the bed for golfers to use as walkways. Some bridges that span the creek are grass-covered. Class.

Tournament professional Jerry Pate calls the greens magnificent with cunning undulations that can be utilized to set up particularly challenging approaches. Shoal Creek will host the 1984 PGA Championship.

SPYGLASS HILL
Pebble Beach, California

For its first five holes, Spyglass Hill is a links course in the truest sense. All of the holes have "island" aspects. That is, the golfer must aim for islands of green on every shot, either patches of fairway amidst sandy wastelands or the greens themselves. After that, the course leaves the seashore, retreats into pine-covered hills and becomes a parkland test. The back-nine challenge is enhanced by three ravines that have been converted into culverts to drain water from the upper slopes. Dams have been built to convert them into water hazards that influence play on three holes.

Spyglass Hill was designed by Robert Trent Jones and opened in 1966. Since the next year it has been part of the triumvirate of courses that host the Bing Crosby National Pro-Am (Pebble Beach and Cypress Point are the others). Author Robert Louis Stevenson lived in the area and it is said that the high dunes there were the inspiration for the "Spyglass Hill" featured in his book, *Treasure Island*.

THE COUNTRY CLUB
Brookline, Massachusetts

American golf has deep roots in The Country Club. It was first organized in 1860, but because of the intervening Civil War has no further history until 1882. Golf was introduced in 1892 when six holes were constructed. Three more were added the next year, and in 1894 the club became one of five charter members of the United States Golf Association.

Another nine was built in 1909, and in 1910 the U.S. Amateur was played here. Since then (through 1982) 10 other national championships have been contested here. Augmented by a third nine in 1927, the club's championship 18 is a combination of holes from all three nines. With extremely tight, timber-lined fairways, small greens and a hilly back nine, the course is a stern test.

When Francis Ouimet, an amateur and former caddie at the club, defeated the English champions Harry Vardon and Ted Ray in a playoff for the 1913 U.S. Open title at Brookline, golf became recognized as a game for the common man in America.

WANNAMOISETT
Rumford, Rhode Island

"Pound for pound," they'll say, "the best boxer today." The same measure can be applied to Wannamoisett, a pocket-watch test with a Big Ben punch. At just 6,630 yards, this Rhode Island course has always held its own. Results of the Northeast Amateur, annually played at Wannamoisett since 1962, bear this out. Wannamoisett's par of 69 (276 for 72 holes) seldom bends to the field, which includes the na-

Play at Spyglass Hill on California's Monterey Peninsula varies dramatically. For five holes it jostles along the Pacific, fraught with sand and rocks. Then it turns inland, starting with the pictured 415-yard sixth, and assumes a parkland nature.

tion's leading amateurs. Among the recent winners are Hal Sutton, John Cook and Scott Hoch, now all successful tournament professionals. Also, in 1931 Tom Creavy won the PGA Championship here.

Wannamoisett is a Donald Ross creation dating from 1898, when nine holes were laid out by Willie Campbell. By 1914 club members voted to hire Ross to design an 18-holer, and the course remains essentially the same today. Tightly woven into only 104 acres, Wannamoisett is considered the longest layout ever built on such a small area of land.

WILMINGTON-SOUTH
Wilmington, Delaware

Greens at Wilmington South are not that difficult to hit in regulation. After all, they are substantial in size, up around the 8,000-square-foot level, and therefore make good targets. But unless the approach is close to the flagstick, the chances of three-putting are good. The greens do not forgive poor putters, for the surfaces are fast and extremely undulating.

This is a Robert Trent Jones course, opened in 1960 when this famous architect was at the height of his fixation with large greens and tees. There are numerous

Small, elevated greens hugged by sand and heavy rough, such as on the 446-yard third hole, characterize The Country Club in Brookline, Mass., a Boston suburb. This is one of the nation's most distinguished clubs, one of five founding members of the USGA in 1894.

bunkers filled with fine, powdery sand in which golf balls often are buried.

Although this Wilmington course, along with the club's North 18, is of fairly recent vintage, the club began at another location in 1902. The original course was good enough to host the 1913 U.S. Women's Amateur. The new facility has hosted the 1971 U.S. Amateur and the 1978 U.S. Boys' and Girls' Junior Championships.

The Wannamoisett Country Club in Rhode Island, designed by Donald Ross, occupies only 104 acres and remains essentially the same since its creation in 1914.

From the back tees, the 16th at Wilmington's South Course plays to 625 yards. In this lovely fall view, the fairway threads through an avenue of oak and maple to a green embraced by numerous sand bunkers. This Delaware facility also has a North Course and has hosted several national championships.

BRITISH ISLES' TOP 25 COURSES

Every summer golfers throughout the world are familiarized with one of the tradition-steeped courses of the British Open, otherwise known as the Open Championship of the Royal and Ancient Golf Club of St. Andrews. This first major event of the game, begun in 1860, was held for 12 years at Scotland's famous Prestwick course. St. Andrews and Musselburgh, also in Scotland, then began sharing in a rotation. It wasn't until the 34th Open that England first got into the act at Royal St. George's in 1894. Altogether the British Open has visited 14 different courses, with the rota, as it is called, consisting of seven or eight courses for the past 30 years. Significantly, all of them are links courses not only out of tradition, but also because they tend to provide the essential element of wind.

It is not surprising that when we asked Golf World of London, our sister publication, to name the top 25 courses in the British Isles, 10 of them turned out to be British Open venues. Those historical courses missing from the list: Musselburgh (which no longer exists), Troon, site of the 1982 event, and the two neighbor courses of Royal St. George's, Prince's and Deal. Both, incidentally, are still championship caliber and are used to qualify contestants for the Open when played at Sandwich.

Interestingly, five of the courses that made the list are in Ireland, which has hosted only one British Open. This is a great tribute to a nation with only about 1/7th of the courses in the British Isles.

While no conscious effort was made by the British selectors to seek geographical dispersion, the 25 are widely scattered across the isles. While the preponderance are links, the inland selections are largely heathland courses built on sand and gravel.

Many outstanding Scottish, English and Irish courses are clustered within a few miles of one another to form constellations of golf, often with one of the famous courses shining brightly among them. One of the exceptions is Gleneagles, whose beautiful courses are in the lowlands of Scotland, miles apart from any others.

All the golfing world knows of Scotland's beautiful courses, more than 300 of them. Two of the best are Gleneagles and Turnberry, hotel golf courses that offer the highest standards of service of any golfing resorts in Europe.

Gleneagles has two breathtaking courses nestled among the Perthshire mountain moorlands, the King's at 6,644 yards and the Queen's at 6,055, both laid out by James Braid just before World War I.

Turnberry, the superb hotel south of Glasgow, overlooks the sea and both its courses, which were completely rebuilt by Mackenzie Ross following World War II. The Ailsa course is the better known, playing 7,060 yards and having been host to many great golfing occasions, including the 1977 British Open. The scenery, especially on the first nine, is spectacular. The ninth, called the "greatest par 4 in golf" by Gene Sarazen, has a tee high among the rocks from which you look down at breaking waves.

If you do not feel up to the challenge of the Ailsa Course—especially off the back tees—the Arran Course, which is 6,350 yards long, is almost as tough and certainly as well kept as its championship sister.

To the north of Turnberry, near Troon, is old Prestwick, considered by some to be rather old-fashioned but by others a supreme test of golf.

Perhaps the most varied concentration of Scottish courses can be found within range of Dundee on the east coast, not far from either Carnoustie or St. Andrews and within a short drive of treelined Rosemount, at Blairgowrie, a precious heavily wooded inland course. Royal Dornoch, near the sea and close to the Highlands, is the most northerly of the famous Scottish resorts with perhaps the most panoramic of views. It

One of the world's most dramatic courses is Ballybunion, on the west coast of Ireland, where vistas such as the 446-yard 11th hole (right) are commonplace.

BRITISH ISLES' TOP 25 COURSES

Ballybunion, Ireland
A fine old links course, wild and magnificent with breathtaking views. A course of real magnitude dominated by natural elements in the form of huge sand dunes with the wind sweeping along the County Kerry coast from the Atlantic. A layout that favors the bold.
Architect: P. Murphy

The Berkshire (Red Course), England
Set in the heart of rural England on rolling heathland with quiet woods of pine, silver birch and chestnut and heather-lined fairways. Unusual feature is six short holes.
Architect: Herbert Fowler

Carnoustie, Scotland
Originally a 10-hole course, it was extended to 18 by Tom Morris and was revamped in 1926 by James Braid. The result is superb. Every hole has its own character and never do more than two holes follow the same direction. One of golf's toughest tests.
Architect: Allan Robertson

Ganton, England
Open heathland course in Yorkshire with several wooded areas and acres of gorse that are spectacular when in summer bloom. The course has some of the deepest and largest bunkers in Britain.
Architect: T. Dunn

Gleneagles (Kings), Scotland
Surrounded by the foothills of the Highlands, the Kings course has views that are superb. Excellent golfing country with rolling terrain, heather, gorse, natural bunkers and towering trees. The greens are on the large side and kept in immaculate condition.
Architect: James Braid and Maj. C.K. Hutchinson

Killarney, Ireland
Henry Longhurst advised on the building of the course, which opened in 1939. His quote "What a lovely place to die" just about sums up the beauty of the setting, surrounded as it is by lakes and mountains. Two or three of the holes are without particular character, but the course has to be seen to be believed.
Architect: Sir Guy Campbell

Muirfield, Scotland
A magnificent test of golf on lovingly cared-for turf. No tricks and rightly proud of its justified "exclusive" tag. A stern, impersonal championship venue loved by all the great players. No wonder Jack Nicklaus named his home course after it. Possibly the fairest links course of all with no trick holes and with hazards clearly visible.
Architect: Tom Morris

Nottinghamshire (Hollinwell), England
Opened in 1900, Hollinwell is a lovely heathland course that meanders through silver birch, oak, gorse and heather. Marvellous history, having been designed by Willie Park Jr.

with bunkers added by J.H. Taylor. A stiff test of golf, which has hosted a number of tournaments.
Architect: Willie Park Jr.

Portmarnock, Ireland
A course of great traditions, laid out in superb, natural country on a peninsula of rolling sand dunes reaching into Dublin Bay. A course to rank with the very best as a test of golf with the wind a constant hazard. Plenty of plateau greens with probably the best short hole in the British Isles (15th).
Architect: George Ross, W.L. Pickeman

Prestwick, Scotland
First home of the Open Championship and the feeling of history is unmistakeable. Time may have overtaken Prestwick and its formidable railway sleepers, but many of the holes are unique and will remain so forever. A premium on accuracy and one or two fairways so narrow that single file is the order of the day. A mighty course!
Architect: Tom Morris

Rosemount, Blairgowrie, Scotland
A marvellous test of straight hitting through pine and birch-lined fairways. Great variety of holes with the 17th being the most memorable. Invariably kept in immaculate condition and quite capable of standing alongside the better-known courses of Scotland.
Architect: Old members helped by Tom Morris

Royal Ashdown Forest, England
Proof that nature can, if given the chance, be the best architect. Here is an unorthodox course without a single artificial bunker, but plenty of trouble with streams, pits, bracken and natural slopes. Heather everywhere and difficult borrows on several greens.
Architect: Unknown

Royal Birkdale, England
One of the fairest links courses with very few blind spots. Great variety of shots needed to tame the course and the setting lends itself to adventurous golf. No domestic tabby of a course, but a full-grown tiger. The fairways are flat, without stance problems and the greens, between sand dunes, give an air of target golf.
Architect: Fred Hawtree

Royal County Down, Northern Ireland
Tom Morris laid this course out at a cost of about $8. Tough test against a backdrop of the Mountains of Mourne. Every hole has its own secluded valley. Truly beautiful course set in heather, gorse and sandhills. Straight driving pays dividends. The slasher is tempted to end it all in Dundrum Bay.
Architect: Tom Morris

Royal Dornoch, Scotland
Inspiring, individualistic old links remotely located 600 miles north of London. When the wind sweeps down, none but the best and the bravest can hope to succeed. Only its remoteness stops it being a great championship venue. World's

northernmost great course, on a level with the Bering Sea and Hudson Bay.
Architect: Tom Morris

Royal Liverpool, Hoylake, England
Second-oldest English links course ranks alongside Carnoustie as the most difficult of the championship greats. Often called the St. Andrews of England. It offers an exacting task with a forbidding opening hole, a gruelling finish and not much comfort in between. The greens are among the best in the world.
Architect: R. Chambers, G. Norns

Royal Lytham and St Anne's, England
Slightly claustrophobic links with never a glimpse of the ocean. A green oasis in a rash of houses and bounded by the railway, but the scene of many great championships. A tough old course, which belies its tranquility. Softer and lusher than a true links and now regarded more as a seaside course.
Architect: G. Lowe

Royal Porthcawl, Wales
The pride of Wales with magnificent views over the Bristol Channel. The opening holes follow the line of the coast, but move inland to where it is more heathlike than links. Final hole is all downhill to the sea. Finding the fairway on some holes is difficult—and only the first of many problems.
Architect: H.S. Colt

Royal Portrush (Dunluce Course), Northern Ireland
A real gem of a course where erratic driving means you are dead. In a category of its own with its hills, hollows and mounds. Magnificent par-3 hole called Calamity—a very apt name. The course is slightly let down by a weak finishing hole, but most people are glad of the rest.
Architect: H.S. Colt

Royal St George's, Sandwich, England
There is a feeling of isolation as the players are dwarfed and lost in towering sandhills. An unforgettable experience providing a golf feast fit for a king. Numerous blind shots make course knowledge imperative just to get back to the clubhouse. Classic links course.
Architect: W. Laidlaw Purves

St Andrews (Old Course), Scotland
The heart and the home of golf. A shrine shaped like a shepherd's crook. Earliest recorded golf played there in 1552 and now, more than 400 years later, it is still a monument to its origin. Seven double greens give an excuse for three-putting from 80 yards.
Architect: Unknown.

Sunningdale (Old Course), England
The perfect heathland course and one of the most distinguished inland courses in the world. Large greens, classically true, in a setting of birch, pine and heather. Bobby Jones once said: "I wish I could take this course home with me."
Architect: Willie Park

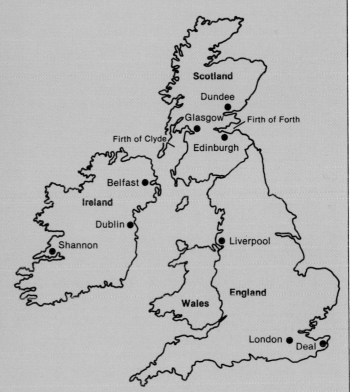

Turnberry (Ailsa Course), Scotland
A most spectacular course, which turns from a friend into a wild savage in wind and rain. Magnificent rocky background with eight of the first 11 holes skirting the ocean's edge. Nightmare course for a hooker and no peace of mind for anyone with other faults.
Architect: Mackenzie Ross (rebuilt after World War II)

Walton Heath (Old Course), England
Real downland turf and an absolute delight for iron shots off the fairway. The rough looks harmless heather until you try to get out of it. A strong, unyielding, but honest course, typical of the man who was professional there for 40 years, James Braid.
Architect: Herbert Fowler

Wentworth (West Course), England
The great Burma Road course, permanent home of the World Match Play Championship. A stirring test of adventurous golf with long carries and tall trees lining both sides of the fairways. Suffered more than a little of late through overuse, but still a mighty course.
Architect: H.S. Colt

was laid out by Old Tom Morris with later modifications by J.H. Taylor.

Some 25 miles to the southwest of central London, in Surrey, there is a strip of sandy, fir-clad land that contains some of the most imitated golf courses in the world. Among them are Wentworth, Sunningdale and Berkshire. Each has two courses.

entworth combines tradition and atmosphere with a modern outlook that makes it Britain's nearest equivalent to the American country club. Part of the tradition are the rhododendron bushes and the silver birches that cover the courses. It also has what many consider the most beautiful clubhouse in England. The pros call Wentworth's West Course the "Burma Road" because of its length and toughness. The shorter East Course (both were designed by H.S. Colt), is as exacting but a little more relenting. Wentworth has been the venue for both the Ryder Cup and World Cup on the West Course, as well as the annual World Match Play Championship.

Step inside Sunningdale's clubhouse and the atmosphere of traditional British golf envelops you. It is the epitome of the true English golf club, where it's the golf that counts, where the men-only bar beside the locker room is full of deep leather arm chairs, where pints of beer are served in traditional tankards.

The Old Course was originally designed by Willie Park in 1900. However, it was later fleshed out and put in its present state by H.S. Colt, who also designed the New Course in 1922.

The Old Course is a marvelous inland layout over the dunes from which elements appear at Pine Valley. The New Course is more open and considered slightly more difficult than the Old and utilizes higher ground that offers commanding vistas. Across the road from the clubhouse is the Ladies Course, 18 holes of the highest quality but run as an independent entity. All in all, Sunningdale is a golfer's paradise and well deserves the reputation it has built up through the years.

The Berkshire courses, situated in the same pine and heather country, give off the same sort of atmosphere as the other two, but in a less sumptuous way. The Red Course is the higher and hillier but, although slightly longer, is not necessarily the more difficult.

The 18th hole of the Blue Course at the Berkshire highlights one of two outstanding layouts created in 1928 by Herbert Fowler. The Red Course is unusual in having six par-3 holes and six par 5s.

One of Scotland's most famous hazards is the Barry Burn at Carnoustie (right), which must be crossed twice on the 18th hole. The incongruous-looking clubhouse is in the background. Treacherous as it is, Carnoustie has brought out the best in such great players as Tommy Armour (below) shown here on his way to the 1931 British Open title.

lmost back-to-back and stretched along the Kent coastline in Southeast England are three courses steeped in history, always a treat to play and true tests of skill. Royal St. George's at Sandwich, established in 1887, has been the scene of countless golfing incidents. One of Britain's best-known professionals, Henry Cotton, recorded his first big-time victory in the 1934 Open with a 283 there and had a round of 65, one of the lowest scores ever in a British Open.

Very near Sandwich is Royal Cinque Ports at Deal. Defended from the encroaching sea by a shingle bank, it is one of England's toughest tests of golf. The most difficult part about it is that the fairways are made of endless bumps and hollows.

Prince's, which shares the same stretch of linksland as Royal St. George's, was founded in 1905, but the bomb work of German planes during World War II almost obliterated it. However, the original architects would have been pleased with the amazing construc-

Here is the spectacular setting of the 13th hole at Ganton, England, from the championship tee (left), with the gorse bushes in full bloom. The great Harry Vardon (above) once served as the professional at Ganton.

tion job done by Sir Guy Campbell and John Morrison, who turned the club into 27 holes of testing and enjoyable golf.

The Deal area is just one of the many great coastal constellations in England, rivaled in many ways by the areas surrounding Royal Birkdale and Royal Lytham in the west.

In Ireland, there is a marvelous cluster of courses within reasonable driving distance of the Shannon Airport: Ballybunion, Killarney, Lahinch, which is not on the 25 greatest list, but well could be, and Waterville Lake also not on the list but well worth a visit.

If ever there were an Irish-sounding name it is Ballybunion; and if ever there were a true Irish seaside links this is it. On the southwest coast of the Shannon estuary facing the blustery Atlantic, far from Ireland's metropolitan centers, Ballybunion is an absolutely beautiful adventure to play.

Royal Portrush, in the very north of Northern Ireland, was the only Irish course to host the British Open, in 1951. The club has three courses, the Dunluce at 6,809

yards being the championship links. The narrow curving fairways and multileveled sandhills make this a fearsome test.

One of the most scenic sections of Ireland is Killarney, an area of almost breathtaking beauty in the southwestern part of the country. Its famous lakes dot the green landscape, scattered among the rolling hills and forests and old mist-covered Irish castles. Killarney Golf Club is more a holiday course than the tough layouts at Portmarnock, Portrush, Ballybunion or Lahinch. It is usually played from the 6,000-yard front tees.

Virtually all of Ireland's courses have very modest clubhouses, no showers or locker rooms of the sort with which Americans are familiar. An exception is the Waterville Lake Hotel and Golf Course on Ireland's famed Ring of Kerry on the southwest coast. It is possibly the longest (7,116 yards, par 73 from the back) course in all Europe. Waterville is a destination itself in the tradition of world-class resorts.

he selections of the top 25 courses in the British Isles were made under the supervision of Peter Haslam, and his staff at Golf World, guided by criteria very similar to those used in the United States except for course conditioning. According to Haslam, ''As some of the candidates were known to be suffering from what was believed to be a temporary demise in this respect, I decided that it should be assumed that care and attention would shortly bring them to peak condition.''

The Golf World selection team consists of the following panelists:

Peter Alliss—Noted golfer, writer, broadcaster and commentator,

Tommy Horton—Tournament professional, former PGA Captain and a member of the European Tour Players Committee.

Peter Dobereiner—Much-traveled columnist of Golf World, golf correspondent of the Observer, The Guardian and *Golf Digest.*

Michael Bonallack—Britain's leading amateur golfer, golf course developer and President of the English Golf Union.

Louis Stanley—Noted golf historian and author of many golf books.

Brian Wilkie—Former Rules official of the European tour.

The elevated fifth green of the King's Course at Gleneagles (above), is one of the few inland Scottish layouts that evokes praise even among links fans. The 167-yard hole is deceptive and a par here is well-earned.

One of the most beautiful golf settings anywhere is Killarney (left), which Henry Longhurst once described as "a lovely place to die." Shown here is the 423-yard eighth hole of the Killeen Course.

The distinctive island bunker that guards the 18th green at Muirfield (below), is hard by the clubhouse that is headquarters of the Honourable Company of Edinburgh Golfers. Walter Hagen (left) scored a memorable victory at Muirfield in the 1929 British Open.

The 14th hole at Portmarnock (above),
when played into a strong wind off the
sea, can seem much longer than its 385
yards. The moods of this great Irish
course can range from sternness to
serenity.

The vast Cardinal bunker, which
dominates the 482-yard third hole at
Prestwick (left), is the course's most
famous feature. The course was designed by Old Tom Morris, shown above
with his son, Young Tom. The two of
them won eight of the first 12 British
Opens.

The large mounds at Royal Birkdale (above), in England, provide a natural amphitheater for spectators, one reason it's a frequent site of the British Open. Peter Thomson (left) won two of his five British Opens here.

No wonder Royal County Down in northern Ireland is the acknowledged favorite of the well-travelled golfing journalist, Peter Dobereiner. This is despite countless blind shots and penal pot bunkers. The players in the foreground are shooting to the fourth green, 211 yards away on the right. The green up and to the left of it serves the 440-yard fifth hole.

Hoylake's 11th (left), a 200-yard shot to an oasis in the dunes, is typical of the course's seaside character. It was at Hoylake that Roberto de Vicenzo (below) scored a popular British Open victory in 1967.

If golf began in Scotland, as most believe, the first game must have been played on just such a sweep of linksland as that at Royal Dornoch (left). In the foreground is the 359-yard par-4 fifth and behind it running along the beach is the 444-yard par-4 11th.

An even more popular British Open winner was native son Tony Jacklin (right), who won in 1969 to break an 18-year streak of triumphs by foreign players. His victory came at Royal Lytham & St. Anne's, whose bunker-strewn eighth hole (below) typifies the course's difficulties.

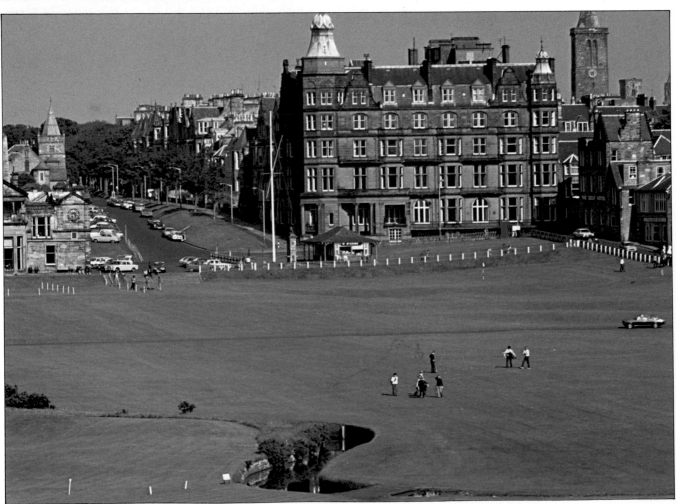

The sweep of Royal St. George's (above), with neighboring Prince's in the distance, was the setting for the 1981 British Open triumph of American Bill Rogers (right), shown giving his caddie a victory hug.

Perhaps the most familiar sight in golf is the 18th green at St. Andrews (left), with the clubhouse at left. Among the historic victories there was that of Tony Lema (below) in 1964.

The fifth hole at Sunningdale (left) is one of the most demanding on the famed course outside London, where Bobby Jones once shot 33-33—66 in what has been called the "perfect" round of golf.

The craggy ninth tee of the Ailsa Course at Turnberry, with the famed lighthouse looking on (below), is one of the great vistas of Scottish golf. It was on the Ailsa that Jack Nicklaus and Tom Watson (right) had their great shootout in the 1977 British Open, won by Watson.

Here is the well-guarded 16th green of the ''Burma Road'' course at Wentworth, in England (below), the annual site of the World Match Play Championship. One of the most successful competitors in the championship has been Gary Player, (left), who won it five times.

Although only 285 yards, the par-4 third at Walton Heath calls for great accuracy. The Herbert Fowler design was the site of the 1981 Ryder Cup Matches, won by the American team, standing left to right: Kite, Rogers, Trevino, Pate, Miller, Lietzke, nonplaying captain Marr, Floyd, Irwin, Nicklaus and Watson; kneeling left to right: Crenshaw and Nelson.

CANADA'S TOP 25 COURSES

The selection of the best golf courses anywhere is an evolutionary process. While change is constant, it is also usually gradual, with new courses taking some years to work their way up the listing. Thus it is all the more remarkable that, in the eight years since *Golf Digest*'s panel selected Canada's 25 best, not one but two new courses have risen to the top.

The courses, both in Ontario, are Glen Abbey Golf Club, designed by Jack Nicklaus and now the permanent home of the Canadian Open, and The National Golf Club, designed by George and Tom Fazio. As previously, the top 25 courses have been grouped together in clusters of five, and the others in the top five are Royal Montreal Golf Club, Hamilton Golf and Country Club and St. George's Golf and Country Club, all of them occupying the same status as in 1974.

Not only were the two new courses absent from *Golf Digest*'s previous list of Canada's top 25 courses, they were only barely in existence. The National was begun

in 1973 and opened in 1974. Glen Abbey, begun in 1974, was opened in 1976.

Glen Abbey once was the estate of Andre Dorfman, a mining millionaire, then was purchased by the Jesuits and operated as a monastery. After the Royal Canadian Golf Association purchased the property from the original developers, the mansion was converted to use as RCGA headquarters and the home of the Canadian Golf Hall of Fame and Museum. Nicklaus designed the course with tournament golf in mind, and from the back tees it is a stern, albeit fair, test. He also had the spectator in mind, and the course offers numerous spots obviously created for optimum viewing.

The National is on the site of the former Pine Valley course, which was purchased by Gil Blechman, Harvey Kalef and Irv Hennick, who brought in the Fazios to redesign it. Blechman, an American who became a Canadian citizen, bought out the other two and now is sole owner.

Unlike Glen Abbey, The National wasn't designed with championships in mind, but the Fazios did create many natural gallery sites that could accommodate up to 50,000 spectators. The course record is 67, shot by Lee Trevino in a Canadian PGA event in 1979. Playing from the members' tees (about 6,640 yards), Trevino birdied the last four holes.

The dean of the list—in fact, the dean of any list in the Western Hemisphere—is Royal Montreal, which was founded in 1873 and is the oldest club west of Britain. Strangled by suburbia after more than a century in

The 423-yard ninth at Hamilton Golf and Country Club (left) typifies the lush, rolling nature of this elegant course.

The rambling clubhouse of the Royal Montreal Golf Club (right), which was founded in 1873 and is the oldest in North America. Shown here are the finishing holes on the Blue and Red Courses, both designed by Dick Wilson.

CANADA'S TOP 25 COURSES

Golf courses within each group are listed alphabetically.

TOP FIVE	Yards	Par
Glen Abbey G.C. Oakville, Ontario	7,133	72
Hamilton G. & C.C. Ancaster, Ontario	6,750	70
National G.C. Woodbridge, Ontario	6,975	72
Royal Montreal G.C. (Blue) Ile Bizard, Quebec	6,487	70
St. Georges G. & C.C. Islington, Ontario	6,797	71

SECOND FIVE		
Capilano G. & C.C. Vancouver, British Columbia	6,562	72
Essex G. & C.C. Sandwich, Ontario	6,645	71
London Hunt & C.C. London, Ontario	7,168	72
Mississaugua G. & C.C. Mississaugua, Ontario	6,860	72
Royal Colwood G. & C.C. Victoria, British Columbia	6,425	70

THIRD FIVE		
Ashburn G.C. (New) Kinsac, Nova Scotia	7,168	72
Banff Springs G.C. Banff, Alberta	6,729	71
Brantford G. & C.C. Brantford, Ontario	6,612	72
Cherry Hill Club Ridgeway, Ontario	6,755	72
Mayfair G. & C.C. Edmonton, Alberta	6,632	70

FOURTH FIVE		
Calgary G. & C.C. Calgary, Alberta	6,462	70
Jasper Park G.C. Jasper, Alberta	6,590	70
Le Club Laval sur-le-lac Ville de Laval, Quebec	6,488	72
Ottawa Hunt & G.C. Ottawa, Ontario	6,581	73
Westmount G. & C.C. Kitchener, Ontario	6,805	73

FIFTH FIVE		
Kanawaki G.C. Caughnawaga, Quebec	6,344	70
Red Deer G. & C.C. Red Deer, Alberta	6,847	72
Riverside C.C. Saskatoon, Saskatchewan	6,608	72
St. Charles C.C. Winnipeg, Manitoba	6,473	72
Shaughnessy G. & C.C. Vancouver, British Columbia	6,555	73

the same location, the club moved and engaged Dick Wilson to design 45 holes of golf. All were open in May, 1959, the centerpiece being the Blue Course, which has huge greens, a minimum of fairway bunkers and a testing finish of four water holes. It is said that a Royal Montreal member can play to his handicap anywhere.

Hamilton, often called Ancaster, which is the name of its location in Ontario, is an elegant, secluded place that is everything a posh country club is thought to be. The course consists of three nines, each—by design—extending 3,375 yards and playing to a par of 35. The West and South Nines were designed in 1919 by H.S. Colt and revisions were made years later by Bill Diddel. C.E. (Robbie) Robinson designed the East Nine in 1974. The Canadian Open was played there twice, in 1930—when Tommy Armour set the course record of 64—and in 1948.

Although St. George's has been around since the late 1920s, when it was designed by Stanley Thompson, it has only had its present name since 1962. It originally was known as Royal York, a hotel course

associated with the Canadian Pacific Railway. The members purchased the course in 1962 and changed its name, then engaged Robbie Robinson to make some alterations in 1967. The club hosted the Canadian Open in 1968 and Bob Charles beat Jack Nicklaus by a stroke with a dramatic birdie on the 18th.

St. George's combines both the finesse game of the past with the power of the present and offers great variety. There are those who consider it the best test of golf in Canada.

Virtually in the same class with the courses already described are those in the second grouping of five. They include Capilano and Royal Colwood in British Columbia, and Essex, London Hunt and Mississaugua, all in Ontario. London Hunt and Royal Colwood were ranked in the top five in 1974.

The setting of Capilano makes it one of the most spectacular courses anywhere. It was laid out by Stanley Thompson on a vast hillside and requires the golfer to play a third of the round down the mountainside, a third across it and the final third uphill. On the

The spectator mounds behind the 14th green indicate Jack Nicklaus' concern for the galleries when he designed Glen Abbey (below), now the permanent home of the Canadian Open.

If ever a picture were worth a thousand words, it would be this classic view of the Banff Springs Hotel and its adjoining golf course. Shown here are portions of the first, second and 18th fairways.

way, at least two holes give the illusion that the golfer is teeing off into downtown Vancouver. Scenery notwithstanding, Capilano, as someone once described it, would be outstanding no matter where it was located.

Another gem is Royal Colwood, which is in Victoria, on Vancouver Island. This beauty dates back to 1913, when it was designed by A.V. Macan, a transplanted Irishman who became one of the top players in the

One of the little-known gems of Canadian golf is the New Course of the Ashburn Golf Club in Nova Scotia (left), whose 10th green is pictured. The course was designed by Geoffrey Cornish and William G. Robinson.

The Toronto skyline provides an unusual backdrop to the fifth hole at St. George's (below), designed by Stanley Thompson in 1928 and for many years known as Royal York.

Pacific Northwest. In 1935 the Duke of Windsor (then the Prince of Wales) played Colwood while on a visit to the neighboring Hartley Castle, and as a mark of his favor, bestowed the title ''Royal'' on the club.

ssex Golf and Country Club started life early in the century as the nine-hole Oak Ridge Golf Club. The club was moved—and its name changed to Essex—in 1911. A final move was made in 1928, and Donald Ross designed the present course. It has undergone some revision over the years, but is substantially the same as Ross left it: a course of moderate length with lots of undulations and a great premium on the approach shot. Jerry Pate won the 1976 Canadian Open at Essex.

London Hunt was founded in 1843, when it was—as the name implies—strictly a hunt club. Its first golf course was built in 1910 on land that now belongs to Western University. The present course was designed in 1960 by Robert Trent Jones with Robbie Robinson as Canadian consultant. Like most Trent Jones courses, London Hunt has big greens and lots of bunkers. It has

been host to a number of championships, including the 1970 Canadian Open, and the course record of 65 was set by Bruce Crampton.

Mississaugua takes its name from the Indian reservation on which it was built back in 1906. George Cumming and Percy Barrett were responsible for the original design, but the course was later remodeled by Stanley Thompson. The Credit River runs through the course and comes into play on 13 holes. Six Canadian Opens have been played here and the winners have included such illustrious names as Walter Hagen, Sam Snead and Gene Littler. The course record of 63 is shared by Larry Ziegler and Chi Chi Rodriguez.

Although the bulk of Canada's estimated 1,100 courses are in and around the population centers of the

It's a demanding approach to the heavily bunkered 17th at The National Golf Club (above), a 428-yard par 4 epitomizing the scenic qualities of the George and Tom Fazio course.

East, some of the more famous are in the western provinces. In addition to the aforementioned Capilano, these include, among others, Stanley Thompson's Rocky Mountain jewels at Banff and Jasper Park. Both layouts are repeaters from the 1974 ranking and are included on merit, of course; it's only incidental that they rank high on any list of most scenic courses.

Golf Digest's selection panel includes golf administrators and professional and amateur players from all parts of Canada. They are listed on these pages along with the ranking of Canada's top 25 courses.

— Ross Goodner

A bird's-eye view of the tree-lined sixth hole at Essex Golf and Country Club in Ontario (left) indicates the type of accurate shots called for on this Donald Ross creation.

223

AUSTRALIA'S TOP 25 COURSES
PLUS NEW ZEALAND

Golf in Australia is both historical and popular. The game was first played in Australia in 1848 by a small group of enthusiasts presided over by Lt. Col. J.H. Ross. They practiced their skills on a plot of ground that was later to become part of the inner city of Melbourne. That was 40 years before the father of American golf, John Reid, made the first joyous swipes at Yonkers, N.Y., establishing the game in the U.S.

By 1855 golf had also been established in Sydney, but it was not until 1882 that the first official golf club was formed there. This was the Australian Golf Club, now at Kensington near Sydney's International Airport. It is a course that today remains one of this nation's great tests—the 1982 site of the prestigious Australian Open, begun in 1904.

An estimated 800,000 Australian golfers enjoy the game on some 1,500 courses. Australians are noted for their love of sports, and the number who play golf reflects this general interest. The clubs stage competitions every weekend, and the courses are usually crowded from dawn to dusk. An island continent dwarfed by the Pacific and Indian Oceans, Australia encompasses three million square miles, almost the area of the continental United States. And although much of the land is uninhabited, the more populated areas boast a wide variety of golf courses, many of them of high caliber. While there are outstanding courses near all the major cities of Australia, the sandy dunesland area north of Melbourne is the home of perhaps the finest cluster on the continent. Among them is the undisputed top golf facility in Australia, the Royal Melbourne courses, designed by Alister Mackenzie. He went on to design such famous courses in the U.S. as the Augusta National and Cypress Point.

Since Joe Kirkwood won the 1920 Australian Open and left for the United States to become golf's first well-known trick-shot stylist, Australia has produced a series of world-class golfers. The acerbic Peter Thomson has been the most successful. Twice the Australian Open winner, Thomson has won five British Opens as well. Norman Von Nida, a three-time Australian winner, is one of the well-known golf teachers. Kel Nagle and

The Australian Golf Club, located in Kensington, New South Wales, is the oldest and longest of the top courses in the country. Since the club's founding in 1882, its current course has undergone many design changes by such well-known architects as Alister Mackenzie and Jack Nicklaus. Measuring some 7,100 yards from the back tees, the course is set in a natural amphitheater.

Overleaf: The Royal Melbourne Golf Club, with its two courses, is unquestionably the finest golfing complex in Australia. Its first course (West) was modified in 1929 by Alister Mackenzie in partnership with Alex Russell, the 1924 Australian Open champion. Apart from deep bunkering, as shown in the photo of the 17th of the West, the real test is the speed of the greens.

AUSTRALIA'S TOP 25 COURSES

1. Australian Golf Club (Kensington, Sydney, New South Wales)

2. Barwon Heads Golf Club (Barwon Heads, Victoria)

3. Commonwealth Golf Club (South Oakleigh, Melbourne, Victoria)

4. Elanora Country Club (Narrabeen, Sydney, New South Wales)

5. Huntingdale Golf Club (East Oakleigh, Melbourne, Victoria)

6. Kingston Heath Golf Club (Cheltenham, Melbourne, Victoria)

7. Kingswood Golf Club (Dingley, Melbourne, Victoria)

8. Kooralbyn Country Club (Kooralbyn, Queensland)

9. Kooyonga Golf Club (Lockleys, Adelaide, South Australia)

10. Lake Karrinyup Country Club (Balcatta, Perth, Western Australia)

11. Metropolitan Golf Club (South Oakleigh, Melbourne, Victoria)

12. Newcastle Golf Club (Fern Bay, Stockton, New South Wales)

13. New South Wales Golf Club (La Perouse, Sydney, New South Wales)

14. Peninsula Country Club (Frankston, Melbourne, Victoria)

15. Royal Adelaide Golf Club (Seaton, Adelaide, South Australia)

16. Royal Canberra Golf Club (Yarralumla, Canberra, A.C.T.)

17. Royal Hobart Golf Club (Seven Mile Beach, Hobart, Tasmania)

18. Royal Melbourne Golf Club (Black Rock, Melbourne, Victoria)

19. Royal Queensland Golf Club (Hamilton, Brisbane, Queensland)

20. Royal Sydney Golf Club (Rose Bay, Sydney, New South Wales)

21. Tasmanian Golf Club (Barilla Bay, Hobart, Tasmania)

22. The Grange Golf Club (Seaton, Adelaide, South Australia)

23. The Lakes Golf Club (Mascot, Sydney, New South Wales)

24. Victoria Golf Club (Cheltenham, Melbourne, Victoria)

25. Yarra Yarra Golf Club (Bentleigh, Melbourne, Victoria)

Jim Ferrier achieved great success in the United States and throughout the world. Today David Graham, 1981 U.S. Open champion, is one of the established stars on the PGA Tour, and many foresee a great future for long-hitting Greg Norman. The Australian summer is from November through April. Prominent American and world golfers are frequent competitors in the Australian Open, Dunlop International and Wills Masters, held late in the year.

Selection of the 25 most challenging and interesting tests of golf in Australia was made and pared down from the top 50 courses named by Australian Golf—*Golf Digest*'s sister publication in Australia. The selection panel, which includes such Australian golfing experts as Guy Wobstenholme, Ted Ball, Ron Luxton, Di Gatehouse and golf writer Tom Ramsey, placed a premium on conditioning, challenge, individual architecture, difficulty and length of each course.

New Zealand, the sister country of Australia with only 3,000,000 people, has more than 400 courses, generally set in countrysides that offer spectacular scenery and challenging shots for the golfer.

Here is another Mackenzie course among the top-rated in the country. Royal Adelaide is recognized for being a searching test of the game of golf, combining the best of classical architecture with a demand for accuracy on virtually every shot. It has been the site of eight Australian Opens—the last in 1962 when Gary Player shot 281 to defeat Kel Nagle by a stroke. The photo is from behind the green on the short, 301-yard par-4 third hole. Veteran Norman Von Nida took a 9 on this hole to lose the Australian Open.

This picturesque shot of play on the Queenstown Golf Club in New Zealand is typical of golf in this thriving country. The courses are relatively short, but they have rolling fairways and small greens against a backdrop of snow-capped mountains.

JAPAN'S TOP 25 COURSES

Golf or "gorufu," which is the colloquial Japanese name for golf, was first played nearly 75 years ago in Japan. "Gorufu fever," however, did not begin rising until the 1950s, as it did in America about the time Arnold Palmer began captivating audiences. Now, gorufu is extremely popular, but golf courses in Japan are for the wealthy. In 1957 the World Cup matches (then known as the Canada Cup) came to Kasumigaseki Golf Club. Japan won the event, a complete surprise to everyone, and a year later sent a team to the World Amateur playoffs at St. Andrews, Scotland. By then, millions of Japanese had begun to patronize the two- and three-tiered driving ranges that sprang up in metro-

The Sagamihara West Course (right), also on the island of Honshu, is built on relatively low-lying land and shows the large greens that are a bench mark of the majority of Japanese architects. Note one of many ponds that dot most of the courses. Sagamihara is one of Japan's top 25 courses.

The Fuji course (below), at the 36-hole Kawana resort on the main island of Honshu near the famous volcano, is typical of the layouts that have been built in the mountainous regions.

JAPAN'S TOP 25 COURSES

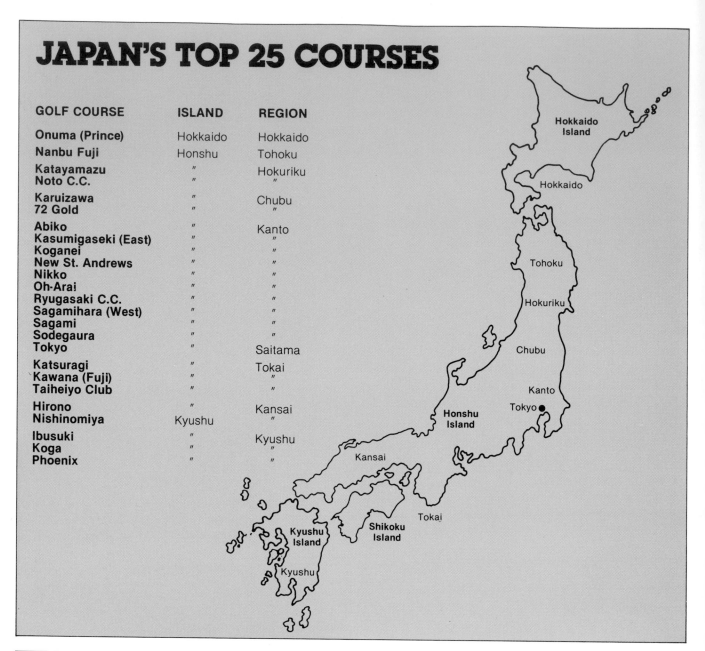

GOLF COURSE	ISLAND	REGION
Onuma (Prince)	Hokkaido	Hokkaido
Nanbu Fuji	Honshu	Tohoku
Katayamazu	"	Hokuriku
Noto C.C.	"	"
Karuizawa	"	Chubu
72 Gold	"	"
Abiko	"	Kanto
Kasumigaseki (East)	"	"
Koganei	"	"
New St. Andrews	"	"
Nikko	"	"
Oh-Arai	"	"
Ryugasaki C.C.	"	"
Sagamihara (West)	"	"
Sagami	"	"
Sodegaura	"	"
Tokyo	"	Saitama
Katsuragi	"	Tokai
Kawana (Fuji)	"	"
Taiheiyo Club	"	"
Hirono	"	Kansai
Nishinomiya	Kyushu	"
Ibusuki	"	Kyushu
Koga	"	"
Phoenix	"	"

The Japanese love their baths and you will find them in virtually every type of hostelry and every golf clubhouse. Here (left) is one of the more unusual ones in an outdoor setting at the exclusive Koganei club outside Tokyo. Golfers head for the baths before the bar.

Robert Trent Jones has established his mark in Japan with the design of one of its top 25 courses (right) called the Onuma (Prince) on the northernmost island of Hokkaido. It is a beautifully scenic, mountainous region that serves as a resort retreat for skiing in the winter season and hiking, boating and golf in the summer. Jones has carved an outstanding course in and around the mountains that features rolling fairways, large slightly elevated greens and a profusion of bunkering.

politan areas. "Gorufu fever" had reached significant proportions.

It is not known how many Japanese golfers never get closer to playing the game than hitting balls at a practice range; those who promote the game estimate as many as 10,000,000 "golfers." The Japan Golf Association reports that there are 1,500,000 established Japanese players. It is a known fact that there are 1,300 golf courses to play on, though, and by comparison, this means Japan has as many as seven times the number of golfers per course as does the U.S., with its 12,000 courses for 15,000,000 golfers.

nly the well-to-do can afford to play. Club memberships average between $10,000 and $300,000 with the prestigious Koganei club in the Tokyo area reported to be at the top of the range. There are very few public courses in Japan. Weekday greenfees are seldom less than $25 and a weekend tee-off time costs at least $50—if you can get one. This explains why many "would be" golfers never get off the practice range.

Most golf courses in Japan are constructed and located in the hilly country because of the critical need for agricultural crops on the existing fields. Then, too, you will find two types of grass on double greens. Korai, similar to our own bermuda, is the tougher and stronger to stand the changeable weather and heavy play. Bent grass is used for winter play.

There exists no established ranking of courses in Japan. The attached list is a compilation from Japanese golf writers and golf experts. They prefer to cite general areas of country where good courses abound rather than individual courses. These regions include the Tokyo suburbs with several top courses, the area of Hirono near the industrial city of Kobe, the beautiful scenic surrounding Mt. Fuji and the southern islands section of Japan with its warm-weather climate.

A photo view of Japan would be incomplete without a typical historic Japanese clubhouse. Shown (right) is the Kaga-Fuigo Country Club, which was built from one of the old Japanese castles with its many levels, upswing roofs and outside stairways.

The Kansai region of Japan on the main island of Honshu near the major cities of Osaka and Kobe has a number of golf courses. Among the more outstanding is the Hirono Golf Club (below). This area is known as the plains region and, as shown in the photo, is relatively flat. The Hirono course is one of the oldest in Japan, having been opened in 1932 and designed by British architect C.H. Alison.

MEXICO AND SOUTH AMERICA

Most of Mexico's best golf is in its southwest section, roughly triangled by Mexico City on the east, Mazatlan on the northwest and Acapulco on the southwest. Both of the latter resort areas are on the Pacific coast. There are, however, pockets of golf in other, scattered, locations such as Cancun off the Caribbean, around Monterey in the northeast section and even a smattering of activity in Baja California, the peninsula that juts southward from California.

Mexico City, the capital, is located in a high valley surrounded by mountains, and has some fine private courses. Most of them will accept visitors during the week, when the traffic is down. It helps to be a member of a club back home, but this isn't crucial. The city's best course is the Club de Golf Mexico, named by Peter Dobereiner as one of the best 50 courses outside the continental limits of the U.S. It cuts its majestic way through groves of cyprus, eucalyptus, pine and cedar. The Country Club of Mexico City and the 36-hole Acozac Golf Club also are worthwhile courses.

Golfers agree that the Guadalajara area offers the best climate for the game. Low humidity and temperatures that seldom stray from the 60-75 degree range is a hard combination to beat. There are four 18-hole courses in the immediate metropolitan area. In Chapala, about 30 miles away, are three more courses.

Quite a few Americans have retired in the area, and many of them have congregated at golf developments such as the Santa Anita Golf Club, an open-fairway course with gorgeous greens. The late Larry Hughes, a Californian, designed many Mexico courses including this one and the nearby San Isidro Country Club, a lovely test replete with elevated greens, deep ravines and astounding scenery. The Atlas Golf Club, designed by Joe Finger, is an imaginative course with some lively inclines. The Guadalajara Country Club is private, with luscious bermuda fairways and bentgrass greens; it can be played by tourists at certain times.

Manzanillo, on the west coast, is the location of Mexico's most talked-about course, the Las Hadas resort 18 designed by Roy Dye. It took forever to be completed; the first nine was opened in 1974, the second in 1981, but the wait was worthwhile. Fairways leap up, down and sideways through a lush tropical setting. Monumental views of Manzanillo Bay can be seen over and around the royal palms, orange and pineapple trees that grace the course. The resort buildings are designed like Arabian minarets, mosques and cupolas. Sensational. There's another course in Manzanillo, the nine-hole Club Santiago.

At Acapulco, with its fabulous Acapulco Bay, resort golf is confined to the two Princess Hotel courses, the side-by-side Acapulco Princess and Pierre Marques layouts. The Princess, designed by Ted Robinson, is

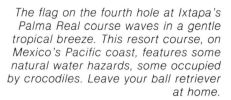

The flag on the fourth hole at Ixtapa's Palma Real course waves in a gentle tropical breeze. This resort course, on Mexico's Pacific coast, features some natural water hazards, some occupied by crocodiles. Leave your ball retriever at home.

Tucked into a mountain valley, the Los Leones course in Chile is one of South America's most attractive courses. Here is the 12th green, fronted by a canal that is at once lovely and intimidating.

San Isidro's course near Guadalajara is dramatically set in a deep valley. A road that leads to the distant clubhouse can be seen on the hillside to the left. One of the course's original developers was the late Bing Crosby, along with Javier Ramirez, a Guadalajara businessman.

level but stiffened by water on 12 holes. The Pierre Marques is a Percy Clifford design, a more rugged test with eight man-made lakes and 55 sand bunkers. Golf's great, but don't miss that view of Acapulco Bay that Frank Sinatra sings about.

At Mazatlan, there is a wonderful beach and many tourist accommodations but only one golf course, the El Cid. It's long enough, 6,712 yards, but on relatively level terrain.

Two other major Mexican resort-area courses are backed by Fonatur, the government's national tourist development fund. They are at opposite sides of the country. Cancun, in the Yucatan's Mayan territory off the Caribbean with its interesting ruins, showcases the Pok-Ta-Pok course completed in 1979. It has wide fairways and little rough, but a constant wind challenges the golfer. On the west coast at Ixtapa is the Palma Real Golf Club, built along a rugged coastline in the foothills of the Sierra Madre mountains. Robert Trent Jones Jr. designed both of these courses.

Although South America has produced a few championship professional golfers—Roberto de Vicenzo of Argentina is the best—this continent has had limited golf development. The few courses that are in operation, however, are delightfully south-of-the-border experiences, what with Spanish-speaking professionals and caddies and tropical settings. South Americans who play golf are usually in the upper class; the game has never reached the masses here.

In Argentina, the 36-hole Jockey Club facility is one of the few on the continent designed by the famed Scottish architect, Alister Mackenzie, who laid out Augusta National, Royal Melbourne and others. The Jockey Club twice has been the site of the World Cup (1962, 1970), the international event that features two-man professional team competition. In Colombia, the Club Los Lagartos in Bogota and the Cali Golf Club are respectable tests. Dick Wilson designed the Lagunita Country Club in Caracas, Venezuela, where the 1974 World Cup was held. Chile's Los Leones and Prince of Wales courses are good tests, as are the Montivideo Country Club in Uruguay, the Los Ineas and Lima courses in Lima, Peru, the Quito Tennis and Golf Club in Ecuador and Brazil's Gavea Golf Club.

Generally regarded as Mexico's most unusual course, the Las Hadas Resort course in Manzanillo is a Roy Dye design that took almost 10 years to complete. This is a view from the tee of the 363-yard, par-4 seventh hole with palms loosely framing the fairway. Many of the holes have multiple tee-placement possibilities that can sharply alter a hole's playability.

ATLANTIC OFF-ISLANDS

Once upon a time fleets of the great European powers—namely Great Britain, France, the Netherlands and Spain—sailed to the tropical islands off America's Atlantic coastline in search of gold. That mission was never realized, for gold was not to be found on these garden isles. What the swashbuckling conquerors found instead, however, were endless strands of white-sand beaches and lush fields on which exotic crops wildly flourished.

For centuries the colonial powers used the native population to grow cash crops—sugar cane, for example—and when the plantation families took a day off, there they were on the beaches, soaking up that gorgeous sunshine.

After World War II the Europeans' influence rapidly waned as the islands gained various degrees of independence, but their cultures have lingered on. Since the late 1950s, golf courses designed by the best architects have proliferated.

Today the American visitor to these Atlantic Off-Islands can enjoy entertaining island golf amidst resort accommodations equal to the best anywhere. On the following pages are descriptions and photographs of what are considered to be the top golf courses on the islands, stretching north to Bermuda and south to Trinidad and Tobago.

Bermuda

Bermuda's most-discussed course is the Mid-Ocean Club, one of the few designed by the American golfing pioneer, Charles Blair Macdonald, winner of the first U.S. Amateur, in 1895. Macdonald had a marvelous site for a course, along bluffs that tower over the Atlantic. Although it is a middling 6,519 yards, Mid-Ocean disturbs good players and reluctantly gives up low scores. The famous fifth, a par 4 that doglegs left over a lake, challenges the player to carry as much of the water as seems possible. The adjacent Castle Harbor course, with its wildly undulating fairways, is a dramatic resort course.

In 1953 Robert Trent Jones revamped Mid-Ocean, and in 1971 he built the Port Royal Golf Course, which some say is the top Bermuda course and which leans against the coast on the opposite side of the island. Its par-3 16th has both a tee and green at the edge of a bluff on the left next to the water. Port Royal is owned

It's a strong uphill shot to the green on Castle Harbour's 18th, a 235-yard par 3. This long-established Bermuda course is hilly from start to finish. It's not long, but hazards threaten just about every off-fairway shot.

by the government and hosts many Bermuda golf championships.

The Bahamas

Celebrated for their lissome beaches and blue-green waters, the Bahamas also offer excellent terrain for golf courses. Fresh water bubbles just beneath the surface on most of these Caribbean islands, and with the tropical climate, grass and other flora, as well as fauna, grow quickly and abundantly. Golf architects also use this water to create hazards that counteract the generally placid levelness of the courses.

On New Providence, where the Bahamian capital of Nassau is located, the South Ocean Golf Club is the leading course. Designed by Joe Lee, this 6,700-yard layout is on high ground that affords a panoramic view of the ocean. Lyford Cay is a demanding 18 through stands of palms that dull any golfer's aggressiveness.

Extremely handsome in appearance, the Emerald and Ruby Courses at the Princess Hotel on the island of Grand Bahama are also severe examinations. The rough is tropical shrubbery growing out of coral.

The four remote courses on the Bahamian out-islands are among the greatest island courses anywhere. On Eleuthera is the Cotton Bay Club, an esthetic treat with excellent greens and designed by Robert Trent Jones. Nearby is the Cape Eleuthera Resort, which features a Von Hagge/Devlin course with plenty of water. One of the others is Great Harbour Cay, a rolling Joe Lee test halfway between Nassau and Freeport. Unfortunately, it is not now operating because of economic setbacks, but one day is certain to return to its

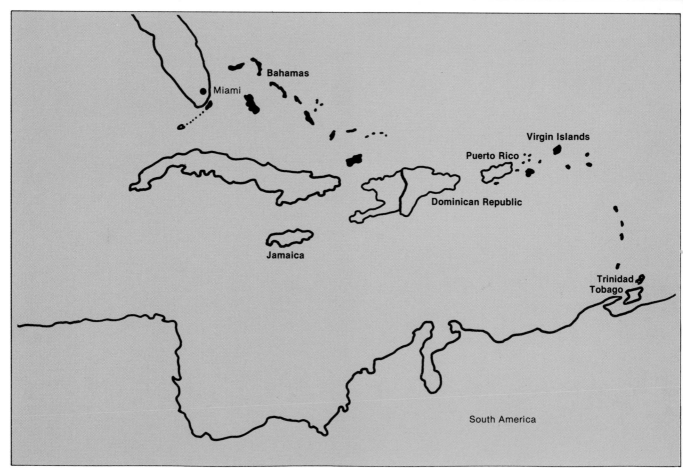

Like most Bermuda courses, Port Royal has a number of holes hard by acquamarine Atlantic waters. This is the par-3 16th at Port Royal, and it's obvious that a shot to the left would not fare well. Port Royal, a government-owned facility, is at 6,900 yards the most demanding test in Bermuda.

rightful position as a great island course with unusual Bahamian elevations. Treasure Cay, on Abaco, is the last course designed by the talented Dick Wilson. It can play up to 7,012 yards and is extremely tight. Don't hit it wayward here.

Dominican Republic

At La Romana on the Dominican Republic coastline are Casa de Campo's two unusual courses, each with sharply different styles as well as backgrounds. Both designed by Pete Dye, the Teeth of the Dog and the Links 18s were built atop coral rock.

Noting that native guinea grass grows on the coral without the benefit of dirt, Dye had the growth cut, then actually shaped the fairways by molding the underlying rock with sledgehammers, pickaxes and chisels. Once this was done, a mixture of sand, soil and cachaza, a by-product of sugar cane and a natural fertilizer, was spread. Voila, golf.

Stretching to 508 yards, the par-5 16th hole at the Cotton Bay Club on the Bahamas island of Eleuthera swaggers by water. Some of the course's 129 sand bunkers can be seen here. This course, designed by Robert Trent Jones, is perched atop a bluff.

Opened in 1972, the Dog features seven holes hard by the rocky ocean beach. These amount virtually to the most seaside holes on any golf course in the world. The 179-yard seventh has a carry over churning water

A rocky surf booms alongside the Teeth of the Dog Course at Casa de Campo in the Dominican Republic. Here the 179-yard, par-3 seventh is played over a sandy expanse to a green that affords no room for error. Golfers below are on the tee of the eighth, also one of the seven "Teeth" holes that hug the coastline.

to a tiny green isolated by sand, bunkers and stubby grass; the 175-yard 13th's green is entirely circled by sand.

In contrast, the Links course, opened in 1977, is all inland on nearly tree-less terrain. It's a Scottish-type course with many large sand deposits preserved to mimic links conditions. Fairways plunge through four-foot-tall guinea grass.

Puerto Rico

Golf course architects from the United States have thoroughly Americanized Puerto Rico's courses—ample fairways and large bunkers and greens are common. Still, they all have individualities. There are seaside and inland tests, there are open and wooded courses and the use of water both as a source of irrigation and hazards adds many challenges to the game.

The most impressive conclave of courses are the four at the Dorado Beach Hotel and the adjacent Cerromar Beach Hotel, each of which operates two 18s. All have been designed by Robert Trent Jones and play to

Dorado Beach East's 13th hole wriggles its way around water and sand hazards to an elevated green fronted by a pond. It's a classic double-dogleg par 5, 540 yards of devilment typical of this Puerto Rico course designed by Robert Trent Jones. There is also a West Course at this famous resort, and both 18s can repel all but the hardiest boarders.

similar yardages—6,500 from the middle tees. The Dorado Beach courses are the oldest, with the first nine completed in 1958, the last in 1966. The area was once a grapefruit plantation and many of these trees remain. The East's 13th, a par 5 that doglegs left before reaching a pond that fronts the green, is the most-discussed hole. Cerromar's courses date from 1971. One is along the ocean and windy, the other is more inland with lovely mountain views.

Another course on Puerto Rico that has earned respect is Palmas Del Mar, a Joe Lee concept with restricted fairways and 11 water holes.

Virgin Islands

The Virgin Islands of St. Croix and St. Thomas, just off Puerto Rico's southeast coast, are small but mighty in the golf derby. Both islands have outstanding courses, tests that also stand up scenery-wise with the best.

St. Thomas' Mahogany Run is the newest, designed by George and Tom Fazio and opened in 1980 with deserved notice. The course is routed through heavy tropical forests and several holes run along a tortuous beach. In fact, some of the seaside holes have greens that seem to teeter over the beaches. Mahogany Run is a complete resort with all the amenities. By contrast, St. Croix' Fountain Valley is simply a fine golf course with no connecting lodge. Set in a valley as its name implies, Fountain Valley sashays through trees and shrubs, many of the flowering variety, with enough ravines and foothills thrown in to grab a golfer's attention. It was designed by Robert Trent Jones, who calls it one of his most handsome creations.

Also on St. Croix is the Buccaneer Beach Hotel's gently rolling, seaside 18, with many sand bunkers and water hazards.

Trinidad/Tobago

Trinidad and Tobago, two islands under the same national flag just off the northeastern coast of Venezuela, offer strikingly different lifestyles. Trinidad is a 1,864-square-mile island that bustles in its historical role as the birthplace of limbo, calypso and the steel

Mahogany Run's 13th and 14th holes are sited along cliffs overlooking the Atlantic Ocean. This is the 13th, a 360-yard par 4 that doglegs left at its conclusion. Mahogany Run is a golf and tennis resort on St. Thomas of the U.S. Virgin Islands and was opened in 1980. The course was designed by U.S. architects George and Tom Fazio.

band. It has one golf course, the Moka Estates 18 at the venerable St. Andrews Golf Club. The course is a short drive from the thriving capital, Port of Spain.

Tiny Tobago, 35 miles west of Trinidad, is only 116 square miles, a somnolent, peaceful place and with the better golf course. This is the Tobago Golf Club, associated with the Mount Irvine Bay Hotel and set in a tropical wonderland. Thousands of coconut palms rustle in the balmy winds. Frigate birds hang in the sky and squads of white egrets are in almost constant motion.

The Tobago course, opened in 1969, features tees so well elevated that the golfer can see the entire fairway of nearly every hole. The fairways are reasonably level and the only sharp climbs are onto some of the tees. Local rules provide that coconuts and palm fronds lying in the numerous bunkers may be removed before play. The course was designed by Englishman John Harris.

Jamaica

Jamaica's Tryall Golf and Beach Club 18 may be one of the most dramatic and demanding island golf courses in the world. Located 14 miles west of Montego Bay, Tryall was opened for play in 1958. Designed by Texan Ralph Plummer, the layout stays close to the coastline for its first nine holes where the wind and sand are the major hazards. The second nine ventures inland onto sloping foothills that lead to a high plateau. Although Tryall measures only 6,324 yards from its longest tees, it is not easily conquerable.

At the other end of the island, in Kingston, is Jamaica's other fine course, the Caymanas Golf Club. This is a cascading, wild one that surges through wooded, hilly terrain. It is often the scene of leading Caribbean golf competitions.

—John P. May

Graceful palm trees and ocean views are stock-in-trade accoutrements of the Mount Irvine Bay Hotel's Tobago Golf Club. But when you're going for a good score at this course, on the island of Tobago, count on a stiff challenge that amounts to 6,793 yards from the back tees.

From its longest tees, the Tryall Golf and Beach Club Course in Jamaica is 6,324 yards. It's a Ralph Plummer design that can show its colors to the best of golfers. Winds often draw a bead on the seaside nine, while hills take their toll on the inland nine.

EUROPE
AND THE MEDITERRANEAN

Golf on the continent of Europe is in many ways quite different from the game in the rest of the western world. Except in the resort areas, it is still largely a game for the very wealthy, the very social, or the very adventuresome. However, this is gradually changing and several new golf courses are on the drawing boards for the 1980s in France, Italy, Switzerland and Germany. An important stimulus to golf on the Continent has been the growth of the European golf tour, an adjunct to the British PGA schedule of events.

Unlike the large golfing nations (United States, Great Britain, Australia and South Africa), the countries of Europe boast relatively little golf near their great capital cities. The area around Paris is the exception with more than 20 courses. Rather, the courses and clubs are widely spread across each nation. In most of Europe, golf is a game of narrow fairways and troublesome rough and woods. It is a game of accuracy, not power. Some of the better-known European courses are situated in or near the ski towns of Austria's Tyrol and the Swiss and French Alps.

Until the late 1960s, little emphasis was placed upon building golf courses of what would be regarded as championship caliber by international standards. At that time a proliferation took place in the resort areas, particularly along the Mediterranean coasts of Spain, Portugal and Morocco. Virtually all of these new facilities were built by professional architects such as Robert Trent Jones, whose organization has a full-time office in Marbella, Spain, and Ron Kirby, an American formerly with Trent Jones who is in partnership with Gary Player. The continent used to be the bastion of such British designers as Commander John Harris and former British Open champion Henry Cotton. The quality of their efforts is often in direct proportion to the funds they are given to work with.

Although Spain and Portugal are today proudly distinctive nations and Morocco is as different from either as Christianity is from Islam, all three show interesting similarities from a golfing viewpoint. It is weather for olives and almonds, and symmetrical rows of olive trees sometimes stitch the landscape as far as you can see. And then there are the mountains that sweep down to the sea, spectacularly along most of the southern coast of Spain, gently at the Algarve in Portugal, abruptly in parts of Morocco.

Golf in any foreign land has special romantic qualities for most Americans. Playing for the first time at St. Andrews, Scotland, is a baptismal experience—something you have heard about since you first took up the game. By contrast, golf along the Mediterranean Gateway is a fascinating incongruity. Here you are swinging away at a golf ball in a setting where the vestiges of one civilization defending itself against another are still widely visible. A thousand years ago, the lands along the Mediterranean and Atlantic coast east and west to Gibraltar as far as soldiers could march were occupied by the Moors. Ruined watch towers and stone embattlements still jut from the horizon.

In 1979, *Golf Digest* commissioned contributing editor Peter Dobereiner, who travels 100,000 miles a year from his base in England, to pick the 50 best courses outside the United States. From that list we have culled his best 15 in Europe and the Mediterranean.

He used three basic criteria in selecting them: esthetics, golfing quality and condition. Says Dobereiner, ''Quite a large proportion of the courses on the list are not of championship quality, mainly because they lack the length to provide the ultimate test considered essential in a championship.''

The straight-away 18th hole at the Penina Golf Club in the Algarve, Portugal, heads toward the hotel on the right and is a classic at 482 yards.

EUROPE/ MEDITERRANEAN'S TOP 15 COURSES

1. El Saler, Valencia, Spain
The late Javier Arana has never received the international recognition that his architectural genius deserves, mainly because he worked exclusively in his native Spain. This course of his is seaside golf at its best, combined with a very special Spanish flavor.

2. Club zur Vahr, Bremen, Germany
Carved through a forest of massive conifers, Vahr combines a superb strategic layout, demanding the widest variety of shots. Architect: Bernard von Limburger.

3. Penina, Algarve, Portugal
Henry Cotton took an unlikely area of paddy fields and created a botanical extravaganza. A monster off the back tees, but swallow your pride and move forward and the course becomes a delight.

4. Den Haag, Netherlands
Justly proud of its reputation as the best links course in continental Europe. The Hague has switchback fairways and some of the most undulating greens to be found anywhere, making golf a sometimes frustrating, but always rewarding, experience. Architect: Sir Guy Campbell.

5. Pevero, Sardinia, Italy
A resort for wealthy holiday makers, but what a tiger of a course for the poor, tired businessman. Blasted out of the boulders and scrub of the macchia country, where brigands once hid from the law, a stray shot spells a lost ball. Magnificent golf. Architect: Robert Trent Jones.

6. Sotogrande (Old), Spain
Artificial lakes, undulating greens of terrifying speed, bunkers of eccentric shapes—these are the Trent Jones trademarks. But here he was in a relatively benign mood and his course is a joy to play and look at. Architect: Robert Trent Jones.

7. Falkenstein, Hamburg, Germany
Hilly country with trees and heather provides faint echoes of Scotland. Architect Harry Colt, who learned his golf at St. Andrews, added to this impression by building large greens. High premium on driving and putting.

8. Quinta do Lago, Algarve, Portugal
Glorious survivor of an ambitious development that went west during the revolution, Quinta is built through wild country of pine and cork oak and is surely destined to become the centerpiece of a fashionable resort. Architect: William Mitchell.

9. Falsterbo, Sweden
Except for the wealth of fine links courses in the British Isles, Falsterbo would surely rank high in European golf for it has a special charm and remoteness that is enhanced by the bird-life and Baltic Sea views. Architect: unknown.

10. Royal Dar es Salam, Rabat, Morocco
A typical Trent Jones course in a Moroccan setting, with flamingos striding disdainfully beside the artificial lakes, but what sets this one apart is the standard of upkeep. Nothing is spared to groom the course, for it literally has to be fit for a king.

11. Noordwijk, Netherlands
This is a rare type of course for it is a modern links, designed and built since World War II, following damage to the original Noordwijksche Club's premises. Pine trees add greatly to the links scenery. Architect: Frank Pennink.

12. Ravenstein, Belgium
Properly the Royal Golf Club de Belgique, this is a mature course in a noble forest where royal personages once hunted wild boar. Superb chateau clubhouse. Architect: George Pannall.

13. Caesarea, Israel
This is the only golf course in Israel to date—the new country has had little inclination or resources for such frivolous development. However, it is a pleasant, links-type course with a refreshing, pioneer spirit among the membership. Architect: unknown.

14. Le Touquet, France
Here we have an agreeable blend of links country with some wooded inland holes over undulating ground. It is an excellent test of golf and for a change the subsidiary forest course is foolish but fun. Architect: unknown.

15. Morfontaine, Senlis, France
Superb sandy subsoil provides the perfect golfing flora of pine and heather for a tight and tricky masterpiece of a course that lacks only length to bring it the accolade of a championship course. Architect: Tom Simpson.

SOUTH AFRICA

Golf in South Africa has come an extraordinary distance since a master putter from Johannesburg named Bobby Locke joined the American tour in 1947 and won four of his first six tournaments. Locke's presence in the U.S. marked South Africa as one of the game's emerging nations. Today, it has arrived. Golf is now a major sport in this vast continental pocket, and its own professional tour is growing in prestige and prominence. Its place in golf history—unusual-facts division—was established early in 1982 at a gargantuan sports resort complex called Sun City, which hosted the game's first million-dollar tournament, won by Johnny Miller in a nine-hole sudden-death playoff with Seve Ballesteros.

Sun City, located in the protectorate of Bophuthatswana, is a dream come true for South Africa's preeminent golf statesman, Gary Player: he co-designed the resort's course at the country club that bears his name. There are three sets of men's tees, and they can extend the course from 5,960 to 7,033 yards. From the back tees, a premium is placed on long, accurate drives and testing second shots to contoured, cloverleaf greens. Since the course borders on a game preserve, finding a baboon in your foursome is a likely event. Denis Watson, a South African who is a standout player on the U.S. tour, says it has the potential to become one of the world's greatest.

The course that still ranks with the pros as the country's most outstanding, though, is Durban Country Club, on the Indian Ocean. There are bush roughs and small greens to make it interesting, says Player, and he once ranked the par-5 third hole as one of the finest in the world. Nearby Royal Durban gets high marks from the players. Located in the infield of a racetrack, there are no trees or other large hazards to block the view of the horseplayers. The course is 6,538 yards and although its rough is nonexistent, its par of 74 is a measure of its testiness.

In the interior of South Africa, Johannesburg is the country's golfing hub. There are more than 80 courses within a 60-mile area, and the pros and amateurs alike rank the Houghton and Royal Johannesburg plants as top of the line. Houghton was founded in 1913 and is a level layout of stately trees and well-kept fairways. "The distances are very misleading," warns Gary Player. "Jack Nicklaus could hardly find a club to hit from 100 yards. Everything he took out of the bag sent the ball too far." Royal Jo-burg, as it is called, has two 18s—the East measuring 6,947 yards and the West at 6,743. The East is perhaps the most demanding course in the area. Unlike most of the country's clubs, this one is private and not generally available for play by visitors. A rising course star in the region is Wanderers

Golf Club, a major sports complex, but smaller than Sun City. The course is short and tight. A modernization program to move the bunkers closer to the greens, undertaken in 1982, raised its unforgiving quotient. Denis Watson claims it as one of his favorites—understandably, because he plays out of this fine establishment. Gary Player also commends the Johannesburg Country Club as the area's best new course.

Over on the Atlantic side of the nation sits the Royal Cape Country Club at Capetown, a sand-and-pipe layout with deep rough and a striking similarity to American courses. It is another favorite of Watson's for that reason.

The Killarney Links, just a few minutes from downtown Johannesburg in the "estate" part of town, is worth special mention because it is so like American layouts. What was originally a working farm has become a 7,000-yard golf challenge, lined with fairway homes on undulating terrain. Translation: you'll hit every club in the bag. The amenities of the new clubhouse leave little to be desired.

But then golf in South Africa leaves little to be desired. Where else can one amuse the monkeys with errant tee shots and play at a place called the Modderfontein Dynamite Factory Golf Club?

It's dynamite all right.

Shown here is an example of the distinctive "fingered" bunkering and greens that are common at South Africa's new Gary Player Country Club course at Sun City in Bophuthatswana. The course, designed by Player and Ron Kirby, was the site of the Sun City Million Dollar Golf Challenge in late 1981, won by Johnny Miller in a nine-hole sudden-death playoff with Seve Ballesteros.

FAR EAST

here once were those who believed that only mad dogs and Englishmen would go out in the noontime heat of the tropics or the midnight cold of the Arctic to beat away at a golf ball. This belief was inspired largely by British colonists, who would play golf wherever they could dig a hole in the ground.

The former British colony, now better known as the nation of India, claims to have the oldest golf course in the world outside the United Kingdom—the Royal Cal-cutta Golf Club, built in 1829 by Scottish troops. More than 150 years later, the Indian Open, a stop on the Asian professional tour, is played here, alternating tournament sites each year with the Delhi Golf Club, in New Delhi. Within the past 10 years, the Royal Calcutta course has been lengthened to 7,053 yards, and the 1982 winning score of 277 attests to its championship quality.

The growth of the Asian professional tour has helped broaden interest in the game, and some of the older

courses have been modernized to bring them up to tournament standards. An example is the Delhi Golf Club itself, which was redesigned in a major way in 1975-'76 by Peter Thomson, the five-time British Open champion from Australia. It was opened for the Indian Open on the Asian circuit in 1977.

Today, the game of golf throughout the Far East has become a strong symbol of sophistication, if not a cult among Oriental royalty, politicians and ranking businessmen. As a result, in the last 30 years many new courses of excellent caliber by international standards have been built.

Some of the most interesting are in Singapore, Thailand, Malaysia and the Philippines. Singapore is an island where modern office buildings merge with ageless sampans in the crowded harbor, and the smells of Madras curries and frangipani blossoms fill the air. The Singapore Island Country Club was formed after Malaysia became independent, merging the former Royal Singapore Golf Club (which came into existence in 1891 when Scottish jute traders were spreading their national game and their trade throughout the Far East) with the former Singapore Island Club.

The Singapore Island Country Club operates today at the two separate original locations: the so-called "Bukit" (which means "hill") and the "Island." Each location has two courses, the best known being the Bukit, site of the 1969 World Cup and the usual venue of the Singapore Open. The courses offer typically British golf in the midst of Asian jungle, for when land was cleared a wide variety of trees were imported from Britain, giving a truly English flavor.

Also in Malaysia is the Selangor Golf Club, virtually in the heart of Kuala Lumpur, the nation's capital. It has two 18-hole courses, both of which are used for the Malaysia Open on the Asian tour, and both of which are lush and beautiful layouts.

Another capital city with great golf is Bangkok, in Thailand. Like Venice, the city is intertwined with drainage ditches, but unlike Venice, on its lowlands are two of the most unusual golf courses anywhere. The most famous is the Royal Bangkok Sports Club, whose golf course is alongside a racetrack, which it occasionally crosses. The newest, called Navatanee, is a country club community developed by Sukum Navapan, president of the Thai Military Bank, and named jointly after his wife Tanee and himself. It was designed by Robert Trent Jones Jr., on land—all 6,500 yards of it—below sea level. Both the clubhouse area and the home of Navapan look like modern castles virtually surrounded by moats. Navatanee is an engineering miracle in converting mush to lush.

The Wack-Wack Golf Club in the Philippines, frequently the site of international matches, is a fine golf course, beautifully landscaped and maintained. It is not as exciting, however, as Luisita in the high country, or the Valley Club, a rolling, modern course designed by Japanese Seichi Inoye, about an hour's drive from Manila.

Indonesia also has a number of interesting courses, including Pondak Indah near Jakarta and Bali Handara on the Island of Bali. Pondak Indah was designed by Robert Trent Jones Jr., built on what were previously rice paddies and where major drainage problems were encountered. Bali Handara was designed by Peter Thomson, who carved nine holes out of an old dairy farm and nine from a tropical rain forest in an old volcanic crater high above the Bali beaches. The course is an hour's drive from the international airport at Denpasar.

Today, mad dogs and Englishmen are not alone in chasing after golf balls in faraway places. They are in the company of millions of golfing enthusiasts from nearly every country in the world, all sharing a common insanity.

Courses in the Far East are often characterized by ancient architecture, such as the mogul burial monument in the background of the fourth tee and third green of the Delhi Golf Club in New Delhi, India.

AMERICA'S TOP 50 PUBLIC COURSES

by Frank Hannigan

Let us now praise courses not famous—the very best of the everyday public courses available to the overwhelming majority of American golfers who seldom get near those acclaimed by *Golf Digest* as "America's 100 Greatest Courses."

A list of 50 excellent public courses accompanies this chapter. It is the result of a written survey and follow-up interviews of four tiers of grassroots golf specialists: the executive directors and secretaries of the 40 regional sections of the PGA of America; the executive directors of 51 state and regional amateur golf associations; and the 101 men and women who make up the USGA's two public links committees.

The experts were asked to recommend only two kinds of courses: Those publicly owned; Those privately owned but operated on a daily-fee basis primarily for nearby residents.

Excluded from consideration, since the intention was to distinguish *everyday* public courses, were those linked to resort hotels, e.g., Pebble Beach and Pinehurst No. 2, and all others built in the hope of attracting revenue from traveling golfers. Also discounted were courses operated by branches of the military services and colleges and universities, which are sometimes but not always open to the public.

According to the National Golf Foundation, the industry-sponsored clearinghouse for information on the business side of the game, about 11 million of the 13 million golfers who play at least 15 rounds a year do so on public courses of one kind or another. The NGF also estimates that slightly more than half of 11,161 "regulation" courses in operation at the start of 1982 were everyday public courses.

But only one such course—Cog Hill No. 4 near Chicago—was deemed worthy enough to be included in

Among the many spectacular views of the Pacific Ocean at San Diego's Torrey Pines is this one looking from the fifth tee on the South Course out across the fourth green.

the most recent biennial revision of "America's 100 Greatest Courses." Is it possible that *Golf Digest*'s distinguished panelists, for their greatest courses list, are an elitist band blind to the virtues of courses for the average, recreational golfer? No. The unfortunate fact is that, by and large the superior courses in this country are those at member-owned clubs. Some others, and not too many at that, are run for profit at resorts, but the quality of those is tenuous because there is an inherent contradiction between the quest for great golf and the profit motive.

So why then bother to publish a list of 50 outstanding public courses? Because:

1. Public courses can be and should be better than they are.

2. Public courses are the wave of the future. The golden age of the proliferation of member-owned courses took place during the 1920s—more than 50 years ago. That age is not going to recur.

3. Celebrating the best of the everyday public courses is an effective way of supporting those agencies and individuals (many of them under siege from bureaucrats who equate fiscal solvency with mediocrity) who do a first-rate job of serving up quality golf to 80 percent of our golfers.

The primary criteria for selection were excellence of design and course conditioning. There is a heavy bias in the direction of daily maintenance because the most common, and justifiable, complaint of the everyday public-course player is that the turf on his course is poor. Fairways are too high, greens are spongy and not cut often enough, and tees are often ratty. Some public courses blessed with good design and with rich tradition, like San Francisco's picturesque Harding Park and the Black Course at New York State's Bethpage Park, have been purposefully excluded because the reports on their current condition are negative.

How difficult a course is from the back tees mattered very little in winnowing down the nominations. Any fool can build a difficult course. All it takes are 18 drab

holes totaling 7,000 yards in length followed by the customary proclamation that it is the newest "monster." No, what the golfer wants is to play his game in a very special environment.

In all likelihood there isn't one golfer in the country who has seen or played as many as 15 of the 50 courses on the list. Thus, there is no basis for a broad range of comparative judgments.

Nevertheless, some everyday courses were so strongly and frequently endorsed that it is reasonable to pick out a select group of 10, scattered throughout the country, to recognize that they are very special, and to say something about their histories, methods of operation and characteristics. These 10 outstanding everyday public courses are presented in alphabetical order:

BROWN DEER PARK GOLF COURSE, Milwaukee.

One of eight regulation courses operated by the County of Milwaukee, the course at Brown Deer Park (which offers a variety of other recreational activities) is an area showpiece. Golf cars are not permitted by the parks commissioners, who opt to forego the extra car revenue in favor of a better course. There is a spacious and homey brick clubhouse. Since it opened in 1929 Brown Deer Park has had the distinction of entertaining the U.S. Public Links Championship three times—in 1951, 1966 and 1977.

COG HILL NO. 4 GOLF COURSE, Lemont, Ill.

Called "Dubsdread," the No. 4 Course of the Cog Hill complex in the western suburbs of Chicago is the capstone of the daily-fee empire of Joe Jemsek, who owns six courses and runs two others under a lease arrangement. Cog Hill No. 4, Jemsek's pride and joy, has been regularly included among the "100 Greatest Courses" and was ranked most recently in the fourth 10. It was designed by architects Dick Wilson and Joe Lee and opened in 1964. The course has huge teeing areas and anyone rash enough to go all the way back on every tee would be playing a course more than 7,300 yards long. The daily green fee is $15. Jemsek leased the course for a week to a local group that entertained the U.S. Public Links Championship in 1970. Later he declined payment on the grounds that everyone—especially himself—had a good time.

EDGEWOOD TAHOE GOLF COURSE, Stateline, Nev.

A handsome course on Lake Tahoe with the High Sierra Mountains as a backdrop. Although in a resort location, it is operated strictly as a daily-fee course. The anything-but-modest green fee of $30 does include a golf car. There are water hazards on 13 holes and the management takes special pride in its slick greens, which suited the USGA just fine when Edgewood Tahoe was first recognized nationally last summer as the host course for the U.S. Public Links. The nearby gambling casinos are a unique neighborhood feature. George Fazio is the architect.

INDIAN CANYON GOLF COURSE, Spokane, Wash.

A traditional and old-fashioned innercity muny course, but one with a special history and quality, In-

AMERICA'S TOP 50 PUBLIC COURSES

FIRST TEN
(In alphabetical order)

	YARDS	PAR	YEAR
Brown Deer Park G. Crse. Milwaukee, Wis.—George Hansen	7,021	71	1929
Cog Hill G.C. #4 Lemont, Ill.—Dick Wilson/Joe Lee	6,911	72	1964
Edgewood Tahoe G. Cse. Stateline, Nev.—George Fazio	6,472	72	1968
Indian Canyon G. Cse. Spokane, Wash.—H. Chandler Egan	6,227	72	1934
Otter Creek G. Cse. Columbus, Ind.—Robert Trent Jones	7,215	72	1964
Plumas Lake G. & C.C. Marysville, Calif.—Don McKee/Bob Baldock	6,180	71	1926
Tanglewood G.C. Clemmons, N.C.—Robert Trent Jones	7,050	70	1958
Torrey Pines G.C. (South) La Jolla, Calif.—Bill Bell Jr.	6,649	72	1957
Wailua G. Cse. Kauai, Hawaii—Toyo Shirai	7,028	72	1960
West Palm Beach C.C. West Palm Beach, Fla.—Dick Wilson	6,789	72	1947

THE OTHER FORTY
(In alphabetical order)

	YARDS	PAR	YEAR
Alvamar Hills G. Cse. Lawrence, Kan.—Bob Dunn	7,209	72	1968
Ancil Hoffman G. Cse. Sacramento, Calif.—Bill Bell Jr.	6,669	72	1965
Arroyo del Oso G. Cse. Albuquerque, N.M.—Arthur Jack Snyder	6,859	72	1965
Bangor Municipal G. Cse. Bangor, Me.—Geoffrey Cornish	6,674	70	1964
Bear Creek G. & R.C. Dallas-Ft. Worth Airport, Tex.—Ted Robinson	6,625	72	1980
Braemar G. Cse. Edina, Minn.—Don Brauer	6,550	72	1964
Bunker Hills G. Cse. Coon Rapids, Minn.—David Gill	6,827	72	1974
Cranberry Valley G. Cse. Harwich, Mass.—G. Cornish/Bill Robinson	6,827	72	1974
Downing G. Cse. Erie, Pa.—J.G. Harrison/F. Garbin	7,213	73	1962
Fall Creek Falls G. Cse. Pikeville, Tenn.—Joe Lee	6,716	72	1972
Flanders Valley G. Cse. Flanders, N.J.—Hal Purdy	6,300	72	1963
Glenview G. Cse. Cincinnati, Ohio—Arthur Hill	6,297	72	1974
Grand Haven G. Cse. Grand Haven, Mich.—W. Matthews/J. Matthews	6,875	72	1965
Grapevine Mun. G. Cse. Grapevine, Tex.—Joe Finger/Byron Nelson	7,022	72	1979
Hershey Parkview G. Cse. Hershey, Pa.—Maurice McCarthy	6,400	72	1931
Hog Neck G. Cse. Easton, Md.—Lindsay Ervin	7,019	72	1976
Hominy Hills G. Cse. Colts Neck, N.J.—Robert Trent Jones	7,059	72	1964
Industry Hills (Eisenhower) Industry, Calif.—Bill Bell Jr.	7,213	72	1979
Kemper Lakes G. Cse. Hawthorn Woods, Ill.—Ken Killian/Dick Nugent	7,092	72	1979
Lawsonia Links G.C. Green Lake, Wis.—William Langford	6,620	72	1929
Mangrove Bay G. Cse. St. Petersburg, Fla.—Bill Amick	6,670	72	1978
Montauk Downs G. Cse. Montauk, N.Y.—Robert Trent Jones	6,860	72	1969
Oak Hollow G. Cse. High Point, N.C.—Pete Dye	6,429	72	1972
Oak Mtn. State Park G. Cse. Pelham, Ala.—Earl Stone	6,911	72	1974
Papago G. Cse. Phoenix, Ariz.—Bill Bell Jr.	7,053	72	1963
Pasatiempo G. Cse. Santa Cruz, Calif.—Alister Mackenzie	6,607	71	1929
Perdido Bay C.C. Pensacola, Fla.—Bill Amick	7,133	72	1962
Pine Ridge G.C. Timonium, Md.—C.A. Hook/L.E. Myerly	6,820	72	1958
Pompano Beach G. Cse. Pompano Beach, Fla.—Robert Von Hagge	6,527	72	1954
Rancho G. Cse. Los Angeles, Calif.—Bill Johnson	6,688	71	1949
Richter Memorial G. Cse. Danbury, Conn.—Ed Ryder	6,750	72	1971
Salem Hills G.C. Northville, Mich.—Bruce Matthews	7,054	72	1963
Sleepy Hollow G. Cse. Brecksville, Ohio—H. Smith/H. Cram/H. Lewis	6,285	71	1923
Spook Rock G. Cse. Ramapo, N.Y.—Frank Duane	7,030	72	1970
Stone Mountain G. Cse. Stone Mountain, Ga.—Robert Trent Jones	6,831	71	1969
Stow Acres C.C. Stow, Mass.—Geoffrey Cornish	6,600	72	1954
Tokatee G. Cse. Blue River, Ore.—Red Robinson	6,775	72	1966
Tumwater Valley G.C. Olympia, Wash.—R.R. Goss/Glen Proctor	7,162	72	1970
Waveland G. Cse. Des Moines, Iowa—Warren Dickinson	6,501	72	1901
Wellshire Municipal G. Cse. Denver, Colo.—Henry Hughes	6,620	72	1926

Architect listed following location of course.

The fifth hole at Tanglewood in Clemmons, N.C., site of the 1974 PGA Championship, is a menacing one. A picturesque old church and graveyard (inset) are adjacent to the course.

dian Canyon was a WPA project during the 1930s. It was laid out by H. Chandler Egan, who also had a hand in the design of Pebble Beach. Egan, an early U.S. Amateur champion (1904 and 1905) was an influential figure on many levels of the game. Indian Canyon, a short (6,227 yards) par-72 layout, is an esthetic wonder, primarily because of thousands of trees—mostly evergreens—and the splendor of Spokane Mountain in the distance. Texan Bill Welch won the U.S. Public Links Championship at Indian Canyon in 1941 and returned 24 years later as the head pro. He's still there.

OTTER CREEK GOLF COURSE, Columbus, Ind.

The course was a 1964 gift to the people of Columbus—37 miles south of Indianapolis—by the Cummins Engine Company. Robert Trent Jones did the design. Columbus welcomes anyone for a daily charge of $10 ($13 on weekends). The total annual rounds is slightly more than 30,000—not at all heavy traffic for a municipal course. Its quality is indicated by its use as the permanent site for the Indiana Amateur Championship.

PLUMAS LAKE GOLF AND COUNTRY CLUB, Marysville, Calif.

Located in the lush Sacramento Valley 20 miles north of Sacramento, Plumas Lake, according to one California golf executive, has the finest and fastest greens in northern California. Its method of operation is unusual in that the City of Marysville owns the land but leases the course for $1 a year to a nonprofit private club, which plows back profits into course improvements. It was originally operated by the city, but was a money-loser until the novel lease arrangement. Anyone can play for $7 on weekdays and $9 on weekends. The course is short but tight.

TANGLEWOOD PARK (West Course), Clemmons, N.C.

When tobacco tycoon Will Reynolds died, he willed his 1,100-acre farm to the people of Forsyth County.

The trustees of Reynolds' estate converted the property into a recreational public park with facilities for boating, fishing and horseback riding. The golf setup is grandiose, with two full-size 18-hole courses and an 18-hole par-3 arrangement. Robert Trent Jones was the architect. Situated eight miles west of Winston-Salem in the rolling hills of North Carolina's Piedmont belt, the West Course was the site of the 1974 PGA Championship, won by Lee Trevino.

TORREY PINES SOUTH COURSE, La Jolla, Calif.

Owned and run by the City of San Diego, Torrey Pines is renowned as the annual site of the Andy Williams PGA Tour stop. The South Course is ranked as the better of two 18-hole layouts, but both offer splendid views of the Pacific Ocean. Torrey Pines is open 365 days a year and the courses endure an astonishing amount of traffic—as many as 185,000 rounds a year. At one time, it was on *Golf Digest*'s "100 Greatest" list. City residents pay green fees of only $4.50; nonresidents pay $6.50.

WAILUA GOLF COURSE, Kauai, Hawaii.

Perched on a coast of Hawaii's "garden island," Wailua is truly a thing of beauty. The back nine has a linksland quality, and two par-3 holes (the 14th and 17th) that overlook the ocean are stunning. That nine was laid out in the 1920s by sugarcane growers who were avid golfers and whose knowledge of mainland courses they derived largely from reading the old American Golfer magazine. A new nine was opened in 1960 after construction supervised by Toyo Shirai, a golf professional of exceptional talents, who remains in charge of the course. Shirai had a less dramatic site to work with because the land left for him had been leveled in World War II by U.S. Marines practicing amphibious landings.

WEST PALM BEACH COUNTRY CLUB, West Palm Beach, Fla.

This delightful city-owned course is set on rolling land, a rarity for inland Florida. It was the first course done entirely by the late Dick Wilson, a talented archi-tect whose major works include Laurel Valley in Pennsylvania and Pine Tree in Florida. Owned by the City of West Palm Beach, the operation offers an annual membership arrangement for city residents, who get unlimited golf for an annual fee of only $230. Outsiders pay a $10 daily fee. The course was a PGA Tour stop in the 1950s, and one of the winners was Arnold Palmer.

The demanding 394-yard par-4 16th at Cog Hill combines the splendor of dramatic bunkering with an intimidating pond. This course, designed by Dick Wilson and Joe Lee in 1964, can be stretched to 7,300 yards from the back tees, one of the reasons it is known as "Dubsdread."

AMERICA'S TOP FIVE COLLEGE COURSES

5

ome of the best-hidden treasures among America's great golf courses are owned and run by colleges or universities. These courses, at least the better ones, often were designed by noted architects, and many times have hosted national championships.

Take for instance the little-known Williams College course in Williamstown, Mass. Williams College can hardly be called a collegiate golf powerhouse, yet its Taconic Golf Club, a beautifully wooded and hilly course designed by Wayne E. Stiles and John R. Van Kleek, has played host to two NCAA Championships, the Women's Amateur, the Massachusetts Amateur and the U.S. Junior.

As good a course as Williams' is, it's not even among the best five collegiate facilities in America, according to a poll of the nation's golf coaches. Here's the top five as selected by those coaches:

1) Ohio State (Scarlet Course), Columbus;
2) Yale Golf Course, New Haven, Conn.;

The 528-yard par-5 seventh hole at Colgate requires an accurate tee shot. In fact, many players keep the driver in the bag on this hole, preferring to tee off with a fairway wood or a long iron. This course hosted the 1977 NCAA Championship, won by the University of Houston.

From the tee of the 441-yard par-4 18th hole at the Stanford University Golf Course the golfer not only gets a superb view of the 18th fairway and green, but the Pacific Ocean as well.

3) Stanford University Golf Club, Stanford, Calif.;

4) University of New Mexico (South Course), Albuquerque;

5) Colgate University (Seven Oaks Golf Club), Hamilton, N.Y.

hio State. When one thinks of golf here, such illustrious names as Jack Nicklaus, Tom Weiskopf, Ed Sneed and John Cook immediately come to mind. For not only were they standouts at Ohio State, they are outstanding on the PGA Tour. One hardly thinks, however, of the equally distinguished name Alister Mackenzie, but he is responsible for designing the remarkable course on which these fine players honed their games in preparation for world-class competition.

Mackenzie designed two courses at Ohio State in 1931 and they were completed by Perry Maxwell using WPA workers four years later—the Scarlet, measuring 7,104 yards with a par of 72, and the Gray, a less-intimidating 6,020-yard par 70. The Scarlet is a typically Scottish course with bunkers to the sides of the greens, not in front. Over the last 10 to 15 years, many trees, most-

ly maple, were added to thwart the wilder hitter. The NCAA Championships have been played here six times, attesting to the course's top-notch quality.

Another prominent architect, Charles Blair Macdonald, designed the prestigious course at Yale University in 1926, and many of Macdonald's trademarks are still evident today. Extremely deep bunkers with wooden steps to walk in and out, severely contoured greens and unusually demanding tee-shot placements all require exacting play from the first drive to the last putt.

Yale's course is ranked in the top five in Connecticut, and at one time secured a spot in America's 100 Greatest listing. Poor maintenance for a while contributed to its demise from the 100 Greatest ranking, but the course is regaining its excellent condition, thanks to a new financial emphasis on its upkeep. The fairways once were cut only every couple of weeks, but now even the rough and the fairways are mowed four times as often.

Under the 32-year guidance of green superintendent Harry Meusel, the Yale course also has undergone extensive revisions. Traps 100 to 175 yards out were filled

in 1942. The NCAA was played at Stanford in 1948, 1966 and 1981.

Another course to host the NCAA is the South at the University of New Mexico. Designed by Robert F. Lawrence and opened in 1967, it can stretch 7,246 yards from the championship tees, and lures the golfer through sage brush, desert sand and trees. The fairways are rolling and the greens are large. The three finishing holes are especially demanding—the 16th, a 459-yard par 4; the 17th, a 250-yard par 3, and the 18th, a 612-yard par 5.

Golf coach Dwaine Knight, who played the tour in the mid-'70s, has produced several current tour regulars, including Brad Bryant and Tom Armour III. In addition to the NCAA in 1976, the course has hosted the Western Junior, The Western Athletic Conference Championships and the William H. Tucker Tournament, the second oldest collegiate event in the U.S.

One of the few times in recent years the NCAA was staged in the East, it was played at Colgate University. The Seven Oaks course was designed by Robert Trent Jones in 1934, one of his first retainers after graduating from Cornell. But because of the Depression the plans sat idle in a drawer until the 1950s. "I went over the land with a friend of mine," Jones recalled recently, "and we laid out the course in two days."

The first nine opened for play in 1957 and the second in 1964. The well-watered course today plays to nearly 7,000 yards, in typical Jones fashion. What is not typical of Jones' style, however, is the striking absence of fairway bunkers. Water comes into play on 13 holes, though, and the greens are heavily trapped. A number of elms have been lost over the years, but many willow, poplar and maple trees have been planted in their place.

In addition to these five venues, there are many good college golf courses, including the University of Michigan Golf Course at Ann Arbor, designed by Mackenzie and Maxwell, and the Duke University Golf Course in Durham, N.C., designed by Robert Trent Jones.

Ironically, some of the best golf colleges don't own courses. The Houston golf team, for instance, which has won eight national titles and produced under coach Dave Williams such tour stars as Bill Rogers, Bruce Lietzke and Keith Fergus, plays on several private courses in the area. Wake Forest, the alma mater of Arnold Palmer, Lanny Wadkins and Curtis Strange, and under coach Jesse Haddock, plays at two nearby clubs.

The raison d'etre for college courses, of course, is student recreation. Most green fees are relatively low and course upkeep relatively lax. The few college gems that stand out, however, would compare favorably with the best courses of any type the game has to offer.

—Roger Schiffman

in and on some holes multiple tees were combined into one. Yale's 18th hole, a winding par-5 dogleg right with a huge mound in the center of the fairway, is perhaps the most demanding. But the most memorable are probably the par-4 fourth with water along the right side and the par-3 ninth over water with a tremendous valley (some call it "Macdonald's Folly") caving into the center of the green. Tommy Armour once labeled these two of the best 18 holes in existence.

At the Stanford University Golf Course, the par 4s leave a lasting impression. Many are 420 to 440 yards and play to every bit of that because the fairways are well watered, minimizing roll. Designer William P. Bell made ample use of San Francisquito Creek, which comes into play on eight holes. The rolling, tight course was opened in 1930 and plays to 6,700 yards and a par of 71.

Perhaps Stanford's most famous golfing alumnus is U.S. Open champion Tom Watson, though his career blossomed after he graduated and went on tour. Also a famous graduate and now a close friend of Watson, Frank D. (Sandy) Tatum won the NCAA Championship

LAST OF THE PERSONAL COURSES

Since the game arrived on this side of the Atlantic the compulsion to own your own golf course—your very own—has overcome titans of American wealth. Many were built, yet only two are known to remain as purely personal preserves. These belong to former U.S. Ambassador to Great Britain, Walter Annenberg, at his Sunnylands estate in Palm Springs, Calif., and to the Rockefeller family on their Pocantico Hills estate near New York City.

The 140-acre Annenberg estate sits concealed from public view behind a 12-foot-high, vine- and shrub-covered fence on some of the most valuable property in Palm Desert. With the main gate obscurely situated at the corner of Frank Sinatra and Bob Hope Drives, the well-protected privacy of the course has aroused some unusual myths. Among them, "Virtually no one plays the course, golf professionals in particular, and it is so impeccably maintained that divot-taking is not permitted."

Indeed, Sunnylands may be the best-maintained golf course over which the least number of rounds are played anywhere. It is where President Ronald Reagan plays what he calls his "annual" game. Three other Presidents also have played Sunnylands—Dwight Eisenhower, Richard Nixon and Gerald Ford—as have many other golfing dignitaries from around the world. At age 73, Annenberg is a steady 16-handicapper, who strikes the ball boldly from the port side and takes a divot almost whenever it is called for.

The myth, however, of the "no-divot rule" is understandable because the course, which is planted with bent greens and Bermuda fairways, is indeed not only perfectly groomed, but beautifully landscaped. It was built in 1962 by none other than Dick Wilson, who constructed three different sets of tees for nine greens. A different name for each hole is justified by the fact that two of the tees are always widely separated. Each of the nines measures approximately 3,000 yards with all of the Wilson characteristics—large greens, beautiful sand bunkers and clever use of water and doglegs.

At the time the course was built, Annenberg personally brought in 875 olive trees and planted a variety of small saplings, which include eucalyptus, Virginia oaks and stone pines. The beautiful landscaping on the course is punctuated with an occasional artistic touch placed there by Annenberg, who is known to possess one of the great art collections in America. Off to the right of the third hole is a beautiful Chinese tea house. Marking the dogleg at the 441-yard fifth is a totem pole, a relic imported from an Indian tribe in British Columbia. The hole, of course, is known as the "Totem Pole." On the seventh, called the "Double Dogleg," the target for the tee shot is a shapely Joshua tree, which Annenberg placed in the middle of one of Dick Wilson's sand bunkers. It has the look of a desert sculpture.

Sunnylands is overseeded with rye in September or October of every year, and Annenberg usually opens it for play December through April when he moves his residence and his office to Sunnylands from Philadelphia, the home of his publishing empire.

The Pocantico Hills course on the Rockefeller estate overlooking the Hudson River was originally a four-hole course built for the use of John D. Rockefeller in late 1899 after he took up golf earlier that year "for his health" at the age of 60. This was expanded to nine holes in 1901. Sometime in the 1930s the Philadelphia firm of Toomey and Flynn added another nine holes.

Rockefeller frequently played on his course with executives of Standard Oil, plus such luminaries as Will Rogers and Harvey Firestone. Robert Trent Jones did considerable remodeling work on the course in the 1970s for use by Laurance Rockefeller. The 18-hole layout is 5,673 yards with several double greens. The Rockefeller family may eventually donate the property as a national monument, with the course remaining intact.

Many golf courses began as personal-use affairs, but have become part of private or public facilities. Others simply have been consumed by today's high costs of labor, maintenance and taxation, or have given way to more profitable land use.

At the turn of the century, Theodore Havemeyer, John Jacob Astor and A.G. Spalding built private courses on their estates. None of them remain. In

The third hole of the Sunnylands estate course, owned by Walter Annenberg, features a Chinese teahouse off to the right of the fairway. Several holes on this private preserve are enhanced with similar "art objects," including totem poles and unusual trees in conspicuous places.

1929, Henry Francis du Pont, great-grandson of E.I. du Pont, employed Devereux Emmet and Albert H. Tull, designers of the Garden City Golf Club and other fine courses of the day, to build a course for him at his Winterthur Estate, near Wilmington, Del. His personal golf pro, Percy Vickers, describes the course as "maybe six strokes harder than the Old Wilmington Country Club course," now called Green Hill. It had 10 greens and 17 tees, providing an 18-hole routing of 6,480 yards that was kept in excellent condition for 34 years, but required a staff of seven in the summer and five in the fall to maintain.

In December, 1963, du Pont leased 141 acres of the golf course for $1 a year to a group of area businessmen, who incorporated it into a new facility called the Bidermann Golf Club. It had cost $59,000 to build.

ow overgrown by weeds and owned by the University of Denver is the personal golf course of Lowell Thomas, built on his estate near Pawling, N.Y. The famed broadcaster, who died at 89 in 1981, entertained numerous celebrity friends at the course, which he called Hammersley Hills Golf (and Hunt) Club. Among those who played there were Presidents Eisenhower and Nixon, longtime neighbor Thomas E. Dewey, Arnold Palmer, Sam Snead and Gene Sarazen.

The course had nine greens and 18 tees providing 18 distinctive holes, measuring 6,300 yards. Robert Trent Jones helped Thomas remodel the course and it

was Jones' idea to use a decimal system for pars, like 3.5, 4.5 and 5.5. A distinctive feature was a monstrous hole measuring 830 yards. The par was 7.5. The greens each had two cups, one the standard 4 1/4-inch size and the other cut at eight inches. The larger cups were added at the suggestion of Sarazen, a Thomas pal, who always contended that golf would be more enjoyable with a bigger putting target. Not surprisingly, those days of designating your own cup size have ended. Within a few years, Walter Annenberg may be the only man left in America who can put a tree in a sand trap without protest from members or the public. His may be the last of the personal golf courses.

THE FRANK COX GAZETTEER

The late Frank Cox was a 14-handicapper who spent most of his days in retirement from the New York Times Company traveling the world over playing golf. He played more than 1,500 courses, 364 in one year! All during his travels, he kept in touch with the editors of *Golf Digest*, writing his impressions or personally dropping in to tell us about his peregrinations, including the time he hit a golf ball off the Great Wall of China. Frank Cox' criteria for judging golf courses were far more subjective than scientific.

One day he reported, ''I played both Firestone courses on the same day, and while I appreciated the South Course for the superb test that it is, I found the North Course with all its water and other difficulties far more exciting. More and more I hear of courses being downgraded as unfair, or too difficult or too long, or with too many blind holes, etc. But I think the game should be big enough to allow for the maximum practical range of challenge to those who wish to sharpen their skills, with appropriate modification by tee placements to satisfy the widest spectrum of player ability. Some think Frenchman's Creek near North Palm Beach, Fla., unfair because of narrow fairways, much water and many traps, but even though it gives me much personal grief, a great satisfaction comes from overcoming difficulties on it.''

On another occasion he said, ''I have found that my own supply of words is clearly inadequate to describe some of the lovely courses I am playing. For example, the Marietta (Ohio) Country Club has a somewhat unexciting first nine, but every hole on the back nine is an exciting picture hole as it winds through the high hills behind the town. The 18th is 410 yards from a high tee to a slightly higher hill for a 200-yard drive, and then the most magnificent view across the town and the Ohio River Valley, with the green straight downhill—even poetry would hardly do the job.'' For the adventuresome golfer we present Frank Cox' Gazetteer of Golf Courses.

UNUSUAL FOREIGN COURSES

P'anmunjom, Korea—on the 38th Parallel. One green with four tees, bordering the minefield between North and South Korea, separated by a high barbed-wire fence. Built to provide the peace-keeping U.N. forces, mostly American, with some recreation facility to relieve the tension and boredom of this rugged outpost.

Muni Golf Course, Manila, Philippines—winds in and out and all around the old fort city. Poor condition but exciting to play.

Royal Nepal Golf Club, Kathmandu, Nepal—at one end of the International Airport, surrounded by the snow-capped Himalayas. Winds around and through small native settlements, where the primitive living goes on more or less oblivious to the golfers, as they dodge the cattle grazing all over the course. Whatever fairways there are, are pockmarked with deep, rugged mullahs or gorges. The greens are all oiled sand, and little boys drag burlap sacks over them to smooth them after putting. A strange mixture of primitive life, magnificent scenery, and the royal and ancient game.

Bucharest Golf Club, Rumania—nine-hole golf club, largely for diplomats, on the outskirts of the city, sandwiched between a network of waterways, with a unique feature being the fourth hole that has a long carry over water, following which a boatman rows the party to the other side to complete the hole and play the fifth. The sixth is back across the water, with the boatman waiting to row the players back to the mainland. Good condition.

Karachi Golf Course, Pakistan—this is a finely laid-out 18 hole course, but there is not a blade of grass anywhere. The tees are built-up earthen mounds compressed into form by rocks and logs; the fairways are compacted brown earth, rather irregularly unlevel to provide long but erratic bounces. It is amazing how soon one can learn to nip the 4-wood and irons for some good-looking shots; the rough is just a rock-and-sand jungle, and the greens are oiled sand, with homemade rakes to

GOLF COURSES IN UNUSUAL LOCATIONS

COURSES SURROUNDED BY OR IN-TEGRATED WITH RACETRACKS:
(some are operated during races, some not):
Vienna Country Club, Vienna, Austria
Gezira Sporting Club, Cairo, Egypt
Penang Golf Club, Penang, Malaysia
Chiang Mai Gymkhana Club, Chiang Mai, Thailand
Royal Bangkok Sports Club, Bangkok, Thailand
Royal Durban Golf Club, South Africa

COURSES PRESENTING OUTSTANDING VIEWS OF GREAT CITIES:
Governor's Island—New York skyline and harbor
Montevideo Country Club—Montevideo, Uruguay
Brightwood Golf and Country Club—Halifax and Dartmouth, Nova Scotia and harbor
Vallee Arriba Country Club—Caracas, Venezuela
Lincoln Park Golf Club—San Francisco and Golden Gate Bridge
Bally Haly Country Club—St. Johns, Newfoundland
East Potomac Park Golf Course—sweeping views of Washington, D.C. highlights
Panama Country Club (old)—Panama City, Panama
Oahu Country Club— Honolulu
Singapore Island Country Club—Singapore
Manila Country Club—Manila and Makati (a suburb of the Philippines)
Gezira Sporting Club—Cairo, Egypt
Monte Carlo Country Club—Monaco and Nice, France
Palm Beach Country Club—Palm Beach, Fla.
Lookout Mountain Country Club—Chattanooga, Tenn.
Bel-Air Country Club, Beverly Hills, Calif.
LaJolla Country Club—LaJolla, Calif.

HIGH-ALTITUDE GOLF COURSES:
Quito Tennis and Golf Club, Equador, (more than 10,000 feet)
La Paz Country Club, Montanillo, La Paz, Bolivia (more than 12,000 feet)
Club de Golf de Mexico, Mexico City (about 7,500 feet)

A GOLF COURSE IN A CLASS BY ITSELF:
Russian Jack Springs Municipal Golf Club, Anchorage, Alaska—this course has a somewhat scenic and interesting layout in the hills behind Anchorage. It's unique and memorable feature is its greens, which are all made of beautiful Astroturf. Unfortunately, they lie on beds of gravel and any ball that lands on them takes off like a rocket. Also this surface will not hold a ball on any slope, so many excellent pitches, chips and putts just roll off. Frustrating! It's the only show in town other than the military courses, so it's treated as just one more hazard of Alaskan golf.

GOLF COURSES WITH UNUSUAL SOUNDS:
Chapultepec Country Club in Mexico City—adjoins the No. 1 army base with a much-stirring band continually playing, which is most helpful to the golfing rhythm.

My Old Kentucky Home State Park Golf Club, Bardstown, Ky.—is a shrine to Stephen Collins Foster and has chimes that play some of his best tunes every 15 minutes, greatly improving the mood of the temperamental.

Glynco Country Club, Brunswick, Ga.—on a site of a former military base within the confines of the Treasury Department's Law Enforcement Training Center on ground leased to the county by the Treasury Department. From the ninth tee you can see patrol training cars chasing one another and hear gunfire from pistol, rifle, and machine-gun ranges, plus roaring motors and screeching brakes.

---

smooth them for putting. It never rains in Karachi, an advantage with mixed blessings.

Ousteen Oslofjord Golf Club—a nine-hole course on a little island in the fjord outside of Oslo. Access is by a little rowboat with an outboard motor that makes trips to the island from the center of the city. There are very few occupants of the island, and the course covers it from one end to the other with an interesting combination of rugged hills and coastlines as the basis for most of the holes. It is considered a private club, the small clubhouse usually unattended and run on the honor system.

Mena House Golf Club, Cairo, Egypt—a nine-hole course literally in the shadow of the pyramids, near the famous Mena House hotel where notable international conferences have been held. The primary feature of the course is the aura of antiquity that hangs over it, but another is that the game is disrupted by a succession of hustlers wanting to sell everything from soda, fruit and souvenirs, to golf lessons. The caddies are equally disconcerting in that almost every shot evokes a stream of

Arabic with the name of Allah prominently featured. Any number of times I couldn't tell whether I had hit a superb shot, or faced total disaster.

Cork Country Club, Cork, Ireland—a beautifully varied course with spectacular views of the broad river that lines it, and many of its holes are played deep in the bowels of an ancient quarry.

John Hay Country Club, Baguio, Philippines—this military camp a mile high in the summer capital of the Philippines features long, sweeping holes, long carries over gullies, and one straight uphill that has about seven terraces to reduce the risk of the ball coming back too far.

Atimaoro Golf Club, Tahiti—has 18 holes through an orange and grapefruit plantation with fine views of the mountains, but the heat and humidity at noon are the worst I've ever felt, and I survived only by long draughts of the grapefruit juice from the greatest grapefruit in the world.

LITTLE-KNOWN GEMS IN THE UNITED STATES

North Redoubt Golf Club, Garrison, N.Y.—got its name from Revolutionary War days when this very rugged area along the Hudson River was one of Gen. Washington's important defensive outposts to defend New York. It has a magnificent view of the River, West Point and Bear Mountain on the opposite side. It has steep palisade-like hills, gorges and dense woods, which make for very exciting golf in largely undisturbed natural beauty.

Manasquan River Country Club, Brielle, N.J.—one of the most scenic courses on the Eastern seaboard. From its high hills there are sweeping panoramas of both the Atlantic Ocean and the inland waterways with their heavy shipping parades, and some unusual golf holes. It is beautifully landscaped with long rows of Japanese cherry trees, laurel, azalea and dogwood.

Wailea Country Club, Maui, Hawaii—has two fine 18s, but the newer course goes up higher in the hills with superb views of much of this very beautiful island. In the strait between Molokai I could see the whales jumping high out of the water. A most exhilarating course.

Here is a scene from the Royal Bangkok Sports Club Golf Course, Thailand. One of the half dozen courses around the world surrounded by or integrated with a racetrack, this par-66 layout runs alongside cricket and hockey fields.

MILITARY COURSES WITH THEIR OWN UNIQUE ATMOSPHERE

U.S. Military Academy Golf Course, West Point—with magnificent views of the Hudson River and long, steep hills that make it ideal for ranger-training exercises.

U.S. Naval Academy, Annapolis, Md.—a gracious course with fine views of the Severn River, Chesapeake Bay, and historic academy landmarks, but sprinkled with high wireless towers for global naval communication.

U.S. Air Force Academy, near Colorado Springs, Colo.—A lovely course in the heart of the Rockies, with a great variety of holes featuring hills, forests and waterways.

Eglin Air Force Golf Club, Florida—a really top-notch course, challenging, hilly, good water holes, about 12 blind greens, but liberal use of giant periscopes and observation platforms, and a push-button motorized cable to assist in walking up one of the steeper hills.

Elmendorf Air Force Base, Anchorage, Alaska—a fine course, considering the elements that have to be contended with, featuring military bridges over the swiftly running streams that wind their way through the course.

Moose Run Golf Club, Fort Richardson (U.S. Army), Anchorage, Alaska—with a very hilly front nine and a fairly level back nine, features bear and moose as special added hazards.

Navy Marine Country Club, Aiea, Hawaii—a hillside course with sweeping views of Honolulu and particularly the Pearl Harbor area.

Marine Base Golf Club, 29 Palms, Calif.—in the high desert but with tremendous underground water supplies that make it a lush oasis in a real hardship training post with temperatures well over 100 degrees.

Avase U.S. Marine Base, Okinawa—a well-maintained lush course, quite hilly, with commanding views of the countryside and shore.

Kadena Air Force Base, Okinawa—adjoining the base airport with spectacular jet exercises and featuring some beautiful cliff and rock formations.

U.S. Coast Guard (Governor's Island), New York Harbor—winds around the old fort on the island. One blind hole into a corner of the fort has a tall mast with a flag to be raised and lowered signaling that the green is in use or clear. An exclusive but exhilarating place to play golf.

Ft. Prevel Golf Course, Gaspe Coast, Quebec, Canada—a former coast artillery fort, with gun emplacements and caves featured on a number of holes, and fine views of the coast.

Fort Lewis, U.S. Army Golf Course, Washington—an excellent course.

ACKNOWLEDGMENTS

Tomorrow's Great Courses

We would like to thank the following architects and their staffs: Geoffrey S. Cornish, Pete Dye, George and Tom Fazio, Joseph S. Finger, Rees Jones, Robert Trent Jones, Robert Trent Jones Jr., Jack Nicklaus, Ed Seay.

We appreciate information provided by the following organizations: United States Golf Association—William Bengeyfield—National Director—Green Section; George Eberl, Managing Editor—Golf Journal; Janet Seagle, Curator and Librarian; National Golf Foundation—Sandra H. Eriksson, Director of Research; Professional Golfers' Association of America.

America's 100 Greatest Courses

Personnel including professionals and assistants, presidents, managers, secretaries and members at many of the clubs gave invaluable help in providing maps, scorecards, crests, data and photographs (separate acknowledgments are included under photo credits): Ronald E. Whitten, co-author with Geoffrey S. Cornish of *The Golf Course,* for review of copy. Special appreciation to Joe Luigs of Crooked Stick Golf Club, Indianapolis and to Red Hoffman of Robert Trent Jones, Inc.

British Isles

Peter Dobereiner; Peter Haslam and staff of Golf World Magazine.

Canada:

Royal Canadian Golf Association—G.R. Hilton, Executive Director; Vera Clow, Secretary-Treasurer; Lorne Rubenstein, Editor Score Magazine; Gil Blechman, The National Golf Club; James R. Lefevre, Capilano Golf and Country Club; James F. Gaquin Jr., former Executive Director RCGA. Selection panel names appear on page 217.

Australia

Editors of Australian Golf Magazine; Tom Ramsey, Australian News Corporation.

Japan

Editors of Asahi Golf Magazine; Editors of Golf Magazine; Editors of Golf Digest Sha; Tak Kaneda.

Mexico and South America

Brazil Office of Tourism.

South Africa

Don Piggott, Director of Marketing, Southern Sun Hotels, Ltd.; Ann Bamrick, Assistant to Don Piggott; Noel Durie, Assist. Manager, Eastern USA; South African Tourist Corporation; A. Lightfoot Walker.

Far East

Dick Severino, freelance golf journalist and photographer.

America's Top 50 Public Courses

Frank Hannigan, Assistant Director Special Projects, USGA.

America's Top Five College Courses

Braden Houston, Golf Coach, Colgate University; James Leach, Director of Communications, Colgate University; Harry Meusel, Course Superintendent, Yale Golf Course.

The Last of the Personal Courses

Walter Annenberg, former ambassador to the Court of St. James'; Catherine Wheeler, Head of Public Relations, Winterthur Museum.

Special Thanks to:

Nick DiDio, Art Director Golf Digest/Tennis, Inc., for designing maps; Bonnie Johnson, Illustrator of maps; Donna Fontaine Meaney, Typesetter; Nikki Richards, Executive Secretary, Golf Digest, for research and coordination; Martin Sylvetsky, Bill Flocco, Brad Louer, for retrieving film, Mary Jane McGirr and Penny Sippel, Golf Digest Librarians; Penny Curcio, Marcia Dawson, Mary Elizabeth Zamboni, Production, Lura Grace Hirsch, indexing.

PHOTO CREDITS

Jacket, Anthony Roberts, **pgs. 2-3,** Steve Szurlej; **8,** Steve Szurlej; **9,** Steve Szurlej; **10,** courtesy of Robert Trent Jones, Inc.; **10,** courtesy of Robert Trent Jones, Jr. (lower photo); **11,** Steve Szurlej; **12,** Steve Szurlej; **13,** Paul Barton; **14,** Steve Szurlej; **14-15,** Steve Szurlej; **16-17,** Tim Ribar; **17,** Brian Morgan, courtesy of Golden Bear, Inc.; **18,** Steve Szurlej; **19,** Bill Knight; **25,** Paul Barton; **26,** UPI; **26-27,** Anthony Roberts; **28,** courtesy of USGA; **28-29,** courtesy of Jack Dunn III of Baltimore C.C. (Five Farms) **30-31,** Anthony Roberts; **31,** Bettman Archives; **32-33,** Anthony Roberts; **33,** Anthony Roberts; **34-35,** Brian Morgan; **35,** Steve Szurlej; **36-37,** Steve Szurlej; **38,** Anthony Roberts; **39,** Steve Szurlej; **41,** Bill Richards; **42,** Wide World Photos; **42-43,** Colo Hayes, courtesy of The Homestead; **45,** courtesy of Champions G.C. (upper photo); **45,** Manuel Chavez; **46-47,** Bill Knight; **47,** Wide World Photos; **48,** Edward Fox; **49,** courtesy of Cog Hill G.C.; **50,** Rich Pilling; **52,** courtesy of Concord G.C.; **53,** AP Wire Photo; **55,** UPI; **56-57,** Roy Attaway; **57,** Steve Szurlej; **60,** Steve Szurlej; **63,** courtesy of Jim Montgomery, Doral C.C.; **64,** John Newcomb; **66-67,** Warren John Grant; **67,** Anthony Roberts; **68-69,** Bill Knight; **69,** courtesy of USGA; **70,** UPI; **70-71,** Steve Szurlej; **72-73,** Steve Szurlej; **73,** Cal Brown; **74,** courtesy of John Abernethy, Lancaster C.C.; **74-75,** Tom Young; **76,** courtesy of Curt Siegel, Laurel Valley C.C.; **79,** R.H. Eichner; **80,** UPI; **80-81,** Anthony Roberts; **82,** UPI; **82-83,** Anthony Roberts; **84,** Brian Morgan; **85,** Steve Szurlej; **86-87,** Brian Morgan; **87,** Tim Ribar; **88,** Brian Morgan; **89,** Brian Morgan; **90-91,** Anthony Roberts; **91,** Wide World Photos; **92,** Steve Szurlej; **94-95,** Steve Szurlej; **96,** Anthony Roberts; **97,** Anthony Roberts (upper photo); **97,** Dick Beattie (lower photo); **98,** George Wilson; **99,** George Wilson; **100-101,** Anthony Roberts; **102,** courtesy of Peachtree G.C.; **103,** courtesy of Red Hoffman, Robert Trent Jones, Inc.; **104,** Anthony Roberts; **105,** Anthony Roberts; **106-107,** Brian Morgan; **108,** courtesy of Peter Tufts; **109,** Roy Attaway; **110-111,** Steve Szurlej; **112,**

Pete Mecca; **113,** Cal Brown; **114-115,** Cal Brown; **116,** courtesy of Western Golf Association; **116-117,** Cal Brown; **118,** Anthony Roberts; **119,** Steve Szurlej; **120-121,** Larry Petrillo; **121,** E.D. Lacey; **122-123,** Tom Doak; **124-125,** Darryl T. Roberson; **126,** George Hurd; **128,** courtesy of Golden Bear, Inc.; **128-129,** Seth Norman; **130-131,** Seth Norman; **132-133,** Steve Szurlej; **134,** Dick Beattie; **134-135,** Steve Szurlej; **136,** Marvin Newman; **137,** courtesy of USGA; **138,** Steve Szurlej; **139,** Steve Szurlej; **140,** Anthony Roberts; **141,** UPI; **142-143,** Anthony Roberts; **144,** AP Wirephoto; **144-145,** Steve Szurlej; **148,** Steve Szurlej; **149,** Anthony Roberts; **150,** Bill Mount; **151,** Bill Mount (upper photo); **151,** Jack Zehrt; **152,** Victor Ruggles; **153,** courtesy of Cedar Ridge C.C.; **153,** Anthony Roberts; **154-155,** Steve Szurlej; **155,** Steve Glick; **156,** courtesy of Colonial C.C.; **156-157,** courtesy of C.C. of Birmingham; **157,** Dr. Donald Sweeny; **158,** Gerry Campbell; **158-159,** Tom Doak; **159,** Anthony Roberts; **160-161,** courtesy of Walt Disney World Company; **162-163,** courtesy of Brandon Advertising Agency; **164,** Charlie Nye; **164-165,** Steve Szurlej; **165,** courtesy of Murray Swafford and Goodyear G. & C.C.; **166,** John Poer Jr. (Greenville C.C.); **168,** courtesy of Hershey C.C.; **170,** Dave Haberle; **170-171,** courtesy of Kemper Sports Management, Inc.; **172-173,** courtesy of Tom Shea Jr., Kittansett Club; **174-175,** Steve Szurlej; **175,** Brian Morgan; **176,** Steve Szurlej; **178,** courtesy of NCR G.C.; **178-179,** Steve Szurlej; **179,** Mike Miller; **180,** courtesy of Olympia Fields C.C.; **181,** Anthony Roberts; **182,** Nicholas Foster; **183,** Anthony Roberts; **184,** Nicholas Demchak; **184-185,** Marty Loken; **185,** Paul Durant; **186,** courtesy of Sea Island; **187,** Ed Maller; **188,** Anthony Roberts; **189,** courtesy of Massachusetts Golf Association; **190,** courtesy of Wilmington C.C.; **190-191,** Allan Halladay; **193,** Dick Severino; **196,** NY Times; **196-197,** Phil Sheldon; **197,** Frank Gardner; **198,** Phil Sheldon (Ganton); **198,** Kadel and Herbert; **199,** W. Croft Jennings Jr.; **200,** Dick Severino; **201,** Rotofotos (Hagen); **201,** Phil Sheldon; **202,** Dick Severino (Portmarnock); **202,** Peter Dazeley (Prestwick); **202,** courtesy of USGA; **203,** Frank Gardner (Royal Birkdale); **203,** H.W. Neale; **204-205,** Anthony Roberts; **206,** Steve Szurlej; **206,** Phil Sheldon (Hoylake); **207,** Barkow (Jacklin); **207,** Anthony Roberts; **208,** Anthony Roberts; **208-209,** Steve Szurlej; **209,** Lester Nehamkin (Lema); **209,** UPI; **210,** Steve Szurlej; **211,** Frank Gardner; **212,** Steve Szurlej; **213,** Steve Szurlej (Wentworth); **213,** Phil Sheldon; **214,** John Mickle; **216-217,** John Briggs; **218-219,** courtesy of Canadian Pacific Hotels, Ltd.; **220,** Dr. D.A. Gillis; **220-221,** John Briggs; **222-223,** Brian Richards; **223,** courtesy of Essex G. & C.C.; **225,** Anthony Roberts; **226-227,** Anthony Roberts; **228,** Peter Parkinson; **229,** Anthony Roberts; **230,** Nikkon Sports Golf; **231,** Tak Kaneda, Asahi Golf and Golf Magazine Japan; **232,** Tak Kaneda, Asahi Golf and Golf Magazine Japan; **232,** Tak Kaneda, Asahi Golf and Golf Magazine Japan; **233,** courtesy of Robert Trent Jones, Jr.; **234-235,** Tak Kaneda, Asahi Golf and Golf Magazine Japan; **235,** Tak Kaneda, Asahi Golf and Golf Magazine Japan; **236-237,** Anthony Roberts; **237,** Anthony Roberts; **237,** courtesy of Shell Oil Company (Los Leones); **238-239,** Anthony Roberts; **241,** Steve Szurlej; **242,** Steve Szurlej; **243,** Howard R. Gill; **244,** Paul Barton; **245,** Bob Gelberg; **246,** courtesy of Mahogany Run; **247,** Peg Bubar; **248-249,** courtesy of Jamaica Tourist Board; **251,** David Hamilton; **253,** courtesy of Southern Sun Hotel Holdings Ltd.; **254-255,** Dick Severino; **256-257,** Anthony Roberts; **258-259,** Don McKenzie and Glenn Dickerson; **260-261,** Brian Morgan; **262,** Angus J. MacDonald; **263,** William Oostenink; **264-265,** Tom Doak; **267,** Steve Szurlej; **270-271,** courtesy of Shell Oil Co.

SELECTION PANEL FOR
AMERICA'S 100 GREATEST GOLF COURSES
The following are members of the regional selection panel who assist the editors of *Golf Digest* magazine in nominating and selecting golf courses in the United States to the list of America's 100 Greatest Golf Courses (pages 21-191). The panel is composed of leading amateur and professional players, and experienced golfing experts from every region of the country.

NATIONAL SELECTORS
Deane Beman, Ponte Vedra Beach, Fla.; Ben Crenshaw, Austin, Tex.; Joseph C. Dey, Locust Valley, N.Y.; Frank Hannigan, Califon, N.J.; Lew Oehmig, Lookout Mountain, Tenn.; Curtis Person, Memphis; John Roberts, Honolulu; Joe Black, Dallas; P.J. Boatwright Jr., Far Hills, N.J.; Fred Brand Jr., Pittsburgh; William Campbell, Huntington, W. Va.; Mark Cox, Lake Park, Fla.; William Hyndman III, Huntingdon Valley, Pa.; Robert Kiersky, Delray Beach, Fla.; Dave Marr, Houston; Dale Morey, High Point, N.C.; Will Nicholson Jr., Denver; Sam Snead, Hot Springs, Va.; Bob Toski, Boca Raton, Fla.; Tom Watson, Mission Hills, Kan.; Herbert Warren Wind, New York City; Gary Wiren, N. Palm Beach, Fla.

STATE SELECTORS
ALABAMA: Elbert Jemison, Birmingham, Hank Johnson, Tuscaloosa; James K. Spader, Birmingham. **ARIZONA:** Joe Porter, Scottsdale; Dr. Ed Updegraff, Tucson. **ARKANSAS:** Charles Wade, Little Rock. **CALIFORNIA:** John Dawson, Palm Desert; Cecil Dees, Glendale; Buddie Johnson, Danville; Steve Menchinella, Fresno; Ron Rhoads, Pacific Palisades; Patrick Rielly, Pasadena; Tal Smith, Oakland; Dave Stockton, Westlake Village; Frank D. Tatum, San Francisco. **COLORADO:** James English, Denver; Paul Runyan, Denver. **CONNECTICUT:** Jerry Courville, South Norwalk; Billy Farrell, Greenwich; W.H. Neale, New Haven. **DELAWARE:** Anthony Dominelli, Wilmington; Ed Richitelli, Newark. **FLORIDA:** Dexter Daniels, Winter Haven; Tom Draper, Boca Raton; Peter Kostis, Boca Raton; James McArthur, Delray Beach; Dr. John Mercer, Sarasota; Don Rossi, North Palm Beach; Larry Smith, Clearwater. **GEORGIA:** Jim Gabrielsen, Atlanta; Davis Love, St. Simons Island. **HAWAII:** Merrill Carlsmith, Hilo; Ronald Castillo, Honolulu. **IDAHO:** Jerry Breaux, Eagle; Tom Sanderson, Sun Valley; Keith Stanwood, Caldwell. **ILLINOIS:** Bill Erfurth, Glencoe; Dick Hart, Clarendon Hills; A.L. (Jim) Miller, Chicago; Bill Ogden, Glenview. **INDIANA:** Sam Carmichael, Martinsville; Mickey Powell, Lebanon; Ed Tutwiler, Indianapolis. **IOWA:** Rodney Bliss Jr., Des Moines; James Rasley, Des Moines. **KANSAS:** Frank Rose, Topeka; Ron Schmedemann, Hutchinson. **KENTUCKY:** Frank Beard, Louisville; Hartcourt Kempt, Louisville; Jim O'Hern, Goshen; John Owens, Lexington. **LOUISIANA:** Bob DeMoss, Monroe; Frank Leach, Lafayette. **MAINE:** Ron Smith, Kennebunk Beach; Haynes Wheeler, Manchester. **MARYLAND:** Ralph Bogart, Chevy Chase; Bill Clarke, Phoenix; Syl Wagasky, Odenton. **MASSACHUSETTS:** Ted Bishop, Boston; Dick Haskell, Weston; James Murphy, Medford; Dick Stranahan, Longmeadow; George Wemyss, Danvers. **MICHIGAN:** Peter Green, Franklin; Glenn Johnson, Grosse Ile; Al Mengert, Birmingham. **MINNESOTA:** Jack Adams, Edina; Neil Croonquist, Edina. **MISSISSIPPI:**

Mickey Bellande, Biloxi; Ben Nelson, Jackson. **MISSOURI:** Bruce Hollowell, Springfield; James Jackson, St. Louis; James Rollins, Columbia. **MONTANA:** Bill Cordingley, Great Falls; Fraser MacDonald, Butte. **NEBRASKA:** Jerry Fisher, Lincoln; John Frillman, Omaha; Del Ryder, Grand Island. **NEVADA:** Bob Cole, Las Vegas; Charles Teel, Las Vegas. **NEW HAMPSHIRE:** Dr. Robert Elliott, Manchester; Dr. Henry Robbins, Portsmouth. **NEW JERSEY:** Gary Danback, Alpine; David Fay, Summit; Larry Mullen, Deal; Norman Scheer, Livingston; Pat Schwab, McAfee; Bob Sommers, Basking Ridge. **NEW MEXICO:** Floyd Doss, Albuquerque; Bill Hicks, Santa Fe; Lee Olson, Anthony. **NEW YORK:** Peter Bisconti, Mount Vernon; Frank Cardi, Rye; James R. Hand, Ossining. **NORTH CAROLINA:** Alfred Goodrich, Goldsboro; Hale Van Hoy, Clemmons; Harvie Ward, Pinehurst. **NORTH DAKOTA:** Lyle Hornbacher, Fargo; Steve Weidner, Fargo. **OHIO:** Jim Flick, Cincinnati; Roger McManus, Hartville; Nick Popa, Columbus; Ed Sneed, Columbus; Frank Wharton, Akron. **OKLAHOMA:** Jim Awtrey, Ardmore; Vince Bizik, Grove; Mark Hayes, Edmond; Jim Lucius, Tulsa. **OREGON:** Jerry Claussen, Albany; Bob Duden, Portland; Dale Johnson, Portland; Joe Much, Monmouth. **PENNSYLVANIA:** Gary Ellis, Pittsburgh; William Power, Doylestown; Jay Sigel, Berwyn. **RHODE ISLAND:** Joe Benevento, East Providence; Norman Lutz, Seekonk, Mass. **SOUTH CAROLINA:** Dean Cassell, Greenville; Bob Galloway, Clover; Happ Lathrop, Columbia. **SOUTH DAKOTA:** Don Platt, Sioux Falls; Dr. Richard Tschetter, Sioux Falls. **TENNESSEE:** Dudley Green, Nashville; Jim Webb, Nashville. **TEXAS:** Jimmy Demaret, Houston; Davis (Spec) Goldman, Dallas; Tom Kite, Austin; Henry Ransom, Wheelock; Webster Wilder, San Antonio. **UTAH:** Bill Korns, Provo; Hack Miller, Salt Lake City. **VERMONT:** Lee Davis, Springfield; John McDonough, Rutland. **VIRGINIA:** Vinny Giles, Richmond; Wallace McDowell, Charlottesville. **WASHINGTON:** Al Jones, Seattle; George Lanning, Tacoma; Skip Nagler, Spokane. **WEST VIRGINIA:** Frank Sluciak, Morgantown. **WISCONSIN:** Steve Bull, Milwaukee; Manuel de la Torre, Milwaukee; Carl Unis, Milwaukee. **WYOMING:** Walter (Pax) Ricketts, Cheyenne; Bernard Spielman, Sheridan.

ARCHITECTS OF THE 100 GREATEST COURSES

Robert Trent Jones (19)—Point O'Woods, Boyne Highlands, Pauma Valley, Spyglass Hill, Wilmington, Peachtree, Atlanta A.C., Bellerive, The Dunes, Goodyear, Greenville, Hazeltine, Old Warson. Co-credit: Oakland Hills, Firestone, Congressional, C.C. of Birmingham, C.C. of Detroit, Eugene.

Donald Ross (13)—Seminole, Pinehurst No. 2, Oak Hill, Inverness, Aronimink, Plainfield, Salem, Wannamoisett. Co-credit: Oakland Hills, Scioto, Bob O'Link, C.C. of Birmingham, Interlachen.

Dick Wilson (12)—Pine Tree, Laurel Valley, Bay Hill, Doral, Coldstream, LaCosta, Meadow Brook, National Cash Register, JDM. Co-credit: Scioto, Cog Hill No. 4, Sea Island.

William Flynn (6)—Shinnecock Hills, Cascades, Cherry Hills, Lancaster. Co-credit: Kittansett, The Country Club.

George & Tom Fazio (5)—Jupiter Hills, Butler National, Champions Jackrabbit, Moselem Springs. Co-credit: Atlanta A.C.

A.W. Tillinghast (5)—Winged Foot, Baltusrol, Quaker Ridge, San Francisco, Baltimore.

Joe Finger (5)—Concord, Cedar Ridge, Colonial (Memphis). Co-credit: Atlanta A.C., Altanta C.C.

Colt and Alison (5)—Co-credit: Pine Valley, Bob O'Link, C.C. of Detroit, North Shore, Sea Island.

Pete Dye (4)—Harbour Town, The Golf Club, Oak Tree, Crooked Stick.

Alister Mackenzie (3)—Cypress Point, Augusta National. Co-credit: North Shore.

Jack Nicklaus (3)—Shoal Creek. Co-credit: Muirfield Village, Mayacoo Lakes.

Perry Maxwell (2)—Prairie Dunes, Southern Hills.

George Thomas (2)—Los Angeles C.C. Co-credit: Riviera.

Desmond Muirhead (2)—Co-credit: Muirfield Village, Mayacoo Lakes.

Joe Lee (2)—Disney World (Palm). Co-credit: Cog Hill No. 4.

Devereaux Emmet (2)—Garden City G.C. Co-credit: Congressional.

Willard Byrd (2)—Co-credit: Atlanta C.C., C.C. of North Carolina.

Fred Hood (2)—Co-credit: The Country Club, Kittansett.

Willie Park (2)—Olympia Fields. Co-credit: Maidstone.

The following have designed, or co-designed, one course on our list: Hugh Wilson (Merion), William and Henry Fownes (Oakmont), Sam Whiting (Olympic), Jack Neville (Pebble Beach), George Crump (Pine Valley), John Bredemus (Colonial), Tom Bendelow (Medinah No. 3), Billy Bell (Riviera), Ralph Plummer (Champions Cypress), Bert Way (Firestone), Herbert Strong (Canterbury), Ellis Maples (C.C. of North Carolina), David Gordon (Saucon Valley), Rees Jones (Arcadian Shores), C.B. Macdonald (Chicago G.C.), William Mitchell (C.C. of New Seabury), Red Lawrence (Desert Forest), Chandler Egan (Eugene), Dave Wallace (Grenelefe), Maurice McCarthy (Hershey), Larry Packard (Innisbrook), Willie Watson (Interlachen), Killian and Nugent (Kemper Lakes), Robert Trent Jones Jr. (Princeville), Ted Robinson (Sahalee), Ed Seay and Gardner Dickinson (Sawgrass).

INDEX

Names of courses, players and architects appear in this index. Photographs are indicated with page numbers in italics.

Onuma (Prince) G. Cse., 232, *233*
Ottawa Hunt & G.C., 216
Otter Creek G.C., 258
Ouimet, Francis, 189
Ousteen Oslofjord G.C., 269
Oyster Reef G. Cse., 13, *13,* 15